INTERCULTURAL COMMUNICATION IN CONTEXTS

INTERCULTURAL COMMUNICATION IN CONTEXTS

Judith N. Martin

Thomas K. Nakayama
Arizona State University

Mayfield Publishing Company
Mountain View, California
London • Toronto

Library of Congress Cataloging-in-Publication Data

Martin, Judith N.
    Intercultural communication in contexts / Judith N. Martin, Thomas
  K. Nakayama.
      p. cm.
    Includes indexes.
    ISBN 1–55934–586–1
    1. Intercultural communication.   I. Nakayama, Thomas K.
  II. Title.
  HM258.M194   1996
  303.48′2—dc20   96–32310
                                                     CIP

Manufactured in the United States of America
10 9 8 7 6 5 4 3 2

Mayfield Publishing Company
1280 Villa Street
Mountain View, California 94041

Sponsoring editor, Holly J. Allen; *production editor,* Lynn Rabin Bauer; *manuscript editor,* Robin Kelly; *text and cover designer,* Carolyn Deacy; *art and design manager,* Susan Breitbard; *photo researcher,* Brian Pecko; *cover artist,* J. W. Stewart; *manufacturing manager,* Randy Hurst. The text was set in 10/12 Janson Text by G & S Typesetters and printed on 50# Text White Opaque by The Maple-Vail Book Manufacturing Group.

BRIEF CONTENTS

CONTENTS

**CHAPTER 3   CULTURE, CONTEXT, AND POWER IN
INTERCULTURAL COMMUNICATION   43**

PREFACE

The field of intercultural communication has been an exciting area of study for the past 50 years; currently, it is undergoing the growing pains of a rapidly maturing field. Those who teach and conduct research in intercultural communication face an increasing number of challenges, and difficult questions often arise: Is it enough to identify differences among people? Are we actually reinforcing stereotypes in emphasizing differences? Is there a way to understand the dynamics of intercultural communication without resorting to lists of instructions? Don't we have to talk about the larger social, political, and historical contexts when we teach intercultural communication?

We wrote this textbook to address these and other questions. Although the foundation of intercultural communication theory and research has always been interdisciplinary, the field is now informed by identifiable and competing paradigms. In this book, we attempt to integrate three different research approaches: (1) the traditional *social psychological* approach that emphasizes cultural differences and how these differences influence communication, (2) the *interpretive* approach that emphasizes understanding communication in context, and (3) the more recent *critical* approach that underscores the importance of power and historical context in understanding intercultural communication.

We believe that each of these approaches has important contributions to make to the understanding of intercultural communication. We begin this book by discussing the more traditional, difference-based, social psychological approach; we then weave in the interpretive and critical approaches, with their greater emphases on context and power.

Throughout, we acknowledge that there are no easy answers to the difficult questions of intercultural communication. Sometimes our discussions raise more questions than they answer. We believe that this is as it should be at this point in time. Not only is the field of intercultural communication changing, but the relationship between culture and communication is—and probably always will be—complex and dynamic.

FEATURES OF THE BOOK

Students usually come to the field of intercultural communication with knowledge about many different cultural groups, including their own. This knowledge comes from television, movies, books, personal experiences, news media, and other sources. But many students have a difficult time assimilating information that does not fit neatly into their pre-existing way of thinking. In this book, we move students slowly to the notion of a dialectical framework for thinking about cultural knowledge. That is, we show that knowledge can be acquired in many different ways—through social scientific studies, experience, media reports, and so on—but these differing forms of knowledge need to be seen dynamically and in relation to each other. Through a number of features, we offer students ways to begin thinking about intercultural communication in a dialectical manner. These features include the following:

- An explicit discussion of differing research approaches to intercultural communication, focusing on both strengths and limitations.
- Attention to history, popular culture, and identity as important factors in understanding intercultural communication.
- "Student Voices"—boxes in which students relate their own experiences and share their thoughts about various intercultural communication issues.
- "Point of View"—boxes in which diverse viewpoints from news media, research studies, and other public forums are presented.
- Incorporation of our own personal experiences to highlight particular aspects of intercultural communication.

In addition, the *Instructor's Resource Manual* includes pedagogical tips, discussion questions, and sample syllabi designed to help the instructor teach the course and handle the challenges that arise because of the controversial nature of much of the material.

OVERVIEW OF THE BOOK

We begin our discussion with a look at the changing dynamics of social life and the impact of such changes on the study of intercultural communication. We consider technological changes, global migration, ethnic conflicts, and other worldwide phenomena that make the study of intercultural communication more imperative than ever.

In Chapter 2 we provide some background on the academic study of intercultural communication and discuss the three principal theoretical approaches that inform the field. We also introduce our own dialectical approach, with its four components of culture, communication, context, and power. In Chapter 3 we elaborate on this framework and explore the relationships among the components and concepts.

Chapter 4 focuses on identity. We first discuss the traditional approach, in which identity is seen as a static concept based on categories like gender and ethnicity. We then present an alternative perspective, showing that identity can be understood as a culturally constructed process. In Chapter 5 we discuss the central place of history in intercultural communication, and we then consider how cultural group histories may contribute to contemporary intercultural communication.

Chapter 6 addresses language, both as a set of components (semantics, syntactics, and so forth) that influence perception of social reality and as a social practice in which power relations are embedded. Chapter 7 explores nonverbal codes and cultural space and their centrality to intercultural communication.

In Chapter 8 we discuss intercultural transitions, focusing first on cultural adaptation, then on the impact of adaptation on identity, and finally on the multiple transitions made by those individuals who live in the borders of cultural contexts.

In Chapter 9 we explore the influence of popular culture on intercultural communication, looking particularly at how people consume popular culture, how they resist it, and how it influences perceptions of other cultures. In Chapter 10 we focus on intercultural relationships, emphasizing that relational development occurs within larger social and political contexts. We look at the role of culture in a variety of relationships, including dating and marriage, gay and lesbian relationships, family relationships, and interethnic relationships.

Chapter 11 discusses the inevitability of conflict in intercultural relations. We look at the context of such conflict—interpersonal, social, political—and suggest new ways of thinking about the relationship between culture and conflict. We also discuss strategies for managing conflict in these various contexts.

Finally, in Chapter 12, we turn to the outlook for intercultural communication. We discuss ethics in intercultural communication, incorporating many of the issues addressed in earlier chapters. We also reinforce the dialectical framework introduced earlier and encourage students to think about their many ways of knowing in a dynamic, relational way.

ACKNOWLEDGMENTS

The random convergence of the two authors in time and place led to the creation of this textbook. We both found ourselves at Arizona State University in the early 1990s. Over the course of several years, we discussed and analyzed the multiple approaches to intercultural communication. Much of this discussion was facilitated by the ASU Department of Communication's "culture and communication" theme. Department faculty met to discuss research and pedagogical issues relevant to the study of communication and culture; we also reflected on our own notions of what constituted intercultural communication. This often meant reliving many of our intercultural experiences and sharing them with our colleagues.

For us, the risks of undertaking a co-authoring project were minimal, because, through our dialogues about intercultural communication, we had established a confident relationship and a strong friendship. The completion of this project is also due to the patience and assistance of our friends and family.

Above all, we must recognize the enduring persistence and faith in us of Holly J. Allen, our editor at Mayfield Publishing Company. Her long contact with Judith lay the groundwork for our collaboration on this project. Holly's encouragement was instrumental in the completion of this book. In addition, we want to thank all the readers and reviewers of the earlier versions of the manuscript. Their comments and careful readings were enormously helpful. In particular, thanks to Rosita D. Albert, University of Minnesota; Carlos G. Alemán, University of Illinois, Chicago; Deborah Cai, University of Maryland; Gail Campbell, University of Colorado, Denver; Ling Chen, University of Oklahoma; Alberto González, Bowling Green State University; Bradford 'J' Hall, University of New Mexico; Mark Lawrence McPhail, University of Utah; Richard Morris, Northern Illinois University; Catherine T. Motoyama, College of San Mateo; Gordon Nakagawa, California State University, Northridge; Joyce M. Ngoh, Marist College; Nancy L. Street, Bridgewater State College; Erika Vora, St. Cloud State University; Lee B. Winet, SUNY Oswego; and Gust A. Yep, San Francisco State University.

Our colleagues provided invaluable assistance as well. We particularly want to acknowledge the advice and guidance provided by Jess Alberts and Sandra Petronio. Graduate students also contributed to the project, including Jola Drzewiecka, Denis Leclerc, Chris Stage, and Anu Chitgopekar. And we thank all of our colleagues for their much needed encouragement, particularly A. Cheree Carlson, Frederick C. Corey, and Michael L. Hecht.

We also want to acknowledge the assistance of the Arizona State University College of Public Programs' Publication Assistance Center. In particular, we are grateful for the work of Chrys Gakopoulos, Jan Nagle, and Janet Soper at the Center, as well as the efforts of Dean Anne L. Schneider, without whom the Center would cease to exist.

We thank our families and friends for allowing us long absences and silences as we directed our energies toward the completion of this book. We want to acknowledge both Ron Chaldu and David L. Karbonski, who did not "go nuclear" despite being saddled with more than their share of redirected burdens. A number of people made it possible for us to take international trips—Kazuko and Tommy Nakayama; Michel Dion and Eliana Sampaïo; and Jerzy, Alicja, Marek, and Jolanta Drzewieccy. We are grateful for their support. Others helped us understand intercultural communication in our communities, especially the staff and students at the Guadalupe Learning Center at South Mountain Community College. We want to thank Dr. Amalia Villegas, Laura Laguna, Felipa Montiel, Cruzita Mori, and Amelia Hernandez.

In spirit and conceptualization, our book spans the centuries and crosses many continents. It has been shaped by the many people we have read about and encountered. It is to these guiding and inspiring individuals—some of whom we had the good fortune to meet and some of whom we will never encounter—that we dedicate this book. It is our hope that their spirit of curiosity, openness, and understanding will be reflected in the pages that follow.

TO THE STUDENT

Many textbooks emphasize in their introductions how you should use the text. In contrast, we begin this book by introducing ourselves and our interests in intercultural communication. There are many ways to think about intercultural interactions. One way to learn more about intercultural experiences is to engage in dialogue with others on this topic. Ideally, we would like to begin a dialogue with you about some of the ways to think about intercultural communication. Learning about intercultural communication is not about learning a finite set of skills, terms, and theories. It is about learning to think about cultural realities in multiple ways. Unfortunately, it is not possible for us to engage in dialogues with our readers.

Instead, we strive to lay out a number of issues to think about regarding intercultural communication. By reflecting upon these issues in your own interactions, and by talking with others about these issues, you will be well on your way to becoming both a better intercultural communicator and a better analyst of intercultural interactions. There is no endpoint from which we can say that we have learned all there is to know. Learning about communication is a lifelong process that involves experiences and analysis. We hope this book will generate many dialogues that will help you come to greater understanding of different cultures and peoples, and the complexity of intercultural communication.

ABOUT THE AUTHORS

The two authors of this book come to intercultural communication from very different backgrounds and very different research traditions. Yet, we believe that these differences offer a unique approach to thinking about intercultural communication. We briefly introduce ourselves here, but we hope that by the end of the book you will have a much more complete understanding of who we are. Simply labeling ourselves does not tell you who we are. Think about how you might describe yourself. Then, as you read this book, apply specific issues to yourself to find out how much information is missing from your initial self-description.

One of the authors, Judith Martin, grew up in Mennonite communities, primarily in Delaware and Pennsylvania. She has studied at the Université de Grenoble in France and has taught in Algeria. She received her doctorate at the

Pennsylvania State University. By background and training, she is a social scientist who has focused on intercultural communication on an interpersonal level and has studied how people's communication is affected as they move or sojourn between international locations. She has taught at the State University of New York at Oswego, the University of Minnesota, the University of New Mexico, and Arizona State University. She enjoys gardening, going to Mexico, and hosting annual Academy Awards parties, and she does not miss the harsh Midwestern winters.

The other author, Tom Nakayama, grew up mainly in Georgia, at a time when the Asian American presence was much less than what it is now. He has studied at the Université de Paris and various universities in the United States. He received his doctorate from the University of Iowa. By background and training, he is a critical rhetorician who views intercultural communication in a social context. He has taught at the California State University at San Bernardino and Arizona State University. He is a voracious reader and owns more books than any other faculty member in his department. He watches TV—especially baseball games—and lifts weights. Living in the West now, he misses springtime in the South.

The authors' very different life stories and research programs came together at Arizona State University. We have each learned much about intercultural communication through our own experiences, as well as through our intellectual pursuits. Judith has a well-established record of social science approaches to intercultural communication. Tom, in contrast, has taken a nontraditional approach to understanding intercultural communication by emphasizing critical perspectives. We believe that these differences in our lives and in our research offer complementary ways of understanding intercultural communication.

Since the early 1990s, we have engaged in many different dialogues about intercultural communication—focusing on our experiences, thoughts, ideas, and analyses—which led us to think about writing this textbook. But our interest was not primarily generated by these dialogues; rather, it was our overall interest in improving intercultural relations that motivated us. We believe that communication is an important arena for those relations to be improved. By helping people become more aware as intercultural communicators, we hope to make this a better world for all of us.

THE NEED FOR IMPROVED INTERCULTURAL COMMUNICATION

We stand at the end of the century with the year 2000 looming before us. We know that we live in rapidly changing times. Although no one can foresee the future, we believe that changes are increasing the imperative for intercultural learning. In Chapter 1, you will learn more about some of these changes and their influence on intercultural communication.

You also stand at the front end of a textbook journey about intercultural communication. At this point, you might take stock of who you are, what your intercultural communication experiences have been, how you respond in those situations, and how you tend to think about those experiences. Some people respond to intercultural situations with amusement, curiosity, or interest; others may respond with hostility, anger, or fear. It is important to reflect on your experiences and to learn how you respond and what those reactions mean.

We also think it is helpful to realize that in many instances people do not want to communicate interculturally. Sometimes people see those who are culturally different as threatening, as forcing them to change. They may feel as if such people require more assistance and patience. Or they may simply think of them as "different." People come to intercultural interactions from a variety of emotional states and attitudes; it is wrongheaded to assume that everyone wants to communicate interculturally. Because of this dynamic, many people have had negative intercultural experiences that influence subsequent intercultural interactions. Negative experiences can range from simple misunderstandings to physical violence. Although it may be unpleasant to discuss such situations, we believe that it is necessary to do so if we are serious about understanding and improving intercultural interaction.

Intercultural conflict can occur even when the participants do not intentionally provoke it. When we use our own cultural frames in intercultural settings, those hidden assumptions can provoke trouble. For example, when renting a small apartment in a private home in Grenoble, France, Judith invited a number of her U.S. friends who were traveling in Europe to stop by and stay with her. The angry and frustrated response that this drew from the landlady came as a surprise. She told Judith that she would have to pay extra for all of the water they were using, that the apartment was not a motel, and that Judith would have to move out if the practice of overnight guests continued. Differing notions of privacy and what it means to rent contributed to the conflict. Intercultural experiences are not always fun. Sometimes they are frustrating, confusing, and distressing.

On a more serious level, we might look at the beating of Rodney King by some members of the Los Angeles Police Department as yet another example of intercultural communication. The subsequent interpretations and reactions of that televised event by different communities of people reflect important differences in our society. The ensuing uprising, which some have called "riots" or "rebellion," was indicative of the tremendous fury among various groups of people who experience life in Los Angeles in very different ways. These are all part of the complexity of intercultural communication. We do not come to intercultural interactions as blank slates; instead, we bring ourselves and our cultures.

Although the journey to developing awareness with intercultural communication is an individual one, it is important to recognize the connections we all have to many different aspects of social life. You are, of course, an individual. But you have been influenced by culture. The ways that others regard you and communicate with you are influenced largely by whom they perceive you to be. By enacting cultural characteristics of masculinity or femininity, for example, you may elicit particular reactions from others. Reflect on your social and individual characteristics; consider how these characteristics communicate something about you.

Finally, there is no list of what to do in an intercultural setting. Although prescribed reactions might help you avoid serious faux pas in one setting or culture, such lists are generally too simplistic to get you very far in any culture and may cause serious problems in other cultures. The study of communication is both a science and an art. In this book we attempt to pull the best of both kinds of knowledge together for you. Because communication does not happen in a vacuum but is integral to the many dynamics that make it possible—economics, politics, technology—the ever-changing character of our world means that it is essential to develop a sensitivity and flexibility to change. It also means that you can never stop learning about intercultural communication.

WHY STUDY INTERCULTURAL COMMUNICATION?

The study of intercultural communication has grown dramatically over the past 50 years. Right now we are living in a particularly exciting period in the development of this field. New means of communication, as well as new ways of thinking about culture and communication, make these last years of the 20th century a truly challenging time.

This book will expose you to the variety of approaches we use to study intercultural communication. We, the authors, also weave into the text our own personal stories to make theory come alive. We hope to link theory and practice to give a much more complete understanding of intercultural communication than either one alone could offer.

The authors of this book bring many intercultural communication experiences to the text. We hope that as you read you will learn not only about both of us as individuals but also about how we think about intercultural communication. Don't be overwhelmed by the complexity of intercultural communication. Not knowing everything that you would like to know is very much a part of this process.

Why is it important to focus on intercultural communication and strive to become better at this complex pattern of interaction? We can present six different reasons; perhaps you can add more.

THE TECHNOLOGICAL IMPERATIVE

In the 1960s, media guru Marshall McLuhan coined the term *global village* to mean a world where communication technology—TV, radio, news services— brings events from the most remote parts of the world. Today, we are connected—via answering machines, fax, E-mail, electronic bulletin boards, and the Internet—to persons we have never met face-to-face (Table 1-1). It's possible not only to communicate with other people via these technologies but also to develop complex relationships with them.

Technology and Human Communication

These monumental changes have affected how we think of ourselves and the way we form intercultural relationships. In his book *The Saturated Self*, psychologist Kenneth Gergen describes the changes that occur as technology alters our patterns of communication. In past centuries, social relationships were confined to the distance of an easy walk and evolved with each technological advance, whether the railroad, the automobile, the telephone, the radio, TV, or movies. These relationships have now multiplied exponentially. We can be "accessed" in numerous ways and be involved simultaneously in many different relationships, all without face-to-face contact. Additionally, family interaction has been radically altered and turned into "microwave relationships"; the nesting place has turned into a pitstop as family members rush from one technological device to another to get their needs met.

TABLE 1-1   THE IMPACT OF TECHNOLOGY ON OUR LIVES

In October, 1995, Nielsen Media Research released a survey about Internet use. The research study polled users in the United States and Canada.

Internet Users	Total Number of People
People who had access to Internet services	37 million
People who had used the Internet in three-month period prior to study	24 million
People who had used the World Wide Web	18 million
People who had purchased products or services over the World Wide Web	2.5 million
People who accessed the Internet every day	7.5 million

Profile of Internet Users	Percent of All Internet Users	Percent of Population
People who are between ages 16 and 34	53%	N/A
People who have incomes that exceed $80,000	25%	10%
People who have college degrees	64%	28%

Source: *Facts on File,* Vol. 55, no. 2868 (1995, November 16).

Gergen makes the case that with the removal of traditional barriers to forming relationships—time and space—these technological advancements lead to "multiphrenia," a splitting of the individual into many different selves. We are available for communication, via the answering machine, fax, and E-mail, where we're not physically present. Gergen writes:

> *The relatively coherent and unified sense of self inherent in a traditional culture gives way to manifold and competing potentials. A multiphrenic condition emerges in which one swims in ever-shifting, concatenating, and contentious currents of being. One bears the burden of an increasing array of oughts, of self-doubts and irrationalities. (1991, p. 80)*

What does this have to do with intercultural communication? Through high-tech communication we come in contact with people who are very different from ourselves, often in ways we don't understand. The people we talk to on E-mail networks may speak languages different from our own, come from different countries, be of different ethnic backgrounds, and have had many different life experiences.

An interesting situation arose recently for one of the authors of this book.

Tom was using an electronic bulletin board when someone posted a message in Dutch. It was met with a flurry of hostile responses as people protested the use of an exclusionary language, one most people couldn't read. A discussion ensued about which languages would be acceptable on the network. The decision reached was that subscribers could post messages in any language as long as there was an English translation. In a subsequent posting, someone from a university in South Africa recommended a book "for those of you who can read Dutch (heh-heh, all four of us)." The remark that accompanied the recommendation was an apparent reaction to the exclusionary sentiment of other subscribers. The use of some languages is given even more privilege in the high-tech communication world, in which we encounter many more people.

Mobility and Its Effect on Communication

Not only do we come in contact with more people electronically these days, we also come in contact with more people physically. Our society is more mobile than ever before. U.S. families move on the average of five times in the lifetime of the family. Of course, there are still communities in which people are born, live, and die in the same small area, but this scenario is less common than ever.

Mobility changes the nature of our society, and it also affects the individuals involved. One of the authors of this book, Judith, remembers moving every few years while she was growing up. She was always facing a new group of classmates at a new school. One year just before going to a new high school, she wrote in her diary:

> *I know that the worst will be over soon. Always changing schools should make me more at ease. It doesn't. I like to meet strangers and make friends. Once I get to know people, it'll be easier. But I always dread the first day, wondering if I'll fit in, wondering if the other kids'll be nice to me.*

Many families move because of divorce. In 1988, only 50% of American youths ages 15–17 years lived with both birth mother and birth father. The rest had other living arrangements: some lived with single parents, step families, or extended families (such as grandparents) or shuttled back and forth between their parents' houses (Howe & Strauss, 1993). Some children commute between different geographical regions of the United States. For example, they might spend the summer with dad in New Jersey and the rest of the year with mother and stepfather in Phoenix.

Families also relocate for economic reasons. A U.S. company might relocate to Mexico and transfer the corporate personnel with the company. Many Mexican workers, on the other hand, cross the border to look for employment in the United States. Germans from the eastern part of Germany move to the western sections of the country seeking social and economic opportunities. Increasing technology and mobility means that we can no longer be culturally illiterate in this shrinking interdependent world.

Rapid changes in technology, demographics, and economic forces mean that you are likely to come into contact with many people of diverse backgrounds. While many of these communication experiences will be in social situations, many other interactions will be in professional or public settings. (© *Chip Henderson/Tony Stone Images, Inc.*)

THE DEMOGRAPHIC IMPERATIVE

The U.S. population has changed radically in the past two decades and will continue to do so in the future. The workforce that today's college graduates enter will differ significantly from the one their parents entered. These demographic changes come from two sources: changing demographics within the United States and changing immigration patterns.

Changing U.S. Demographics

The changing demographic characteristics of the U.S. workforce have been described in a well-known study conducted by the Hudson Institute, published as *Workforce 2000* (Johnson & Packer, 1987). According to this study, by the 21st century the U.S. workforce will be older than it is now, with a mean age of 36. There will also be more women working; 48% of the workforce will be female, compared to 30% in the 1950s. The workforce will also be more ethnically and racially diverse.

What accounts for these changes? The workforce will be older because the Baby Boomers (people born from 1946 to 1964) are aging. More women are in the workforce for several reasons. Economic pressures have come to bear; more women are single parents, and even in two-parent families it often takes two incomes to meet family expenses. Secondly, the women's movement of the 1960s

TABLE 1-2 THE WORKFORCE OF THE 21st CENTURY		
Population Group	**Percent of Population**	
	1970	2000
Between the ages of 35 and 54 years	48%	51%
Women	29%	47%
Ethnically diverse (non-White)	11%	15%

Source: W. B. Johnston and A. E. Packer, *Workforce 2000* (1987), p. 94.

and 1970s resulted in more women seeking careers and jobs outside the home. Finally, the workforce is more ethnically and racially diverse—in part, simply because there are more minorities now than before, but also because of civil rights efforts that have provided more opportunities for minorities in business and industry (Table 1-2).

Changing Immigration Patterns

The second source of demographic change is different immigration patterns. Although the United States has often been thought of as a nation of immigrants, it is also a nation that established itself by subjugating the original inhabitants. It is also a nation that prospered while forcibly importing millions of Africans to perform slave labor. These other aspects of national identity are equally important in understanding contemporary society.

Today, immigration looks to change significantly the social landscape. Until the 1960s, most of the immigrants to the United States came from Europe. This changed in the 1980s and 1990s. Of the one million immigrants who now enter the United States every year, 90% are from Latin America and Asia. According to a study by the Population Reference Bureau (1993), by the middle of the next century the United States will be a global society in which nearly half of all Americans will be from today's racial and ethnic minorities—primarily African Americans, Asians, Hispanics, and Native Americans (Wright, 1993). It's not hard to see that the United States is becoming more heterogeneous.

This heterogeneity presents many opportunities and challenges for the student of intercultural communication. The tension among these heterogeneous groups, as well as fear on the part of the politically dominant groups, must be acknowledged. California's Proposition 187, which passed in the November 1994 election, excludes nondocumented immigrants from receiving medical and social services. This proposition remains highly controversial and led to protests and court challenges. The subsequent California Civil Rights Initiative, which goes to vote in the autumn of 1996, would further extend the challenges to diversity by eliminating many affirmative action programs. The opportunities of a culturally diverse society should also be noted. Diversity can expand our horizons of what is possible—linguistically, politically, socially—as many different lifestyles and ways of thinking are brought together.

To get a better sense of the situation in the United States today, let's take a look at our history. As mentioned above, the United States has always been a nation of immigrants. When Europeans began arriving on the shores of the New World, an estimated 8–10 million Native Americans were already living here. The ancestors of these natives probably began to arrive via the Bering Strait at least 40,000 years earlier. The outcome of the encounters between these groups—the colonizing Europeans and the native peoples—is well known. By 1940, the Native American population of the United States was reduced to an estimated 250,000. Today, there are about 1.9 million American Indians (and 542 recognized tribes) living in the United States (Bureau of the Census, 1990; U.S. Government Printing Office, 1994).

Relationships between residents and immigrants—between oldtimers and newcomers—have often been filled with tension and conflict. In the 19th century, Native Americans sometimes were caught in the middle of European rivalries. During the War of 1812, for example, Indian allies of the British were severely punished by the United States when the war ended. In 1832, the U.S. Congress recognized the Indian nations' right to self-government, but in 1871 a congressional act prohibited treaties between the U.S. government and Indian tribes. In 1887, Congress passed the Dawes Severalty Act, terminating Native Americans' special relationship with the U.S. government and paving the way for the removal of Native Americans from their land.

As waves of immigrants continued to roll in from Europe, the more firmly established European—mainly English—immigrants tried to protect their way of life, language, and culture. James Banks, a U.S. history specialist, identifies various conflicts throughout the nation's history (1991). Many of these conflicts are not uniquely American but are imported from European conflicts. In 1729, for example, an English mob prevented a group of Irish immigrants from landing in Boston. Conflicts between the English and the Irish continued on the North American side of the Atlantic. A few years later, another mob destroyed a new Scots-Irish Presbyterian church in Worcester, Massachusetts. In these acts we can see the Anglocentrism that characterized early U.S. history. Later, northern and western European characteristics were added to this model of American culture. Immigrants from southern, central, and eastern Europe were expected to assimilate into the so-called mainstream culture—to jump into the "melting pot" and come out "American."

In the later 19th and early 20th centuries, an anti-immigrant, nativistic movement propagated violence against newer immigrants. In 1885, 28 Chinese were killed in an anti-Chinese riot in Wyoming; in 1891, a white mob attacked a Chinese community in Los Angeles and killed 19 people; in 1891, 11 Italian Americans were lynched in New Orleans in an anti-immigrant riot.

Nativistic sentiment was well supported at the government level. In 1882, Congress passed the Chinese Exclusion Act, officially prohibiting anyone who

Many people fear the negative impacts of immigration without also considering the quantitative, statistical evidence that highlights the measurable benefits of increased immigration. W. B. Johnson and A. E. Packer, authors of a study on the future of the U.S. workforce, point out the benefits of immigration, not only to the White population, but for minorities as well.

> *One particularly important concern with immigration is its impact on the job prospects of native minorities. Although the evidence is not definitive, the results of one statistical analysis of 247 metropolitan areas concluded that black unemployment rates are not increased by a rise in the proportion of Mexican immigrants in a local labor market. These results suggest that, to some extent, immigrants are complementary to, rather than in competition with, native minority workers.*
>
> *In fact, it is plausible that residents of areas that experience significant influxes of immigrants will benefit rather than suffer from the new workers. This will be particularly likely over the long-run. Census data and other studies have shown that, over 10 or 20 years, the earnings of immigrants and their offspring will equal or exceed those of native-born Americans with similar characteristics.*
>
> *Despite the evidence of economic benefits, immigration has always triggered negative emotional reactions from natives, and the current concerns with the "loss of control" of U.S. borders are continuing this tradition.*

Source: W. B. Johnson and A. E. Packer, *Workforce 2000* (1987), pp. 93–94.

lived in China from emigrating to this country. In 1924, the Johnson-Read Act and the Oriental Exclusion Act established extreme quotas on immigration, completely excluding the legal immigration of Asians. According to Ronald Takaki, these 1924 laws "provided for immigration based on nationality quotas: the number of immigrants to be admitted annually was limited to 2 percent of the foreign-born individuals of each nationality residing in the United States in 1890" (1989, p. 209). The nativistic sentiment increasingly shifted to debates centering around race, where it was argued that economic and political opportunities should be reserved for Whites, not just native-born Americans. By the 1930s, southern and eastern European groups were considered "assimilatable" and the concept of race assumed new meaning. All of the so-called White races were now considered one, and racial hostilities could now focus on non-White ethnic groups, such as Asian Americans, Native Americans, and Mexican Americans, who were perceived as non-White (Banks, 1991).

Economic conditions make a big difference in attitudes toward foreign workers and immigration policies. During the Depression of the 1930s, Mexicans and Mexican Americans were forced to return to Mexico to free-up jobs for other ("White") Americans. When prosperity returned in the 1940s, Mexicans were welcomed back as a source of cheap labor. This type of situation occurs all over the world. Algerian workers are alternately welcomed and rejected in France, depending on the condition of the French economy and the need for imported labor. "Guestworkers" from Turkey have been subjected to similar uncertainties in Germany. Indian workers in Kenya, Chinese immigrants in Malaysia, and many other workers toiling outside their native lands have suffered the vagaries of fluctuating economies and see-saw immigration policies.

The tradition of tension and conflict between cultures continues to this day. The conflicts that occur across Southern California exemplify many aspects of the demographic changes in the United States. We often imagine Hollywood and Los Angeles as the California dream portrayed in popular TV shows and movies. Such images sometimes prevent us from seeing the kinds of intercultural tensions like those manifested in the Los Angeles riots that followed the jury trial of the police officers accused of beating Rodney King.

The tensions in Los Angeles among Latinos, African Americans, Korean Americans, and European Americans can be examined on a variety of levels. Some of the conflict is due to different languages, values, and lifestyles. Some African Americans resent the success of recent Korean immigrants—a reaction that follows the pattern throughout history. The conflict may also be due to the pattern of settlement that results in cultural "enclaves": Blacks in south-central Los Angeles, Latinos in Englewood and east Los Angeles, Koreans in the "Miracle Mile," and Whites on the west side of the city. Some of the conflict may be due to the economic disparity that exists among these different groups. These groups mostly come in contact during the day in schools, businesses, hospitals, with different languages, histories, and economic conditions. This presents great challenges for our society and for us as individuals.

The challenge becomes to look beyond the Hollywood images, recognizing the disparities, diversity, and differences and to try to apply what we know about intercultural communication. Perhaps the first step is to realize that the melting pot metaphor probably never was viable; it probably was never possible for everyone to assimilate into the United States in the same way. Today we need a different metaphor, one that reflects the racial, ethnic, and cultural diversity that truly exists in our country. Perhaps we should think of the United States as a "salad," in which each group retains its own flavor and yet contributes to the whole. Or we might think of it as a tapestry, with many different strands contributing to a unified pattern.

However, the United States is hardly a model of diversity. Many countries are much more ethnically diverse than the United States. For example, Nigeria has 200 ethnic groups and Indonesia has a similar number. Nigeria was colonized by the British, and boundaries forced many different groups artificially into one nation-state, which caused many conflicts. The diverse groups in Indonesia, in contrast, have largely co-existed amiably for many years. Diversity, therefore, does not necessarily excuse intercultural conflicts.

Fortunately, most individuals are able to negotiate day-to-day activities in schools, businesses, and other settings, in spite of cultural differences. Diversity can even be a positive force. Demographic diversity in the United States has given us tremendous linguistic richness and culinary variety. Diversity has given us the resources to meet new social challenges, as well as domestic and international business opportunities.

Our gender, class, and race all influence our position in society and also influence us to have a different understanding of social life. We all have different social realities based on what we were taught, and this fact makes communication between people very challenging. I believe that nowadays we come into contact with people of all types of backgrounds and nationalities more often than we did years ago. We find people of different standpoints at the workplace, at social events, at the grocery store, and so on. With all of these diverse people suddenly brought into contact with each other every day of their lives, it is extremely hard to take the time to treat everyone as individuals. Instead, we make categories based on our past experiences and from our different standpoints. This makes our lives simpler, but it also breeds stereotyping and prejudice. The categories that we make are not based on our past experiences and our different standpoints, but also on what we hear from other sources and from the examples that the media give us.

—Tara

THE ECONOMIC IMPERATIVE

Increasingly more of the U.S. economy depends on global markets. James Fallows, a U.S. journalist, writes about his experiences living in Japan in the mid-1980s when the Japanese economy was booming. He points out that in 1986 Japan surpassed the United States as an international creditor. A year later the per capita income in Japan surpassed that in the United States. In 1988, a Japanese bank overtook Citibank and the Bank of America to become the largest bank in the world. A year after that the eleven largest banks in the world were all Japanese; the shares listed on the Tokyo Stock Exchange were worth twice as much as all of the shares on the New York Stock Exchange (Fallows, 1989).

Many management experts have examined Japanese business practices for ways to increase U.S. productivity (Vogel, as cited in Fallows, 1989). One of the strengths they identify is the Japanese belief in effort for its own sake. Japanese employees work longer hours and sometimes produce better products simply as a result of persistence. This trait also pays off in schools: Japanese students score higher on standardized exams than do American students. Fallows compares the U.S. and Japanese values:

> *Of course there are areas in which American culture encourages pure effort. Political campaigns, athletic teams, fledgling businesses. . . . But in the foreseeable future, cooperation, self-discipline, and self-denial will come much more naturally to the Japanese than to Americans. (Fallows, 1989, p. 46)*

The point is not whether these traits are right or wrong, but that for Japan they are right. Fallows continues by pointing out that Americans have other traits that serve us well. For example, our demographic heterogeneity and our "talent for disorder" provide challenges and strengths that the Japanese do not possess.

Here is one view of affirmative action that emphasizes the need for considering the contradictory character of this issue. Note how the author, Bernardo Ferdman, resists a simplistic resolution or position on the issue. He asks that we search for ways to maintain civil rights rather than view affirmative action as a battle.

It may be much more fruitful to see the debate as one over what constitutes fairness in dealing with ethnic differences. When we look at it this way, we can see that American society seems to be caught in a bind.

On the one hand, to assess the presence and the extent of racial and ethnic discrimination, and to ensure group-level equity, we must take people's group memberships into account. Thus, to ignore people's race or ethnicity can be seen as patently unfair. On the other hand, recognition and consideration of racial and ethnic group membership can be experienced as discriminatory, and even as calling into question, for example, the qualifications of individuals whose group membership are highlighted. Thus, to notice people's race or ethnicity can also be seen as unfair. . . .

[T]hese views represent the elements of a paradox. In the individualistic view, we emphasize the commonalities among us and thus the importance of treating everyone alike, and we believe it is only when we let group labels get in the way that we discriminate.

In the group view, we emphasize the difference among ethnic and racial groups and thus the importance of being sensitive to these in dealing with others. We believe that expecting the same behavior and values from everyone is discriminatory.

How can these seemingly contradictory values be reconciled: The solution to the paradox does not lie in convincing the advocates of whatever perspective we more strongly disagree with that they are wrong. It is more likely to lie in giving up the type of thinking that says that one side must "win." Both perspectives are integral to American thinking and practice regarding civil rights and in their various versions find proponents among all parties to the issue. . . . When looked at this way, we can see that the individual must be valued and *group rights must be protected. . . .*

We must be more conscious of this tension inherent in the nature of an ethnically and racially diverse society and learn to better live with it. We could do so by acknowledging that ethnicity and culture are not extraneous to what makes individuals unique. Rather, they are important aspects of the person—all persons. . . .

There is no middle ground between these paradoxical visions of fairness, yet we must live according to both of them if we are to uphold the values of individual and group freedom. . . . I hope that we can give up the battle mentality and find mutually acceptable ways to maintain civil rights.

Source: Bernardo M. Ferdman (assistant professor at SUNY-Albany), *Sunday Times Union*, Albany, NY (1989, September 17), p. D3.

Some people often think that studying intercultural communication is necessary only if they are going to be living in a foreign country. Given the importance of culture and capital, corporations do not always want to send executives abroad. Think about how the shifting needs of corporations will create the necessity for different intercultural skills, not necessarily overseas. What might these new intercultural needs look like?

> *At a time when the reality of a global economy has never been more obvious, the ranks of international executives in U.S. companies should be swelling.*
>
> *That's not what's happening.*
>
> *Instead, the number of Americans who see themselves as international executives is actually decreasing. More than half of the international companies surveyed in a recent study concede they are unsuccessful in filling key overseas posts.*
>
> *Of even greater significance for America's budding international executives is the discovery that about three-fourths of those U.S. companies say they plan to fill future overseas positions with foreign nationals rather than with Americans.*
>
> *The reasons are as complex as the global economy itself, according to a recent study by the Harvard Business School and Amrop International, an international executive-search firm.*
>
> *Clearly, part of the reason is cost. Relocation costs for an American executive and family can climb to more than $300,000, excluding training and development.*
>
> *Hiring locally eliminates that cost, as well as sky-high monthly rents for executive apartments and houses that can easily run from $8,000 to $12,000 a month in cities such as Tokyo. It also eliminates other costs, such as expensive international schools for children and annual allowances for food and clothing that often come with overseas compensation packages.*

Source: Ronald E. Yates, "U.S. International Executives Corps' Ranks Are Thin," *The Arizona Republic* (1994, March 28), p. E4.

To compete effectively with other nations, we need to understand how business is conducted in other countries. We need to be able to negotiate deals that are advantageous to the U.S. economy. However, U.S. businesses are not always willing to take the time and effort to do this. For example, U.S. automobile manufacturers do not produce automobiles with right-hand drive, which would enable them to enter markets in nations like Japan.

Cross-cultural trainers in the United States report that Japanese business personnel often spend years in the United States studying English and learning about the country before they decide to build a factory here or invest money. The Japanese are known for their emphasis on long-term goals. In contrast, many American companies provide no training before sending their workers overseas and expect business deals to be completed very quickly with little regard for cultural idiosyncrasies.

The following excerpt is from an article in a Thai newspaper by journalist Jennifer Sharples. Note that "modernization" does not mean "westernization." Thailand is becoming increasingly industrialized, which may give the landscape a Western appearance. But we should not ignore the cultural differences that reside within the landscape.

The apparent westernization that many foreigners see occurring in Thailand can be very misleading, because despite modern, well-equipped offices that equal—if not surpass—anything found in New York or London, this doesn't mean that the staff necessarily see things from the western perspective.

Come to that, there are also many value differences between the various countries of Asia; Thailand, Singapore, and Japan, for example, all have very different ways of operating in the workplace, which means cross-cultural sensitivity is the name of the game.

Dr. Viboonpon Poonprasit of Thammasat University's Faculty of Political Science, who has been involved in cross-cultural training for many years, says: "Because Thailand is developing well economically, many foreigners believe that western ways prevail. Little do they realize that they are faced with deep-rooted traditional values. Expatriates often believe they can work the way they would back home and believe among other things that Thais are nonassertive and noncompetitive.

"Thais, on the other hand, expect foreigners to know some of their basic cultural values such as kreng jai *(showing consideration for others) and* jai yen *(keeping calm or cool), but foreigners frequently make the mistake of ignoring these niceties, since they don't expect these things to create a big issue in the workplace.*

"Thailand having remained independent was never exposed to western values. But many Thais realize the need to compete globally and we have to adapt to international trade and business practices.

"This means having to be assertive and decisive, while retaining some Thai characteristics such as kreng jai. *In cross-cultural training courses, we tell Thais to be more flexible and to learn the western system as well as the Thai; much depends on how Thai-oriented the boss is, of course."*

Source: Jennifer Sharples, "A Cross-Cultural Conundrum," *Bangkok Post Sunday Magazine* (1995, May 28–June 3), pp. 10–11.

It may be interesting to speculate on why people in the United States are far more concerned with Japanese investments in the United States than they are with much larger investments from countries like Britain and the Netherlands. Perhaps we need to recognize the role of the media and the historical significance of racial difference in the United States to understand why we focus on Japanese investors instead of British and Dutch investors.

There are many influences that shape intercultural communication interactions. In this photo of Jews in an Arab section of Jerusalem, notice the Israeli soldier with the gun, the father's glance, and the child. Given the many forces that structure our world, it is often difficult to overcome barriers to intercultural communication. Larger social and cultural conflicts are often a part of intercultural interaction. (© George Mars Cassidy/ Tony Stone Images, Inc.)

THE PEACE IMPERATIVE

The bottom line is: Can individuals of different genders, ages, ethnicities, races, languages, and cultural backgrounds live together and get along on one planet? The history of humankind is not very optimistic on this point. Contact among different cultural groups—from the earliest civilizations until today—often leads to disharmony. One has only to look at world politics to see examples of intergroup strife. For example, consider the ethnic struggles in Bosnia and the former Soviet Union; war between the Hutu and Tutsi groups in Rwanda; and racial and ethnic struggles and tension in neighborhoods in Boston, Los Angeles, and other U.S. cities.

Some of these conflicts are tied to histories of colonialism around the world, in which European powers placed diverse groups—differing in language, culture, religion, or identity—together as one state. For example, the union of Pakistan and India was imposed by the British; eventually Pakistan struggled for independence from India. The tremendous diversity—and historical antagonisms—within many former colonies must be understood in the context of histories of colonialism.

It would be naive to assume that simply understanding something about intercultural communication would end war, but these problems do underscore the need for individuals to learn more about groups of which they are not members. Ultimately, people, not countries, negotiate and sign peace treaties.

An example of how individual communication styles may influence political outcomes can be seen in the negotiations between Saddam Hussein and George Bush during the Gulf War. Many Middle East experts assumed that Saddam Hussein was not ready to fight, that he was merely bluffing, using an Arabic style of communication. This style emphasizes animated exaggeration and conversational form over content (Patai, 1983). Arab communication specialists emphasize that during conflict situations, Arab speakers may threaten the life and property of their opponents with no intention to carry out the threats. Rather, Arab speakers use threats to buy time and intimidate their opponents. Declaratory speeches given by U.S. leaders (which contained such expressions as "We will find the cancer and cut it out") seemed mundane to Arab listeners. Verbal exchanges, regardless of the different speech styles, often take the place of physical violence (Griefat & Katriel, 1989).

However, we always need to consider the dialectic between individual and societal forces in studying intercultural communication. Although communication on the interpersonal level is important, we need to remember that individuals often are born into and are caught up in conflicts that they neither started nor chose and yet are impacted by the larger societal forces.

THE SELF-AWARENESS IMPERATIVE

One of the most important reasons for studying intercultural communication is the awareness it brings to our own cultural identity and background. This is also one of the least obvious reasons. Peter Adler, a noted social psychologist, observes that the study of intercultural communication begins as a journey into another culture and reality and ends as a journey into one's own culture.

Examples from the authors' own lives come to mind. Judith's earliest experiences in public school made her realize that not everyone wore "coverings" and "bonnets" and "cape dresses," the clothing worn by her Amish/Mennonite family. She realized that her family was different from most of the other people she came in contact with. Years later, when she was teaching high school in Algeria, a Muslim country, she realized something about her religious identity as a Protestant. December 25 came and went and she taught classes with no mention

*I have spent three years in the United States seeking an education. I am from Sin-
gapore, and I believe that in many ways both countries are similar. They are both
multicultural. They both have a dominant culture. In the United States the dominant culture is White, and in Singapore it is Chinese.*

*Coming to the United States has taught me to be more aware of diversity.
Even though in Singapore we are diverse, because I was part of the majority there
I didn't feel the need to increase my level of intercultural awareness. In the United
States I became a minority, and that has made me feel the need to become more
culturally competent.*

—Jacqueline

of Christmas. Judith had never thought about how special the celebration of
Christmas was or how important the holiday was to her. She then recognized on
a personal level the uniqueness of this particular cultural practice.

When Tom, who is of Japanese descent, first started elementary school, he
attended a white school in the segregated U.S. South. By the time he reached
the fourth grade, schools were integrated, and some African American students
were intrigued by his very straight black hair. At that point, he recognized a connection between himself and the Black students, and a kernel of self-awareness
began to develop about his identity. Living in increasingly diverse worlds, we
can take the opportunity to learn more about our own cultural backgrounds and
identity and what makes us similar and different from people we interact with.

THE ETHICAL IMPERATIVE

Living in an intercultural world presents challenging ethical issues that can be
addressed by the study of intercultural communication. Ethics may be thought
of as principles of conduct that help govern the behavior of individuals and
groups. These principles often arise from communities' perspectives on what is
good and bad behavior. Some are stated very explicitly. For example, the Ten
Commandments teach that it is wrong to steal, tell a lie, commit murder, and so
on. Many other identifiable principles arise from our cultural experience that
may be less explicit—for example, that people should be treated equally and that
people should work hard.

A subject of interest to intercultural communication scholars is what happens when two ethical systems collide. Ethical principles are often culture-
bound, and intercultural conflicts arise from varying notions of what is ethical
behavior. Sociologist Donald Kraybill, in *The Riddle of Amish Culture* (1989),
provides examples of how cross-cultural clashes over ethical issues have been negotiated through the years. Part of the Amish *Ordnung* (code of order) is a

In the corporate world in Bangkok, the new year beginning on January 1st (as opposed to the Thai New Year or the Chinese New Year) is a time of giving gifts to valued customers. The company I worked for was real big on ethics, which was nice; they wanted to treat everyone equally and be fair in their business dealings, which was good, but they took it too far. During New Year's, companies usually give gifts to their customers as a way of saying thanks for their patronage. The gift you give depends on the customer's place in society and the amount of business they do with your company. What I hated is that this company (an American company) viewed that as unethical, as some form of a bribe. We could only go out and buy one item in bulk, and we'd have to give the same gift to all of the customers. I was so embarrassed to give those gifts. I hope the customers knew that I worked for an American company that just didn't understand the way things were done in Thailand.
—Chris

strong belief in simplicity and the rejection of modern conveniences such as electric lights. Because of the hazard this code presented, the Commonwealth of Pennsylvania in the 1970s required the Amish to put bright lights and reflective orange triangles on their horse-drawn buggies.

For people who detest publicity, these requirements were most unwelcome. Flashing lights and bright triangles mocked the modest spirit of Gelassenheit *(self-surrender). But acknowledging the need for safety and respecting the public welfare, the Amish agreed to use them. (Kraybill, 1989, p. 67)*

Kraybill describes the resolutions of other clashes including OSHA (Occupational Safety and Health Administration) requirements that forbad Amish men to wear their traditional broad-brimmed hats on construction sites and regulations forcing children to go to school and Amish men to participate in the military. Kraybill stresses that, although some of these issues may not seem like ethical dilemmas to most contemporary Americans, they are important cultural symbols to the Amish; their communities have remained intact because these issues were negotiated with the greater U.S. society—that is, because the Amish did not give in to the U.S. government.

Another ethical dilemma is the clash over standards of conducting business in multinational corporations. The U.S. Congress and the Securities and Exchange Commission consider it unethical to make payments to government officials of other countries to promote trade. (Essentially, such payment smacks of bribery.) However, in many countries, government officials are paid in this informal way instead of being supported by taxes (Howell, 1982). What is ethical behavior for the personnel in multinational subsidiaries?

The study of intercultural communication should not only provide insights about understanding cultural patterns but also help us address these ethical issues involved in intercultural interaction. First, we should be able to judge what is ethical and unethical behavior given variations in cultural priorities. Second, we should be able to identify guidelines for ethical behavior in intercultural contexts where ethics clash.

Another ethical issue concerns the application of intercultural communication scholarship. Everett Kleinjans, an international educator, stresses that intercultural education is different from some other kinds of education: Although all education may be potentially transformative, learning as a result of intercultural contact is particularly so in that it deals with very fundamental aspects of human behavior. Learning about intercultural communication sometimes calls into question the very core of our assumptive framework and challenges existing and preferred beliefs, values, and patterns of behavior.

Sometimes communities lose their cultural uniqueness because of intercultural contact. When visiting the Navajo Nation, one of the authors, Judith, heard an older Navajo woman lamenting the fact that many of the young people no longer followed the Navajo traditions. By contrast, one reason the Amish have remained culturally intact is that they have resisted contact with outside communities. Other communities, such as some Native Americans, have had contact forced on them. Another example of the transformative power of intercultural contact is international students who come to the United States and do not return, usually acquiring U.S. values and a U.S. lifestyle.

As in other areas of communication, there are ethical issues about the application of our knowledge. What constitutes ethical and unethical applications? Michael Paige and Judith Martin (1996) give examples of dubious applications of intercultural scholarship. One questionable practice concerns people who pursue the study of intercultural communication in order to proselytize others without their consent. (Some religious organizations conduct Bible study on college campuses for international students under the guise of English conversation lessons.) Another questionable practice is the behavior of cross-cultural consultants who misrepresent or exaggerate their ability to deal with complex issues of prejudice and racism in brief one-shot training sessions.

SUMMARY

In this chapter, we have identified six reasons for studying intercultural communication: the technological imperative, the demographic imperative, the economic imperative, the peace imperative, the self-awareness imperative, and the ethical imperative. Perhaps you can think of some other reasons. We have stressed that the situations in which intercultural communication takes place are complex and present great challenges for us. Unfortunately, there are no easy answers.

We have presented some questions that will be addressed in the following chapters as we continue our study of communication and culture. What is the next step? Now that we have identified some of the reasons to study our topic, we can look at how scholars and professionals have tackled this area of study. In

Chapter 2, we describe three approaches to the study of intercultural communication and give examples of what each approach contributes.

REFERENCES

Adler, P. S. (1975). The transition experience: An alternative view of culture shock. *Journal of Humanistic Psychology, 15*, 13–23.

Banks, J. (1991). *Teaching strategies for ethnic studies.* Needham, MA: Allyn & Bacon.

Fallows, J. (1989). *More like us: Putting America's native strengths and traditional values to work to overcome the Asian challenge.* Boston: Houghton Mifflin.

Gergen, K. (1991). *The saturated self: Dilemmas of identity in contemporary life.* New York: HarperCollins Basic Books.

Griefat, Y., & Katriel, T. (1989). Life demands *musayara:* Communication and culture among Arabs in Israel. In S. Ting-Toomey & F. Korzenny (Eds.), *Language, Communication and Culture: International and Intercultural Communication Annual* (Vol. 13, pp. 121–138).

Howe, N., & Strauss, B. (1993). *13th gen: Abort, retry, ignore, fail?* New York: Vintage Books.

Howell, W. S. (1982). *The empathic communicator.* Belmont, CA: Wadsworth.

Johnson, W. B., & Packer, A. E. (1987). *Workforce 2000: Work and workers for the twenty-first century.* Indianapolis: The Hudson Institute.

Kleinjans, E. (1975). A question of ethics. *International Education and Cultural Exchange, 10*, 20–25.

Kraybill, D. B. (1989). *The riddle of Amish culture.* Baltimore: Johns Hopkins University Press.

McLuhan, M. (1967). *The medium is the message.* New York: Bantam.

Paige, R. M., & Martin, J. N. (1996). Ethics in intercultural training. In D. Landis & R. Bhagat (Eds.), *Handbook of intercultural training.* Newbury Park, CA: Sage.

Patai, R. (1983). *The Arab mind.* New York: Scribner.

Takaki, R. (1989). *Strangers from a different shore.* New York: Penguin.

Wright, M. W. (1993, March 25). Study: Nation's minorities on rise. *Tribune Newspaper,* Tempe, AZ, p. A5.

THEORETICAL APPROACHES TO INTERCULTURAL COMMUNICATION

In this chapter, we describe how the study of intercultural communication got started in the United States. People have pondered the complexities of communication among peoples of different cultures for many centuries. And scholars in many different disciplines, including cultural anthropology, linguistics, and literature, have written about aspects of intercultural encounters. However, only recently did intercultural communication become a formalized and defined area of study. Why did this happen in the United States? How did this field of study evolve as part of communication rather than anthropology or psychology? In the following sections, we explore the development of this subdiscipline and then outline three contemporary perspectives that recognize contributions from other disciplines. In the final section of this chapter, we outline our approach, which integrates the strengths from all three contemporary perspectives.

THE HISTORY OF THE STUDY OF INTERCULTURAL COMMUNICATION

E. T. Hall and the Foreign Service Institute

The study of intercultural communication in the United States can be traced to post–World War II, when business and government were expanding and rebuilding globally. Government and business personnel working overseas often found that they were ill-equipped to deal with the challenges of working among people of different cultures. The language training they received, for example, did little to prepare them for the complex challenges of working abroad.

In response to this situation, the U.S. government passed the Foreign Service Act in 1946 and established the Foreign Service Institute. The Institute hired Edward T. Hall and other prominent anthropologists and linguists (including Ray Birdwhistell and George Trager) to develop "predeparture" courses for overseas workers. Intercultural training materials were scarce, so they developed their own. In so doing, the Institute theorists formed new ways of looking at culture and communication. Thus, the field of intercultural communication was born.

An Innovative Approach to Culture and Communication

Nonverbal Communication   The Institute emphasized the importance of nonverbal communication and applied linguistic frameworks to study nonverbal aspects of communication. The studies concluded that nonverbal communication varied from culture to culture just as language varied. E. T. Hall pioneered this systematic study of culture and communication with *The Silent Language* and *The Hidden Dimension*, which influenced the new field of study. In *The Silent Language*, for example, Hall introduces the notion of proxemics, the study of how people use personal space to communicate. According to his observations, people from contact cultures (found in South America, the Mediterranean, and southern Europe) stand close together and touch frequently when they interact, whereas noncontact people (for example, British and Japanese) maintain more space and touch less often.

In *The Hidden Dimension*, Hall elaborates his study of proxemics and identifies four personal distance zones (Intimate, Personal, Social, and Public) at which people interact. These zones are based on his observations of Americans, mostly in the northeastern part of the United States. Hall describes the sensory input and other characteristics of each zone and suggests that people know which distance to use depending on the situation. He explains that each cultural group has its own set of rules for personal space and that respecting these cultural differences is critical to smooth communication.

Application of Theory   The staff at the Foreign Service Institute (FSI) found that government workers were not interested in theories of culture and communication; rather, workers wanted specific guidelines for getting along in the countries they were visiting. Hall found that workers "could tolerate only a few theoretical statements, although they paid attention to concrete details, real occurrences and were able to learn from them by drawing their own generalizations" (Leeds-Hurwitz, 1990, p. 269). Hall's strategy in developing materials for these predeparture training sessions was initially to observe variations in cultural behavior. At the FSI he was surrounded by people of many different languages and cultures, and he found himself

> as though pulled by hidden strings to hold myself, respond, and listen in quite different ways. I noted that when I was with Germans, I would (without thinking) hold myself stiffly, while with Latin Americans I would be caught up and involved. (Leeds-Hurwitz, p. 269)

He gradually compiled sets of "microcultural" observations. For example, he might have observed that Italians tend to stand close to each other when conversing, or that Greeks use lots of hand gestures when interacting. In contrast, he might have observed that Chinese use few hand gestures in conversations. He then would confirm his observations by consulting members of different cultural groups. Also, when he visited government and business workers overseas, he paid close attention to the particular cultural problems these people experienced.

In his training materials and scholarly essays, Hall offered few generalizations about communication. Instead, he focused on documenting examples of intercultural interaction. This practical approach suited FSI's client needs—and has had a long-lasting effect on the field of intercultural communication. Today, most textbooks in this discipline still focus on practical guidelines and barriers to communication.

This emphasis on the application of theory has spawned a parallel "discipline" of cross-cultural training. Cross-cultural training began with the FSI staff who trained diplomats. It expanded to include overseas training for students and business personnel in the 1960s and 1970s. During the next two decades, it grew to include diversity training, increasingly popular in modern corporations. Diversity trainers facilitate intercultural communication among various gender, ethnic, and racial groups, mostly in the corporate or government workplace (Landis & Bhagat, 1996). Two professional training organizations—the Society for Intercultural Education, Training, and Research (SIETAR International) and the International Division of the American Society for Training and Development (ASTD)—promote intercultural communication. Their memberships include many professional trainers who can trace their interest and knowledge to the contributions of Hall and his colleagues at the FSI.

Emphasis on International Settings   Early scholars and trainers in intercultural communication defined *culture* narrowly, primarily as "nationality." Scholars mostly compared middle-class U.S. citizens to residents of other nations. Trainers tended to focus on helping middle-class professionals become successful overseas. They rarely looked at ways to help ethnic groups within the United States to interact more effectively with each other.

In the 1960s and 1970s, some scholars in the field began to study interracial interaction. In fact, one of the first intercultural communication textbooks, *Transracial Communication* (Smith, 1973), focused on communication between Whites and Blacks in the United States. However, during the 1980s, the focus returned to international contexts and only recently shifted again to domestic applications.

Why, when the United States was fraught with civil unrest in the 1970s, did scholars in this field focus primarily on international contexts instead of domestic cultures? There are several explanations. One is the legacy of Hall and the early emphasis of the FSI on helping overseas personnel. Another explanation is the increasingly common foreign ownership of private industry in the United States. Finally, most scholars who studied intercultural communication were themselves middle-class and educated; they gained their intercultural experience through international contexts such as the Peace Corps, the military, or business abroad.

Interdisciplinary Focus   The scholars at the Foreign Service Institute came from many different disciplines, including linguistics, anthropology, and psychology. In their work related to communication, they drew from theories pertinent to their specific discipline. Contributions from these fields of study blended to form an integrated approach that continues to the present day.

Linguists help us understand the importance of language and its role in intercultural interaction. They describe how languages vary in surface structure and are similar in deep structure. They also shed light on the relationship between language and reality. Two well-known linguists, Edward Sapir and Benjamin Whorf, formulated a theory to describe how perceptions are influenced by the particular language we speak. This theory is known as the Sapir-Whorf hypothesis. An example of the phenomenon it explores is the use of formal and informal pronouns. French and Spanish, for instance, have both formal and informal forms of the pronoun *you*. (In French, the formal is *vous* and the informal is *tu;* in Spanish, the formal is *usted* and the informal is *tu*.) By contrast, English makes no distinction between formal and informal usage. One word, *you*, suffices in both situations. Such language distinctions affect our culture's notion of formality. Linguists also point out that learning a second or third language can enhance one's intercultural competence. Language learning provides insights into other cultures and expands our communication repertoire.

Anthropologists help us understand the role that culture plays in our lives and the importance of nonverbal communication. Anthropologist Renate Rosaldo encouraged scholars to consider the appropriateness of cultural study methods. Other anthropologists have followed Rosaldo's lead. They point out that many U.S. and European studies reveal more about researchers than about the subjects. Many anthropological studies of the past concluded that the people studied were inferior, particularly in studies of non-Europeans. To understand this phenomenon, science writer Stephen Jay Gould argues that "we must first recognize the cultural milieu of a society whose leaders and intellectuals did not doubt the propriety of racial thinking—with Indians below whites, and blacks below everyone else" (1993, p. 85). The so-called scientific study of other peoples is never entirely separate from the culture in which the researchers are immersed. In his study of the Victorian era, for example, Patrick Brantlinger notes that "evolutionary anthropology often suggested that Africans, if not nonhuman or a different species, were such an inferior 'breed' that they might be impervious to 'higher influences'" (1986, p. 201). These conclusions reveal more about the cultural attitudes of the researchers than they do about the people they studied. An interdisciplinary focus can help us view this type of knowledge in a more comprehensive manner—in ways relevant to bettering the intercultural communication process, as well as the production of knowledge.

Psychologists such as Gordon Allport help us understand notions of stereotyping and how prejudice functions in our lives and in intercultural interaction. In his classic study, *The Nature of Prejudice*, he describes how prejudice can develop from "normal" human cognitive activities, like categorization and generalization. Other psychologists, such as Richard Brislin and Dan Landis, reveal how variables like nationality, ethnicity, personality, and gender influence our communication (Harman & Briggs, 1991).

Whereas the early field of intercultural communication was characterized as interdisciplinary, it became increasingly centered in the discipline of communication. Nevertheless, the field continues to be influenced by interdisciplinary contributions, including ideas from cultural studies, critical theory, and the more traditional disciplines of psychology and anthropology. At present, we can identify three broad approaches that characterize the study of culture and communication within the field of communication (B. J. Hall, 1992; Gudykunst & Nishida, 1989; Wiseman, 1995). All three approaches reflect a blend of disciplines.

THREE APPROACHES TO STUDYING INTERCULTURAL COMMUNICATION

Three contemporary approaches to studying intercultural communication are the social science (sometimes called functionalist) approach, the interpretive approach, and the critical approach (Table 2-1). These approaches are based on different fundamental assumptions about human nature, human behavior, and the nature of knowledge (Burrell & Morgan, 1988). Each one contributes in a unique way to our understanding of the relationship between culture and communication. We can learn from each one while recognizing its limitations. These approaches vary in their assumptions about human behavior, their research goals, their conceptualization of culture and communication, and their preferred methodologies.

To examine these three approaches, let us start with a situation that illustrates a communication dilemma. In the early 1990s, Walt Disney Corporation opened its European "Disneyland" near Marne-la-Vallée, just outside of Paris. This corporate venture was plagued with problems from the beginning; by 1994, it was deeply in debt. *Newsweek* writer Jolie Solomon observed:

> *Euro Disney has fallen far short of the dream. A stunning 19 million people have visited the park since it opened, a fact the company trumpets with devotion. But it isn't enough. The guests don't spend enough time or money at the park, and no one will buy the hotels Euro Disney had built and planned to sell. Euro Disney is drowning in debt, and its stock has plunged. (Solomon, 1994, p. 34)*

Many explanations were offered for the problems at Euro Disney, now called Disneyland Paris. Analysts attributed the troubles to everything from lack of sunshine in this part of France to cross-cultural misunderstandings and French resistance to the cultural imperialism of the U.S. Disney conglomerate. Although the problem was due in part to a failing economy (a recession occurred just after the park opened), a significant part of the problem was culture-based. We will use three approaches to analyze the situation and explain the problem. In so doing, we will also outline the characteristics of these three approaches and provide other examples for exploring the approach. We also discuss the contributions and limitations of each perspective to the study of intercultural communication.

The Social Science Approach

The social science approach (also called the functionalist approach) was most popular in the 1980s. It is based on research in psychology and sociology. This approach assumes a describable external reality. It also assumes that human behavior is predictable and that the researcher's goal is to describe and also predict behavior. Researchers who take this approach use quantitative methods. Usually they gather data by questionnaire, but sometimes they observe subjects firsthand.

TABLE 2-1	THREE APPROACHES TO INTERCULTURAL COMMUNICATION		
	Social Science (or Functionalist)	**Interpretive**	**Critical**
Discipline on which approach is founded	Psychology	Anthropology, sociolinguistics	Various
Research goal	Describe and predict behavior	Describe behavior	Change behavior
Assumption of reality	External and describable	Subjective	Subjective
Assumptions of human behavior	Predictable	Creative and voluntary	Changeable
Method of study	Survey, observation	Participant observation, field study	Textual analysis of media
Relationship of culture and communication	Communication influenced by culture	Culture created and maintained through communication	Culture as a site of power struggles
Contribution of the approach	Identifies cultural variations; recognizes cultural differences in many aspects of communication, but often does not consider context	Emphasizes that communication and culture and cultural differences should be studied in context	Recognizes the economic and political forces in culture and communication, that all intercultural interactions are characterized by power

Social science researchers assume that culture is a variable that can be measured. Culture influences communication much the same as a personality trait does. The goal of this research, then, is to predict specifically how culture influences communication.

Methods   To understand the Disneyland Paris fiasco, social science researchers would try to identify cultural differences between French and U.S. communication and then predict success or failure based on these cultural differences. Let's see how this might work. There are many examples of how cultural patterns collided in the operation and management of the theme park. Disney management and French employees differed in their approach to rules and regulations. Disney has a strictly regulated corporate culture: Employees cannot wear heavy makeup, grow beards or mustaches, or let their fingernails grow longer than 0.2 inches; employees are encouraged to smile. Also, Disney management mandates that lines waiting for rides should be orderly and that grounds be fastidiously maintained. Finally, there was the issue of eating and drinking. According to one journalist's account, the French were stunned to

This photo of Disneyland Paris might easily be confused with Disneyland in Tokyo or Disneyland in the United States. Although each Disneyland may appear similar there are important cultural differences at each location that need to be recognized. These differences are important to understanding intercultural communication. *(© Chad Ehlers / Tony Stone Images, Inc.)*

discover that there was no beer or wine at the theme park. Also, "unlike Americans, who will wander around, hot dog in hand, Europeans seemed determined to eat at a set time" (Solomon, p. 38).

The rules and cultural patterns imposed by Disney clash with French values—a singular distrust of conformity, a disrespect for mandated procedures, and a love of style and savoir faire. As E. T. Hall and Mildred Hall explain:

> *The French are impatient with conformity because they don't like to follow the crowd. . . . Procedures are taken less seriously in France than in the United States. . . . Procedures tend to bore the French; they think they inhibit their creativity and impinge on their individuality. They tend to be disrespectful of the law. (Hall & Hall, 1990, p. 106)*

On the other hand, some things—like eating and drinking well—do require the proper form.

> *A French meal is a work of art, a composition not unlike a painting. Everything must fit together to create a perfect arrangement: the different courses of the meal, the cuisine, the wines, the service, the flowers, the setting. (Hall & Hall, p. 107)*

Formal meals are not a Disney priority. The theme park is not set up to accommodate the dining expectations of French patrons.

Finally, there is the notion of smiling. U.S. service industries value smiling more than the French do. French reporters from the French newspaper *Libération noticed this curious phenomenon of smiling, which, they said, quite unsettled home-grown [French] visitors. One of the French staff confided to them, they reported, "the foreigners are used to being smiled at, but the French don't understand it. They think they are being taken for idiots." (Rees, 1992, p. 58)*

Several contemporary research programs illustrate the social science approach. One such program is headed by William Gudykunst, a leading communication researcher. Gudykunst tried to discover if people from different cultures varied in their strategies for reducing uncertainty on first encounter. He found that strategies varied depending on whether people were from individualist or collectivist cultures (Gudykunst, 1983; Gudykunst & Nishida, 1984). For example, many people in the United States, which has an individualist orientation, ask direct questions when interacting with acquaintances. In cultures that have a more collectivist orientation, people are more likely to use an indirect approach.

The communication accommodation theory is the result of another social science program. In this program, researchers have attempted to identify how and when individuals accommodate their speech and nonverbal behavior to others during an interaction. Researchers posit that in some situations individuals will change their communication patterns to accommodate others (Gallois, Giles, Jones, Cargile, & Ota, 1995). Individuals are likely to adapt during low-threat interactions or situations in which they see little difference between themselves and others. The underlying assumption is that we accommodate when we feel positive toward the other person. For example, when we talk to international students, we may speak more slowly, enunciate more clearly, use less jargon, and mirror the other's communication. We also may adapt to regional speech. For example, when Tom, one of the authors of this book, talks with someone from the South, he starts to "drawl" and use words like *y'all.* Of course, it is possible to overaccommodate; for example, if a European American speaks Black English to an African American, this may be perceived as over-accommodation.

Many social science studies explain how communication styles vary from culture to culture. Dean Barnlund, a well-known intercultural communication scholar, compared Japanese and U.S. communication styles. He identified many differences, including how members of the two groups give compliments and apologies. Although people in both countries seem to prefer a simple apology, U.S. residents tend to apologize (and compliment) more often, and Japanese prefer to *do* something whereas Americans tend to *explain* as a way to apologize.

Another group of social science studies investigated how travelers adapted overseas. They tried to predict which travelers would be the most successful. These researchers found that a variety of factors—including age, gender, language, preparation, and personality characteristics—influenced how well someone adapted (Kim, 1988).

Strengths and Limitations   Many of these social science studies have been useful at identifying how communication varies from group to group. They also have identified some of the psychological and sociological variables in the communication process. However, this approach is limited. Many scholars now realize that human communication is often more creative than predictable, and that reality is not just external but that humans also construct reality. We cannot identify all of the variables that affect our communication. Nor can we predict exactly why one intercultural interaction seems successful and others do not.

Scholars also recognize that some methods used in this approach are not culturally sensitive; sometimes researchers are too distant from the phenomena or people they are researching. In other words, researchers may not really understand the cultural groups they are studying. For example, suppose we conducted a study that compared self-disclosure in the United States and Algeria using the social science perspective. We might distribute Jourard's self-disclosure measure (a common instrument used in U.S. research) to students in both countries. However, we might not realize that the concept of self-disclosure does not translate exactly between the United States and Algeria. Algerians and U.S. residents may have different notions of this concept.

To overcome these kinds of problems, social scientists have developed strategies for achieving equivalence of measures. A leading cross-cultural psychologist, Richard Brislin (1993), has written extensively on guidelines for cross-cultural researchers. He has identified several types of equivalencies that researchers should establish, including conceptual equivalence and translation equivalence. For example, when conducting cross-cultural studies literal translations are inadequate. To establish translation equivalence, research materials should be translated several times, using different translators. Materials that proceed smoothly through these multiple steps are considered translation equivalent.

Researchers can establish conceptual equivalence by making sure that the notions they are investigating are similar at various levels. For example, the notion of problem solving is one aspect of intelligence that may be conceptually equivalent in many cultures. Once this equivalence is established, researchers can identify culture-specific ways in which problem solving is achieved. In the United States, and western Europe, good problem solving might mean quick cognitive reasoning. In other cultures, it might be slow and careful thought (Serpell, 1982). Establishing these equivalencies allows the researcher to isolate and describe what distinguishes one culture from another.

The Interpretive Approach

The interpretive approach gained prominence in the late 1980s among communication scholars. One interpretive approach, founded in sociolinguistics, is the ethnography of communication (Hymes, 1974). Ethnographers of communication are devoted to descriptive studies of communication patterns within specific cultural groups. Interpretive researchers assume that reality is not just external to humans but also that humans construct reality. They believe that human experience, including communication, is subjective. They also believe that human behavior is creative, not determined or easily predicted.

There are many ways of studying and learning about cultural patterns that are different from our own. One way is by interviewing other people, which is this young woman's approach as she talks to a member of the Old Order Brethren in Manheim, Pennsylvania. What are some of the strengths and weaknesses of interviewing as a research strategy? (© *Jeff Greenburg/PhotoEdit*)

The goal of the interpretive researcher is to understand and describe human behavior. (Predicting behavior is not a goal.) Whereas the social science perspective tends to see communication as influenced by culture, the interpretivist sees culture as created and maintained through communication (Carbaugh, 1996). This type of research uses methods derived from anthropology and linguistics: field studies, observations, and participant observations. (A researcher engaging in participant observation contributes actively to the communication processes being observed and studied.) It also assumes that the researcher will be intimately involved in the research and may become good friends with members of the communities he or she is studying.

Another example of interpretive research is the rhetorical approach, perhaps the oldest communication scholarship, dating back to the Greeks in the 5th century B.C. Rhetoricians typically examine and analyze texts or public speeches. They try to interpret the meanings of texts or oral discourses in the contexts in which they occur.

Cross-cultural psychologists use the terms *etic* and *emic* to distinguish the social science and interpretive approaches. These terms were borrowed from linguistics, *etic* stemming from phon*etic* and *emic* from phon*emic*. Social science research usually searches for universal generalization. In this way it is "etic." By contrast, the interpretive research approach usually focuses on understanding communication patterns from the inside of a particular cultural community or context. Researchers try to describe patterns or rules that individuals follow in particular contexts. They tend (though not always) to be more interested in describing cultural behavior in one community, rather than in making cross-cultural comparisons.

Methods   How would an interpretive researcher investigate the Euro Disney context? One such study was conducted by a team of communication researchers, headed by Professor John Jarvis. The researchers obtained permission to live at the theme park for a month. They trained as new employees (called "castmembers") and conducted informal interviews and conversations with employees. Their goal was to "try to see the meanings Euro Disney employees were making of their experience in the Park as clearly as possible from their own perspective" (Jarvis, 1995, p. 2). They also supplemented their participant observations with formal interviews, to "ground themselves in the official version of Disney culture as it is perceived by managers and top executives in the Park" (p. 2).

They discovered serious workplace conflicts between U.S. and non-U.S. corporate culture at Disneyland Paris. Through their interviews and participant observations, they found that management and workers operated with conflicting values. They found that the French workers resented the U.S. Disney "culture" being forced on them—being told they had to smile and be enthusiastic. Workers also resented the assumption that management and workers could be friends. France has a long history of bad relations between workers and bosses.

These interpretivists discovered some of the same findings that a social science researcher might have, although they approached it in a unique way. They did not assume that because French and U.S. cultures are different they would find different outcomes. They simply began the project with a general research question and tried to understand the Disneyland Paris experience from the point of view of the participants (Jarvis, 1995). In addition, because of their involvement they also had experiential data on which to base their interpretations. Essentially, they lived through the intercultural conflict that occurred in this community.

Other examples of interpretive research are studies investigating the communication patterns in many different groups—from the Burundi in Africa and the Athabascan in Northern Canada to cultural groups within the United States. An example is Gerry Philipsen's study of the communication patterns of men and women in a working class neighborhood of Chicago called Teamsterville (Philipsen, 1990). Philipsen discovered that men in this community consider speaking to be important only in some situations. For example, Teamsterville males speak when asserting male solidarity but not when asserting power and influence in interpersonal situations. That is, they are more likely to talk when they are with their equals, their buddies, than when they are with their children or with superiors. With superiors or subordinates, other forms of communication are appropriate. With children, for example, they are more likely to use gestures or disciplinary action instead of speech. When they are with someone of higher status, such as a school principal, they may seek out a mediator—for example, the neighborhood priest—rather than speak directly to the principal.

Another interpretive study is Donald Carbaugh's (1990) analysis of the communication rules on a U.S. TV talk show. Carbaugh watched and analyzed many hours of the *Donahue* show and concluded that the way guests and audience members talked reflected notions of self. He identified the following four communication rules of interacting as exhibited on the program:

1. The preferred communication style is to present the self through opinions.
2. Participants have the right to present themselves.
3. Participants' right to speak, and their presentations, are respected.
4. The audience prefers individualistic rather than universal opinions.

Carbaugh then shows how these rules reflect the European American notions of personhood and identity, based on a cultural value of individualism.

Molefi Asante's (1987) notion of Afrocentricity provides another example of the interpretive approach. Asante emphasizes that describing the communication rules of a given people must be grounded in the beliefs and values of that particular group. Whereas most scholarly studies in communication are based on European research perspectives, he suggests that this frame of reference is not applicable to African American communication.

Afrocentricity involves five assumptions that people of African descent share. These are:

1. A common origin and experience of struggle

2. An element of resistance to European legal procedures, medicines, and political processes

3. Traditional values of humaneness and harmony with nature

4. A fundamentally African way of knowing and interpreting the world

5. A value for communalism

Communication scholars have used this framework to understand various aspects of contemporary African American communication. For example, Garner (1994) stresses the strong oral tradition of African Americans and identifies rhetorical assumptions that include indirection, improvisation and inventiveness, and playfully toned behavior. These assumptions underlay communication in many African American contexts, including rapping, playing the dozens (an aggressive verbal contest, often involving obscene language), and signifying (the verbal art of insult, in which a speaker jokingly talks about, needles, and puts down the listener).

Janice Hamlet (1994) explains the unique qualities of African American preaching in similar terms. She emphasizes the strong participative nature of the call and response and ties this style to the cultural emphasis on emotionalism, interaction, spiritualism, and the power of the spoken word in Black churches. In this way, the Bible is interpreted by Black preachers in the contexts of African American culture and experiences. Both Garner's and Hamlet's studies are descriptive of particular communication patterns of one cultural group. Both scholars use emic methods in trying to describe communication in a way that reflects and captures the cultural experience and lives of African Americans.

Strengths and Limitations The utility of the interpretivist approach is that it provides an in-depth understanding of communication patterns in particular communities because it emphasizes investigating communication in context. We learn more about African American communication in religious contexts and popular U.S. communication in TV talk show contexts than we would know by passing out a questionnaire with general questions on African American and European American communication.

The limitation of this approach is that there are few interpretivist studies of *intercultural* communication. Interpretive scholars typically have not studied what happens when two groups come in contact with each other. However, there are some comparative studies, including Jarvis's study of Disneyland Paris and Charles Braithwaite's study that compares rules for silence in 15 different communities (Carbaugh, 1990).

A second limitation is that the researchers often are outsiders to the communities, which means that they may not represent accurately the communication patterns as seen by the members of that community. For example, consider Renate Rosaldo's study of the cultural practices of the Ilongot in the Philippines, particularly of their practice of headhunting. Rosaldo's initial descriptions attempt to document the expressed connection between grief and headhunting.

Reflecting back on his own work, Rosaldo (1989) describes how his earlier limited understanding changed when his own wife fell to her death from a mountain trail during one of their trips to the Philippines. During his intense mourning for his wife, he came to understand better the link between grief and headhunting, which he had described in naive academic terms. As Rosaldo explains, he became an "insider" to the experience of grieving and rage. He tells of the intense anger he felt at the death of his wife, and the rage that he needed to deal with in the grieving process. He realized that headhunting was a symbolic process meant both to vent anger at death and to re-establish order in the Ilongot community.

Rosaldo subsequently reread studies of his own ethnic (Latino) community and reinterpreted the studies as an insider. His new interpretations overcame the scholarly descriptions' limitations. Such opportunities are rare, though.

The Critical Approach

A third approach includes many assumptions of the interpretive approach. That is, critical researchers believe in subjective (not objective) reality. They also emphasize the importance of studying the context in which communication occurs. However, they usually focus on macrocontexts—for example, the political and social structures that influence communication. Critical scholars, unlike most social science and interpretive scholars, are interested in the historical context of communication (Putnam & Pacanowsky, 1983).

Critical scholars are always interested in understanding the power relations in communication. Identifying cultural differences is important only in relation to power differentials. In this perspective, culture is seen as a site of struggle, a place where multiple interpretations come together, but where there is always a dominant force. The goal of critical researchers is not only to understand human behavior but to change the lives of everyday communicators. Researchers assume that by examining and writing about how power functions in cultural situations, the average person will learn how to resist forces of power and oppression.

The methods preferred by critical scholars are usually textual analyses. That is, they generally analyze cultural "products," such as media (TV, movies, journalistic essays), rather than observing or participating in face-to-face interactions or conducting surveys.

Methods   In analyzing the Disneyland Paris situation, a critical scholar might see the theme park as a site of cultural struggle. On the one hand, the Disney leadership considers the exportation of Disney icons (Mickey Mouse; Donald Duck; Main Street, U.S.A.; Fantasyland; and so on) as benign international trade that represents the "American Dream," originality, and a universal human innocence (Eisner, 1991, p. 39). On the other hand, many French see Disneyland Paris as the worst example of cultural imperialism, a "cultural Chernobyl." They feel as if the Disney icons are imposed on them, as if Disney is taking over and replacing existing French cultural values such as love of literature, the French style of savoir faire, savoir vivre. It would even seem that French cultural values and Disney values are diametrically opposed.

In *Le Figaro*, Jean Cau of the Académie Française describes Euro Disney as

*this horror of cardboard, plastic, atrocious colors, solidified chewing gum construc-
tions, and idiotic folk stories that come straight out of cartoon books for fat Americans. It is going to wipe out millions of children . . . mutilate their imagination.
(Rees, 1992, p. 57)*

Cau's view is shared by others and reflects that of the late French premier
Georges Clemenceau. Michael Eisner, president and CEO of Disney, quoted
Clemenceau as stating that, "America is one nation in history that has gone
miraculously directly from barbarism to degeneration without the usual interval
of civilization" (Eisner, 1991, p. 41).

Critical scholars might also analyze public relations of Disney. According to
some French journalists, Disney's approach was very heavy handed; they cite as
evidence the fact that the Disney people controlled access to information and
rarely returned phone calls. They also maintained strict regulations about interviews, requiring that interview requests be made in writing and that a representative from the Disneyland Paris communication team always be present
(Fawcett, 1992, p. 14). The skirmishes are instructive examples of the resistance
that U.S. pop culture meets from intellectuals in some countries where it is con-
sumed avidly by mass audiences (Rudolph, 1991, p. 48).

Critical scholars might analyze the aspects of U.S. culture and history being
exported and represented as the "American experience." For example, the theme
park attraction Frontierland includes the "Rustler Roundup Shootin' Gallery,"
and the "Cottonwood Creek Ranch." Critical scholars might examine what it
means to present an era of American history typified by the Western expansion.
They also might analyze whose point of view is being represented. Does the attraction portray the experience of Native Americans, Asian Americans, working
class European Americans?

A current example of critical scholarship is Janice Peck's (1993/94) analysis
of a series of *Oprah Winfrey* segments on racism. Peck identifies three discourses
about racism: liberal, therapeutic, and religious. The liberal discourse emphasizes the individual's response to racism and can result in a double bind: Although individual rights must be respected, racism also violates others' rights.
The therapeutic discourse sees prejudice and stereotyping as simple operations
of human thinking, which can be corrected through education. The religious
discourse about racism relies on the notions of "understanding" and equality before God. Here, racism is seen as a lack of understanding, a failure to recognize
others as divine creations.

Peck's point is that these three ways of talking about racism are all individual-
centered and place all of the responsibility on individual actions for subjective
change. She emphasizes that these discourses fail to focus on many of the root
causes of racism—social structures and practices such as redlining, the banking
practice of automatically denying home mortgage loans to people who live in
specific areas.

Another example of a critical study is Tom Nakayama's analysis of the movie
Showdown in Little Tokyo, which depicts two Los Angeles police officers investigating a murder. One is European American; the other is of mixed European

Asian American heritage. Nakayama's analysis shows that the movie's narrative, its use of camera shot sequences, and other aspects of the movie favor the European American character over the Asian American character. For example, the European American police officer is portrayed as more physically attractive. This character is the one who gets the love interest.

Nakayama emphasizes that this type of relationship between majority and ethnic characters in movies is so prevalent in our everyday culture that we don't ever question the superiority of Whites. We identify with this dominant view of the world, even though it is one that an increasing number of people in the United States do not share.

Strengths and Limitations   The critical approach emphasizes the power relations in intercultural interactions and the importance of social and historical contexts. However, one limitation is that it does not focus on face-to-face intercultural interaction. Rather, most critical studies focus on popular media forms of communication—TV shows, music videos, magazine advertisements, and so on. Also, this approach does not allow for much empirical data. For example, Janice Peck did not measure the audience reaction to the *Oprah Winfrey* segments; her essay merely analyzes these TV discourses.

A final limitation is that critical studies rarely focus on international contexts. Mostly, they study culture and communication in domestic settings. In part, this may be so because it is difficult to understand the role of power in intercultural interactions—for example, when U.S. residents and Japanese interact. The social, historical, and political ramifications are indeed complex.

A DIALECTICAL APPROACH TO UNDERSTANDING CULTURE AND COMMUNICATION

The authors of this book see the social science, interpretive, and critical approaches as operating in interconnected and sometimes contradictory ways. A dialectical approach accepts these contradictions and ambiguities in a "yin and yang" manner.

This is the approach we have taken in this book. We see that cultural reality is both objective and subjective. Culture influences and is influenced by communication. It is also an arena where power struggles are played out. Communication is individual and it is also social.

We assume that we can learn something from each of the three approaches. Our understanding of intercultural communication has been enriched by all three approaches. Combining the three, as our Disneyland Paris example shows, provides us with a rich and extensive understanding of the problems and challenges of this and other intercultural ventures. And research findings can actually make a difference in the everyday world.

From the social science perspective, we see how specific cultural differences might predict communication conflicts. From an interpretive investigation, we have the opportunity to confirm what we predict in a hypothetical social science study. This was the case with the Disneyland Paris example. The employees and the management at the theme park interpreted their experience as conflictual. In fact, the research findings actually led to modifications in the training and management at Disneyland Paris (Jarvis, 1995). The Disney management adopted a more French approach to training and provided more historical background when presenting the Disney philosophy. By taking a more collaborative intercultural approach, conflicts were reduced and training ran more smoothly. The critical approach on Disneyland Paris raises some questions about the issue of exporting popular culture and challenges us to examine our assumptions about the neutrality of intercultural experiences.

Employing these different perspectives is like taking pictures of a room from different angles. No single angle or snapshot gives us the truth, but taking pictures from different angles gives a more comprehensive view of the room. The knowledge we gain from any of these approaches is enhanced by the knowledge gained from the other approaches.

The approach taken for this book combines the three approaches and emphasizes four components to consider in understanding intercultural communication. These are culture, communication, context, and power. Culture and communication are the foreground, but context and power are the backdrop against which we can understand intercultural communication.

The Component of Culture

Culture is often considered the core concept in intercultural communication. One characteristic of culture is that it functions largely at a subconscious level. Trying to understand one's own culture is like trying to explain to a fish that it lives in water. Therefore, we often cannot identify our own cultural backgrounds and assumptions until we encounter assumptions that are different from our own.

Consider the following example. During a trip to Paris, one of the authors of this book, Tom, learned about a U.S. cultural pattern of shopping. In France, cultural norms dictate that shoppers greet the shopkeeper before they begin to gather items. In shopping, he realized that the U.S. norm is to simply start shopping. All facets of French life have what is sometimes called *la forme de la politesse*, or a structured way of manners. As Louis-Bernard Robitaille explains in a Montreal magazine:

> *In France, there are an infinite number of rites, terms, and manners that must be assimilated, known and scrupulously respected if one has any intention of surviving in this society.* (En France, il y a en nombre infini des rites, des usages, et des manières qu'il faut assimiler, qu'il faut saisir, et qu'il faut respecter scrupuleusement si l'on a l'intention de vivre en société; *1995, p. 68*)

Culture has been defined in many ways—from a pattern of perception that influences communication, to a site of contestation and conflict. Because there are many acceptable definitions of culture, and because culture is complex, it is important to reflect on the centrality of culture in our own interactions. The next chapter examines more fully the various definitions and explanations of culture.

The Component of Communication

The second component, communication, is as complex as culture. The defining characteristic of communication is meaning, and communication occurs when individuals attach meaning to behavior. However, meaning gets constructed in more than just the communication event. Meaning depends on the way in which words are used and on the meanings they conveyed in previous communication encounters. Also, although we may intend to communicate particular messages, we may also convey unintended messages.

We define *communication* as the symbolic processes of human interaction. One of the primary features of communication is that it is social: It is organized and produced in relation to a social structure that favors particular forms, speakers, and audiences over other communicative forms, speakers, and audiences. When we examine communication, we can study the ways in which meaning is constructed according to the social organization. In other words, we can try to understand what kinds of meanings are generated, by whom, and for what purposes.

Communication is the use of language and other systems of symbols. As such, it is like *discourse*. Because communication requires participants to become involved, it is a social practice. We cannot interpret things in any way we please; to do so would make communication impossible. Yet, our adherence to the social systems of communication does not mean that we cannot maneuver and bend the rules to create new understandings in the communication process. Unlike computer languages, human communication allows for a wider range of messages to be constructed. In intercultural communication, this is central to the ways that we communicate with others and how they use communication.

The Context of Communication

Context is important because it often defines and sets up expectations for the communication that occurs. Context can be seen as physical, social, or political. Consider, for example, the contextual expectations for weekend dress (a form of nonverbal communication) at the office. On weekends, professors might come to work at the office in shorts and t-shirts. However, in the same location during the work week, the context changes and expectations are different. Throughout this book, we examine different kinds of contexts and their influence on intercultural communication.

The Element of Power in Communication

Power pervades every communication event, although it is not always evident or obvious how power influences communication and what kinds of meanings are constructed as a result. For example, in contemporary society cosmetic companies have a vested interest in a particular image of female beauty that involves purchasing and using makeup. Advertising encourages women to feel compelled to participate in this cultural definition. What happens if someone decides not to buy into this definition? Regardless of the woman's individual reasons for not participating, other people are likely to interpret her behavior in ways that may not match her own individual reasons. What her unadorned face communicates is understood against a backdrop of society's definitions—that is, the backdrop developed by the cosmetics industry.

Power in this sense should be thought of in broad terms. Dominant cultural groups attempt to perpetuate their positions of privilege in many ways. However, subordinate groups can resist this domination in many ways, too.

Cultural groups can use political and legal means to maintain or resist domination. But these are not the only means of invoking power relations. Groups can negotiate their various relations to culture through economic boycotts, strikes, and sit-ins. Individuals can subscribe (or not subscribe) to specific magazines or newspapers, change TV channels, write letters to government officials, or take action in other ways to change the influence of power.

SUMMARY

The study of intercultural communication in the United States began with the Foreign Service Institute, established in 1946. It drew from different disciplines and emphasized practical ways to facilitate communication among cultural groups. Three contemporary study approaches developed from the different disciplines. These are the social science approach, the interpretive approach, and the critical approach. Combined, these three approaches form the dialectical perspective, based on four touchstones that provide a framework for thinking about intercultural communication: culture, communication, context, and power.

The next chapter describes more fully the two most important elements, culture and communication, and examines how these two interact with issues of context and power to form our understanding of intercultural communication.

REFERENCES

Allport, G. W. (1979). *The nature of prejudice*. Reading, MA: Addison-Wesley.

Asante, M. K. (1987). *The Afrocentric idea*. Philadelphia, PA: Temple University Press.

Barnlund, D. C., & Yoshioka, M. (1990). Apologies: Japanese and American styles. *International Journal of Intercultural Relations, 14*, 193–205.

Berry, J. W. (1980). Introduction to methodology. In H. C. Triandis & J. W. Berry (Eds.), *Handbook of Cross Cultural Psychology: Vol. 2. Methodology* (pp. 1–28). Needham Heights, MA: Allyn & Bacon.

Braithwaite, C. (1990). Communicative silence: A cross cultural study of Basso's hypothesis. In D. Carbaugh (Ed.), *Cultural Communication and intercultural contact* (pp. 321–328). Hillsdale, NJ: Lawrence Erlbaum.

Brantlinger, P. (1986). Victorians and Africans: The genealogy of the myth of the dark continent. In H. L. Gates, Jr. (Ed.), *"Race," writing and difference* (pp. 185–222). Chicago: University of Chicago Press. (Original work published in 1985)

Brislin, R. (1993). *Understanding culture's influence on behavior.* Fort Worth, TX: Harcourt Brace Jovanovich.

Burrell, G., & Morgan, G. (1988). *Sociological paradigms and organizational analysis.* Portsmouth, NH: Heineman.

Carbaugh, D. (1990). Communication rules in Donahue discourse. In D. Carbaugh (Ed.), *Cultural communication and intercultural contact* (pp. 119–149). Hillsdale, NJ: Lawrence Erlbaum.

———. (1996). *Situating selves: The communication of social identities in American scenes.* Albany, NY: State University of New York Press.

Eisner, E. (1991, Fall). *NPQ,* pp. 39–41.

Fawcett, K. (1992, Dec.). *IABC communication world,* 13–16.

Gallois, C., Giles, H., Jones, E., Cargile, A. C., & Ota, H. (1995). Accommodating intercultural encounters: Elaborations and extensions. In R. L. Wiseman (Ed.), *Intercultural communication theory* (pp. 115–147). Newbury Park, CA: Sage.

Garner, T. (1994). Oral rhetorical practice in African American culture. In A. González, M. Houston, V. Chen (Eds.), *Our voices: Essays in culture, ethnicity and communication* (pp. 81–91). Los Angeles: Roxbury Publishing.

Gould, S. J. (1993). American polygeny and craniometry before Darwin: Blacks and Indians as separate, inferior species. In S. Harding (Ed.), *The "racial" economy of science: Toward a democratic future* (pp. 84–115). Bloomington: Indiana University Press. (Original work published in 1981)

Gudykunst, W. B. (1983). Uncertainty reduction and predictability of behavior in low and high context cultures. *Communication Quarterly, 31,* 49–55.

———. (1985). The influence of cultural similarity, type of relationship and self-monitoring on uncertainty reduction processes. *Communication Monographs, 52,* 203–217.

Gudykunst, W. B., & Nishida, T. (1984). Individual and cultural influences on uncertainty reduction. *Communication Monographs, 51,* 23–36.

———. (1989). Theoretical perspectives for studying intercultural communication. In M. F. Asante & W. B. Gudykunst (Eds.), *Handbook of international and intercultural communication* (pp. 17–46). Newbury Park, CA: Sage.

Hall, B. J. (1992). Theories of culture and communication. *Communication Theory, 1,* pp. 50–70.

Hall, E. T. (1959). *The silent language.* Garden City, NY: Doubleday.

Hall, E. T. (1966). *The hidden dimension.* Garden City, NY: Doubleday.

Hall, E. T., & Hall, M. (1990). *Understanding cultural differences.* Yarmouth, ME: Intercultural Press.

Hamlet, J. (1994). Understanding traditional African American preaching. In

A. González, M. Houston, & V. Chen (Eds.), *Our voices: Essays in culture, ethnicity and communication* (pp. 100–103). Los Angeles: Roxbury Publishing.

Harman, R. C., & Briggs, N. E. (1991). SIETAR survey: Perceived contributions of the social sciences to intercultural communication. *International Journal of Intercultural Relations, 15,* 19–28.

Hymes, D. (1974). *Foundations in sociolinguistics: An ethnographic approach.* Philadelphia: University of Pennsylvania Press.

Jarvis, J. (1995). *Euro Disneyland Paris cultural research project.* (Report No. 2). Pittsburgh, PA: Robert Morris College.

Kim, Y. Y. (1988). *Communication and cross-cultural adaptation.* Philadelphia: Multilingual Matters.

Landis, D., & Bhagat, R. (1996). *Handbook of intercultural training* (2nd ed.). Thousand Oaks, CA: Sage.

Leeds-Hurwitz, W. (1990). Notes on the history of intercultural communication: The Foreign Service Institute and the mandate for intercultural training. *The Quarterly Journal of Speech, 76,* 262–281.

Nakayama, T. K. (1994). Show/down time: "Race," gender, sexuality, and popular culture, *Critical Studies in Mass Communication, 11,* 162–179.

Peck, J. (1993/94). Talk about racism: Framing a popular discourse of race on Oprah Winfrey, *Cultural Critique, 27,* 89–126.

Philipsen, G. (1990). Speaking 'like a man' in Teamsterville. In D. Carbaugh (Ed.), *Cultural communication and intercultural contact* (pp. 11–20). Hillsdale, NJ: Lawrence Erlbaum.

Pike, R. (1966). *Language in relation to a united theory of the structure of human behavior.* The Hague: Mouton.

Putnam, L. (1983). The interpretive perspective. In L. Putnam & M. Pacanowsky (Eds.), *Communication and organizations: An interpretive approach.* Newbury Park, CA: Sage.

Rees, J. (1992, May 11). The mouse that ate France. *National Review,* pp. 57–61.

Robitaille, L.-B. (1995, April 15). La terre de la grande complication. *L'actualité,* pp. 67–69.

Rosaldo, R. (1989). *Culture and truth: The remaking of social analysis.* Boston: Beacon.

Rudolph, B. (1991, March 25). Monsieur Mickey. *Time,* pp. 48–49.

Serpell, R. (1982) Measures of perception, skills and intelligence: The growth of a new perspective on children in a third world country. In W. Hartrup (Ed.), *Review of child development research, 6.* Chicago: University of Chicago Press.

Smith, A. L. (a.k.a. Asante, M. K.) (1973). *Transracial communication.* Englewood Cliffs, NJ: Prentice-Hall.

Solomon, J. (1994, February 14). Mickey's trip to trouble. *Newsweek,* pp. 34–39.

Wiseman, R. L. (Ed.) (1995). *Intercultural communication theory.* Newbury Park, CA: Sage.

CHAPTER THREE

CULTURE, CONTEXT, AND POWER IN INTERCULTURAL COMMUNICATION

The context in which communication occurs is an important factor in intercultural communication. This is a photo of Vienna, Austria. In what ways do you think this context (an urban, German-speaking city with a long and varied history) would be different from where you live? How would cultural expectations be different? *(© Adam Woolfitt/Woodfin Camp and Associates)*

In the last chapter, we looked at the brief history of intercultural communication studies, examined three theoretical approaches, and identified four important issues to consider in our approach to intercultural communication. In this chapter, we continue discussing these four issues, which are culture, communication, context, and power. We also discuss their interrelatedness as a foundation for examining intercultural communication.

WHAT IS CULTURE?

Culture is a word that we are all familiar with but that is difficult to define. The late British writer Raymond Williams wrote that culture "is one of the two or three most complicated words in the English language" (1983). Its complexity indicates the many ways in which it influences intercultural communication (Williams, 1981).

Culture is more than just a part of the practice of intercultural communication. How we think about culture frames our thinking about intercultural communication. For example, if we think that culture is defined by nation-states, then communication between a Japanese and an Italian would be intercultural

There are many different definitions of culture. Here are a few of the most common ones, as given by prominent anthropologists. These show the range and some of the contradictions of various meanings.

> *Culture is the learned, socially acquired traditions and lifestyles of the members of a society, including their patterned, repetitive ways of thinking, feeling and acting (i.e., behaving). . . . Some anthropologists, however, restrict the meaning of culture exclusively to the mental rules for acting and speaking shared by members of a given society. These rules are seen as constituting a kind of grammar of behavior. Actions are then regarded as "social" rather than "cultural."*
> —M. Harris, *Cultural Anthropology* (1983), p. 5.

> *Looking across at our primate relatives learning local traditions, using tools, and manipulating symbols, we can no longer say comfortably that "culture" is the heritage of learned symbolic behavior that makes humans human.*
> —R. M. Keesing, "Theories of Culture," p. 42 in *Language, Culture, and Cognition* (1981), edited by R. W. Casson.

> *It is not all of what an individual knows and thinks and feels about his world. It is his* theory of what fellows know, believe, and mean, *his theory of the code being followed, the game being played, in the society into which he was born.*
> —R. M. Keesing, p. 58.

> *Culture lends significance to human experience by selecting from and organizing it. It refers broadly to the forms through which people make sense of their lives, rather than more narrowly to the opera or art of museums.*
> —R. Rosaldo, *Culture and Truth: The Remaking of Social Analysis* (1989), p. 26.

> *We refer to "a culture" (as we might refer to "a society") meaning an autonomous population unit defined by distinctive cultural characteristics or shared tradition. . . . It may also refer to a system of values, ideas and behaviors which may be associated with one or more than one social or national group (e.g., "black American culture," "Western culture," and so on. . . .) We may also speak of the "personal culture" of a single individual. In these usages the term identifies not a population unit but a system of ideas, beliefs and behaviors which the anthropologist isolates for the purposes of his study.*
> —C. Seymour-Smith, *Macmillan Dictionary of Anthropology* (1986), pp. 65–66.

communication because Japan and Italy are nation-states. By this definition, an encounter between an Asian American from North Carolina and an African American from California would not be considered intercultural communication because North Carolina and California are not nation-states.

In this chapter, a singular definition of culture is not being advocated. Any one definition is too restrictive. This term has many definitions; these different definitions offer flexibility to ways of approaching intercultural communication.

By and large, social science researchers do not focus on culture per se but on the influence of culture on communication. In other words, the concern of such studies is on communication differences due to culture. Such researchers give little attention to the ways that culture is conceptualized or seen to function. Culture is simply an effect of difference. Research from an interpretive perspective focuses more on cultural contexts and communication rules that are generated or followed within these contexts.

Although these studies are helpful in understanding many aspects of intercultural communication, we believe it is necessary to investigate how we think about culture, not simply as researchers but as practitioners as well. We therefore have broadened our scope to consider different views of culture. In each of the following conceptualizations, think about how this view would influence intercultural communication.

High Culture and Low Culture

Nineteenth-century essayist and poet Matthew Arnold, who expressed concern with protecting "civilization," defined culture as "the best that has been thought and said in the world." Arnold's view of culture emphasizes quality. Many Western societies distinguish "high culture" from "low culture."

High culture refers to those cultural activities that are often the domain of the European elite or the well-to-do: ballet, symphony, opera, great literature, and fine art. These activities are sometimes framed as international because supposedly they can be appreciated by audiences in other places, other cultures. Their cultural value is seen as transcendent and timeless. To protect these cultural treasures, social groups build museums, symphony halls, and theatres. In fact, universities devote courses, programs, even entire departments to the study of aspects of high culture.

Low culture is often seen in opposition to high culture. Low culture refers to the activities of the non-elite: music videos, game shows, wrestling, stock car racing, graffiti, TV talk shows. Traditionally, these activities are considered unworthy of serious study—hence, of little interest at museums or universities. The cultural values embedded in these activities are considered neither transcendent nor timeless. They are provincial in the sense that they often do not speak to those in other cultures.

The elitism reflected in the distinction between high and low culture is indicative of larger tensions in Western social systems. The second half of the 20th century, though, has seen a breakdown in this distinction. Rapid social changes propelled universities to alter their policies, for example. These changes also affect how we study intercultural communication.

The wake of the turbulent 1960s brought to the university an interest in ethnic studies, women's studies, and gay and lesbian studies. These areas of study did not rely on the earlier distinctions between high and low culture. Rather, they contributed to the rethinking of this cultural framework by arguing for the legitimacy of other cultural forms that traditionally would have been categorized as low culture.

Although the distinction between high and low cultures has broken down, it has not disappeared. University administrators and academics quickly realized what was at stake in the challenge to high culture and its entrenchment in the university. What we study and how we study it has significant implications for how we think about the world. The biases of high culture prevail: In most academic settings, some works are favored and others are shunned. Although this practice is weaker, it continues to reinforce a particular view of the world in which European elite culture dominates.

Shared and Learned Patterns of Beliefs

Anthropological Definitions of Culture Traditional intercultural communication studies have been influenced mostly by definitions of culture proposed by anthropologists and psychologists. Of the two disciplines, anthropology is more concerned with definitions. Even so, the definitions proposed are numerous and varied. In 1952, two anthropologists, Arthur Kroeber and Clyde Kluckhohn, categorized and integrated about 150 definitions. Some definitions, for example, emphasized culture as a set of patterns of thought and beliefs; others emphasized culture as a set of behaviors. Some definitions focused on the nonmaterial aspects of human life whereas others focused on the material aspects of societies. The proliferation of definitions has not diminished (Baldwin & Lindsley, 1994).

Anthropologist Clifford Geertz's definition of culture was probably the most widely accepted early in his field. It also has been adopted in communication studies.

> [Culture] denotes an historically transmitted pattern of meaning embodied in symbols, a system of inherited conceptions expressed in symbolic forms by means of which men communicate, perpetuate and develop their knowledge about and attitudes toward life. (Geertz, 1973, p. 89).

The traditional concept of culture continues to be the learned, shared patterns of belief and behavior. A more recent definition of culture reflects Geertz's influence:

> (1) that set of capacities which distinguishes Homo sapiens *as a species and which is fundamental to its mode of adaptation; (2) the learned, cumulative product of all social life; (3) the distinctive patterns of thought, action, and value that characterize the members of a society or social group. (Winthrop, 1991, p. 50)*

Psychological Definitions of Culture Geert Hofstede, a noted social psychologist, has defined culture similarly, as the "programming of the mind" and as the "interactive aggregate of common characteristics that influence a human group's response to its environment" (Hofstede, 1984, p. 21). The social psychological definition of culture is centered in the mind of the individual. Hofstede explains his notion of culture as a computer program:

*Every person carries within him or herself patterns of thinking, feeling, and poten-
tial acting which were learned throughout [his or her] lifetime. Much of [these
patterns are] acquired in early childhood, because at that time a person is most
susceptible to learning and assimilating. (Hofstede, 1991, p. 4)*

Hofstede goes on to describe how these patterns are developed through interactions in the social environments and with various groups of individuals, first
with family and people in the neighborhood, at school, at youth groups, at college, and so on. Culture becomes a collective experience because it is shared
with people who live in and experience the same social environments.

To understand this notion of "collective programming of the mind," Hofstede and other scholars studied organizational behavior in IBM subsidiaries in
53 countries around the world. Their studies included two different data col-
lections: the first one in 1967 to 1973, the second phase from 1985 to 1987.
Through this extensive research, Hofstede identified five areas of common
problems. Although the problems are shared by different cultural groups, answers to the problems varied from country to country. The problem types are
identified as follows:

1. Power distance: social inequality, including the relationship with authority
2. Individualism versus collectivism: orientation toward the individual or
   groups
3. Femininity versus masculinity: the social implications of having been born
   male or female
4. Ways of dealing with uncertainty, controlling aggression, and expressing
   emotions
5. Long-term versus short-term orientation to life

Hofstede then investigated how these various cultural values influenced corporate behavior in many different countries.

Both the anthropological and the psychological approaches to understanding culture have been influential in the social science perspective to intercultural
communication. These approaches have helped us identify patterns of beliefs
related to communication. They tend to focus on the nation-state or ethnic
group level of culture; cultural patterns of interest are those that are shared by
members of these groups.

Definitions Borrowed from Ethnography

Ethnography of communication is a specialized study within the communication field. It defines cultural groups rather broadly. Talk show participants and
Vietnam War veterans are two examples of cultural groups. Communication
scholar Donal Carbaugh (1988) suggests that it is best to reserve the concept of
culture for patterns of symbolic action and meaning that are *deeply felt, commonly
intelligible, and widely accessible.*

Patterns that are deeply felt must be sensed collectively by members of the cultural group. Gathering around the coffee machine at work every morning, for example, could be a cultural pattern, but only if the activity holds symbolic significance or evokes feelings that extend beyond itself. Then the activity more completely exemplifies a cultural pattern. For example, suppose that gathering around the coffee machine each morning symbolized teamwork, or the desire to interact with colleagues. To qualify as a cultural pattern, the activity must have the same symbolic significance. That is, all members of the group must find the activity meaningful in about the same way. Finally, all participants must have access to the pattern of action. This does not mean that all persons must use the pattern; it only means that the pattern is available to them.

Communication theorist Gerry Philipsen extends Carbaugh's notion of culture by emphasizing that these patterns must endure over time and are passed on from person to person. Philipsen writes:

> *Culture . . . refers to a socially constructed and historically transmitted pattern of symbols, meaning, premises, and rules. . . . A cultural code of speaking, then, consists of a socially constructed and historically transmitted system of symbols and meanings pertaining to communication—for instance, symbols "Lithuanian" or "communication" and their attendant definitions; beliefs about spoken actions (that a man who uses speech to discipline boys is not a real man); and rules for using speech (that a father should not interrupt his daughter at the dinner table). (1992, pp. 7–8)*

These definitions of culture suggested by Philipsen are influenced by communication ethnographer Dell Hymes's framework for studying naturally occurring speech in depth and in context. The framework comprises the following eight elements: scene, participant, end, act sequence, key, instrumentality, norm, and genre. In this sequence, the terms form the acronym *SPEAKING*. Chapter 6 of this text explores Hymes's framework further. The point is that by analyzing speech using this descriptive framework we can gain a comprehensive understanding of the rules and patterns followed in any given speech community.

Culture as a Contested Zone

The arrival in the 1960s of British cultural studies, which held a critical perspective, brought profound changes to the ways we think about culture and study communication. Originally motivated largely by the establishment of the Centre for Contemporary Cultural Studies at the University of Birmingham, cultural studies was fiercely multidisciplinary and committed to social change. Proponents believed that divisions between disciplines were arbitrary and ideological, and that no single discipline held all of the methods and theories needed to generate rich understandings of cultural phenomena. British cultural studies was conceived as having a commitment to social change. Stuart Hall (not related to Edward Hall), an early and enduring figure in cultural studies, envisioned the

You can probably notice many differences among the people in this cultural group despite not having communicated with them. What symbols and nonverbal communication influence your assumptions about them? You are likely to encounter many people who are culturally different from you in everyday life—what influences your decisions about which cultural expressions are more acceptable or less acceptable? (© *Michael Newman/PhotoEdit*)

group's work as drawing on intellectual resources to help understand everyday life and its antihumaneness.

The desire to make academic work relevant to everyday life sparked a newness in other fields. Most people, in fact, want to find the connections between what they learn in books and what is occurring in contemporary society. In any case, this view led to the reconfiguration of the role of the university in society.

Cultural studies began in Britain but spread to Australia, Latin America, and other parts of the world. Due to differing cultural and political situations, the specific construction of cultural studies differs from place to place. In the United States, cultural studies developed mainly within departments of communication (Grossberg, 1993).

The influence of cultural studies in communication has been profound. In many ways, it has far surpassed that of ethnic studies. The cultural studies movement presented a significant challenge to the distinction between high culture and low culture. In fact, it argued that low culture was far more significant because it captured the contemporary and dynamic everyday representations of cultural struggles. Low culture was subsequently renamed *popular culture*. As a result of this hierarchy inversion, formerly overlooked cultural phenomena such as television soap operas and music videos became important areas of study.

You can probably sense that the concept of *culture* that emerged from this area of inquiry differed markedly from the concept of culture in social science research or even in interpretive research. Culture is a contested site or zone. As such, it is a particularly crucial arena for understanding the struggles of various groups—Native Americans, Asian Americans, African Americans, Latinos, women, gays and lesbians, working class people, and so on—as they attempt to negotiate their relationships and well-being within U.S. society.

By studying the communication that springs from these ongoing struggles, we can better understand several intercultural concerns. Consider, for example, Proposition 187 in California. The proposed law denies basic social services, such as health care and education, to undocumented immigrants. The controversy surrounding the passage of this proposition illustrates the concerns of many different cultural groups.

To think about culture as a contested site opens up new ways of thinking about intercultural communication. After all, the people from a particular culture are not identical. Any culture is replete with numerous cultural struggles. When we use terms such as *Chinese culture*, or *French culture*, we gloss over the heterogeneity, the diversity, that resides in that culture.

Yet, the ways in which cultures are heterogeneous are not the same elsewhere as compared to the United States. It would be a mistake to map our structure of differences onto other cultures. How sexuality, ethnicity, gender, and class function in other cultures is not necessarily the same or even similar to their function in the United States. By viewing any culture as a contested zone or site of struggle, we can understand the complexities of that culture; we can become more sensitive to how people in that culture live.

WHAT IS COMMUNICATION?

The essence of communication is meaning. *Communication is a process, not a product.* It is not a singular event but is ongoing. It relies on other communication events to make sense. When we enter into communication with another person, we simultaneously take in messages through all our senses of sight, smell, and hearing. These messages are not discrete and linear, but happen simultaneously, with blurry boundaries of beginning and end.

Communication is a set of constructed meanings. That is, each message has more than one meaning; often, there are many layers of meaning. For example, the message *I love you* may mean, "I'd like to have a good time with you tonight," "I feel guilty about what I did last night without you," "I need you to do me a favor," "I have a good time when I'm with you," or "I want to spend the rest of my life (or at least the next few hours) with you."

Communication involves the use of shared symbols. The words we speak—or the particular combination of letters we write or gestures we make—have no inherent meaning. Rather, they gain their significance from an agreed-upon meaning. When we use symbols to communicate, we assume that the other person shares our symbol system. We assume that he or she takes the meaning that we intend. When individuals come from different cultural backgrounds and experiences, this assumption may be faulty.

Communication is both nonverbal and verbal. We communicate not only by words but also by our behaviors. Thousands of nonverbal behaviors (gestures, postures, eye contact, various facial expressions, and so on) involve shared meaning. Powerful social symbols—for example, flags, national anthems, and Disney logos—also communicate meaning nonverbally.

THE RELATIONSHIP BETWEEN CULTURE AND COMMUNICATION

The relationship between culture and communication is complex. They are interrelated and reciprocal. As anthropologist Edward Hall claimed, culture is communication and communication is culture.

How Culture Influences Communication

Intercultural communication scholars use the broad frameworks from anthropology to identify and study cultural differences in communication. For example, researchers Kluckhohn and Strodtbeck (1961) studied contemporary Navajo and descendants of Spanish colonists and Anglo-Americans in the Southwest. They extended Geertz's earlier work, which emphasized the centrality of cultural values in understanding cultural groups.

Values are the most deeply felt, zero-order beliefs shared by a cultural group. They are the beliefs of what ought to be, not what is. Equality, for example, is a value shared by many people in the United States. It is a belief that all humans are created equal, even though we acknowledge that in reality there are many disparities, such as in talent, access to material goods, and so on.

Kluckhohn and Strodtbeck suggested that members of all cultural groups must answer the following important questions:

What is human nature?

What is the relationship between humans and nature?

What is the relationship between humans?

What is the preferred personality?

What is the orientation toward time?

According to Kluckhohn and Strodtbeck, there are three possible responses for each question. The range of answers to these questions is shown in Table 3-1. For example, the question of the relationship between humans and nature may be answered in three ways. The response chosen by a particular society reflects

TABLE 3-1   VALUE ORIENTATIONS

Range of Values

Human nature	Basically good	Mixture of good and evil	Basically evil
Relationship between humans and nature	Humans dominate	Harmony between the two	Nature dominates
Relationships between humans	Individual	Group-oriented	Collateral
Preferred personality	"Doing": stress on action	"Growing": stress on spiritual growth	"Being": stress on who you are
Time orientation	Future-oriented	Present-oriented	Past-oriented

Source: Adapted from Kluckhohn and Strodtbeck, *Variations in Value Orientations* (1961).

the dominant value orientation of that society. These responses represent deeply held beliefs about the way the world should be, not necessarily the way it is. The questions and their responses become a framework for understanding broad cultural differences between societies.

Let's see how this works by using the human and nature relationship as an example. In the dominant U.S. society, humans seem to dominate nature. We can see evidence of this in many ways. Clouds are seeded if rain is needed. Rivers are rerouted and dammed to meet needs for water, recreation, and power. Births are controlled by medication. We make snow and ice for the recreational pleasures of skiing and skating. Of course, not everyone in the United States completely agrees that humans should dominate nature. Conflicts between environmentalists and land developers often center on disagreements over this value orientation.

In a society that believes mainly in the domination of nature over humans, decisions are made differently. Families may be more accepting of the number of children that are born naturally. There is less intervention in processes of nature, fewer attempts to control what is seen as the natural order.

A belief in the value of humans living in harmony with nature, rather than one dominating the other, is held by many Native American groups. In this value orientation, nature is respected and enjoyed, and it plays an integral part in the spiritual and religious life of the community.

It is important to note that not everyone in the society holds the dominant value. Representation follows a normal distribution pattern, with most people clustered near the mean but with many spread at various distances around the mean.

Kluckhohn and Strodtbeck's framework has provided a way to map and contrast broad cultural differences between various groups. It can also serve as a way of analyzing cultural differences. Intercultural conflicts are often due to differences in value orientations. For example, past-oriented people may feel strongly that it is important to consider how things were done in the past. For them, the past and tradition hold answers. Values often conflict in projects in which

Holidays are significant ways of enacting and transmitting culture and cultural values across the generations. For example, Kwanzaa is an important holiday for many African Americans. What holidays does your family celebrate? What cultural values are being transmitted in those celebrations? *(© Lawrence Migdale/Tony Stone Images, Inc.)*

future-oriented individuals (such as many people from the United States) may show a lack of respect for traditional ways of working.

Based on his cross-cultural study of IBM subsidiaries, Hofstede (1984) suggested a framework for understanding broad cultural differences in values. Some societies value individualism, for example, whereas others value collectivism. The cultural differences pertaining to these values distinguish the two types of societies. Individualism, often cited as a value held by European Americans (Bellah, Madsen, Sullivan, Swidler, & Tipton, 1985), places importance on the individual rather than the family or work teams or other groups. It is often cited as the most important of European American cultural values. By contrast, people from collectivist societies place importance on extended families and group loyalty.

The values in each type of society influence patterns of communication. For example, individualistic societies tend to value direct forms of communication and support overt forms of conflict resolution. People in collectivist societies may employ less direct communication and more avoidance-style conflict resolution.

One limitation of this framework is that it tends to "essentialize" people. In other words, people tend to assume that a particular group characteristic is the essential characteristic of a given person at all times and in all contexts. For ex-

Just out of college, I went to Japan and lived with a family for a few months. I vividly remember the sense of shock upon realizing the gap between my Japanese homestay family's perception of my status, power, and role compared to my own view of the situation. I had seen the experience as a chance for them to show and teach me various facets of Japanese home life and, reciprocally, as a time for me to study my language books and appreciate them. And I tried to learn as much as I could from Ken, their son, whom I considered a role model. One day, however, after what I suppose was a lengthy period of frustration on her part, my Japanese mother took me aside and said, "You seem to look for learnings behind each of Ken's actions, Douglas-san, but remember that since you are older it is you who must teach and be the responsible one."
—Douglas

ample, we might mistakenly assume that parents who encourage their 20-year-old son to leave home are selfish; we might instead recognize this trait as characteristic of an individualistic society.

How Communication Influences Culture

Just as culture influences communication, it also is enacted through communication. Scholars of cultural communication describe how various aspects of culture are enacted in speech communities *in situ*, or in contexts. They seek to understand communication patterns that are situated socially and give voice to cultural identity. Specifically, they examine how the cultural forms and frames (terms, ritual, myth, and social drama) are enacted through structuring norms of conversation and interaction. The patterns are not connected in a deterministic way to any cultural group.

Researcher Tamar Katriel (1990) examines "griping," a communication ritual that takes place among middle-class Israelis. Using the SPEAKING framework (scene, participant, end, act sequence, key, instrumentality, norm, and genre), Katriel analyzes the ritual in the following way: The griping topic must be one related to the domain of public life, the purpose of the griping is not to solve the problem but to vent pent-up tensions and to affirm the shared reality and togetherness of being Israeli. The ritual is a deeply felt, widely accessible pattern that affirms the cultural identity of Israelis. Although individuals belonging to other cultural groups may gripe, the activity may not be done in this systematic cultural way and may not fill the same function.

The *instrumentality* (or *channel*) in griping is face-to-face, and the *scene* (or *setting*) usually is a Friday night gathering in a private home. *Participants* usually are friends, casual acquaintances, or even strangers, but not real outsiders. (Katriel describes an embarrassing incident, when a couple of gripers discover that one of the group is a visiting Jew, not a native Israeli.) The *key*, or tone, of this ritual is one of plaintiveness and frustration. The *act sequence* comprises an

55

initiation phase, when someone voices a complaint. This is followed by the acknowledgment phase, when others comment on the opener. Then a progression of subthemes follows. Finally, during the termination phase, everyone intellectually sighs and agrees that it is a problem: "It's no joke, things are getting worse all the time," the participants might say.

It is possible to compare different ways in which cultural norms and forms such as griping enact aspects of the culture and construct cultural identity. For example, although Katriel is not interested in making cross-cultural comparisons, she does allude to the difference between the Israeli griping ritual and a similar communication ritual that many White, middle-class U.S. residents engage in (Katriel & Philipsen, 1990). The communication ritual is a form of close, supportive, and flexible speech aimed at solving a personal problem and affirming participants' identities. It is initiated when people "sit down and talk about it," acknowledge the problem, and together negotiate a solution. Katriel identifies similarities in these two rituals: They both fill the function of dramatizing major cultural problems and provide a preferred social context for the venting of problems and frustration; they also provide a sense of community identity (Katriel, 1990).

A related approach from cultural communication studies sees culture as performative. If we accept this metaphor, then we are not studying any external (cultural) reality. Rather, we are examining how persons enact and represent their culture's worldviews. For example, in Gerry Philipsen's (1992) study of Teamsterville, men enact their gender (cultural) roles by remaining silent in many instances, engaging in talk mainly with peers, not with women or children.

Culture as Resistance to Dominant Society

Resistance is the metaphor used in cultural studies to conceptualize the relationship between culture and communication. Borrowing this metaphor, we can try to discover how individuals use their own space to resist dominant society. For example, we might study the floating bars in New York City, warehouses where people meet (clandestinely and illegally) for a night or two, exchange money, party, and then disappear. The "establishment" does not obtain a liquor license or pay taxes. In this way, people are circumventing the system. We can interpret their behavior as resistance to the dominant cultural system.

THE RELATIONSHIP BETWEEN COMMUNICATION AND CONTEXT

Traditionally, context is created by the physical or social aspects of the situation in which communication occurs. For example, communication may occur in a classroom, a bar, or a church; the physical characteristics of the setting influence the communication. People communicate differently depending on the context. Context is not static or objective, and it can be multilayered. Context

It is often difficult to distinguish what is "natural" from what is "cultural." In this selection, author bell hooks tells us how she negotiated her way through one cultural practice related to fashion. Consider what aspects of cultural domination she is resisting and notice how gender is intertwined with culture.

> *GOOD HAIR—that's the expression. We all know it, begin to hear it when we are small children. When we are sitting between the legs of mothers and sisters getting our hair combed. Good hair is hair that is not kinky, hair that does not feel like balls of steel wool, hair that does not take hours to comb, hair that does not need tons of grease to untangle, hair that is long. Real good hair is straight hair, hair like white folks' hair. Yet no one says so. No one says your hair is so nice, so beautiful because it is like white folks' hair. We pretend that the standards we measure our beauty by are our own invention—that it is questions of time and money that lead us to make distinctions between good hair and bad hair. . . .*
>
> *For each of us, getting our hair pressed is an important ritual. It is not a sign of our longing to be white. It is not a sign of our quest to be beautiful. We are girls. It is a sign of our desire to be women. It is a gesture that says we are approaching womanhood. It is a rite of passage. . . . Secretly I had hoped that the hot comb would transform me, turn the thin good hair into thick nappy hair, the kind of hair I like and long for, the kind you can do anything with, wear in all kinds of styles. I am bitterly disappointed in the new look.*
>
> *A senior in high school, I want to wear a natural, an afro. I want never to get my hair pressed again. It is no longer a rite of passage, a chance to be intimate in the world of women. The intimacy masks betrayal.*

Source: bell hooks, "Black Is a Woman's Color," *Callaloo*, 12:2.

may consist of the social, political, and historical structures in which the communication occurs.

The social context is determined on the societal level. Consider, for example, the controversy over the Calvin Klein (CK) ads that use young adolescents. The controversy takes place in a social context that says that pedophilia is perverse or immoral. This means that any communication that encourages or feeds that behavior or perspective, including advertising, is deemed wrong by the majority of residents. However, pedophilia is not considered wrong in all societies in all periods of history. To adequately interpret the CK ads, we have to know something about the current feeling and meanings attached to pedophilia wherever the ads are displayed.

The political context in which communication occurs includes those forces that attempt to change or retain existing social structures and relations. For example, to understand the acts of protesters who throw blood or red paint on people who wear fur coats, we must consider the political context. In this case, the political context would be the ongoing informal debates about animal rights and cruelty to animals farmed for their fur. In other countries or in other time

Many of the Thai managers I spoke with while doing research on American companies in Thailand stressed to me that when working with Thais one needed to be very aware of relationships and the hierarchy in which they exist. A Thai woman I spoke with, who was the secretary to the company's American president, provided this example of the need for attention to the details of relationships:

> *I believe in the United States it is common for a boss to ask the secretary to request some materials from another person or to call people and tell them the boss wants to see them. In the United States, you all look at each other as equals. It is not so important what someone's title is, their age, or time with the company. In Thailand, those things are very important. For example, my boss, who is an American was always asking me to go call so-and-so and request a meeting or go talk to so-and-so and get some reports from them. By having me do this, the Thais were wondering several things: Why should we deal with her; she is just a secretary, and have I done something wrong that the boss does not want to talk with me? Finally, I got my boss to understand that when he had a request for someone—especially someone who was high-ranking in the company, someone who was much older than me or had been with the company longer than me—I would write a short note to that person, he would sign it, then I would pass the note along. That way, everyone's face was saved, their positions were recognized, and the boss came across as showing that he cared about his personal relationship with everyone. Mind you, I can run over and ask others of my same rank, age, or time with the company for any information or a meeting, but it is important to show respect toward those in high positions.*
> —Chris

periods, the protesters' communicative act would not make sense or would be interpreted in other ways.

We also need to examine the historical context of communication. For example, the meaning of a college degree depends in part on the reputation built in the past. Why does a Harvard degree communicate a different meaning than a degree from a small state university? Harvard's reputation relies on history—the large endowments given over the years, the important persons who attended and graduated, and so forth.

THE RELATIONSHIP BETWEEN COMMUNICATION AND POWER

Power is pervasive in communication interactions. We often think of communication between individuals as being between equals, but this is rarely the case. In large part, power comes from social institutions and the roles we occupy in those institutions. For example, in the classroom there is temporary inequality, with the instructor having more power. He or she sets the course requirements, gives grades, determines who speaks. In this case, the power rests not with the individual instructor but with the role that he or she is enacting.

Power is dynamic. It is not a simple one-way proposition. Students in a classroom, for example, are not powerless. They may assert and negotiate their power. Also, the typical power relationship between instructor and student often is not perpetuated beyond the classroom.

The disempowered may negotiate power in many ways. Employees in a large institution can find ways to reposition themselves or gain power. Students may sign their advisors' signature on their registration schedules if they don't have time to see their advisors.

Power is complex, especially in relation to institutions or social structure. Some inequities (such as gender, class, or race) are more rigid than those created by temporary roles such as student or teacher. The power relations between student and teacher, for example, are more complex if the teacher is a woman challenged by male students. We really can't understand intercultural communication without considering the power dynamics in the interaction.

SUMMARY

In this chapter, we have identified several different approaches to understanding culture, communication, context, and power. Each approach has implications for understanding intercultural communication. Culture can be viewed as:

1. Deep-seated patterns of learned, shared beliefs and behaviors
2. Deeply felt, commonly intelligible, and widely accessible patterns of symbolic meaning
3. Contested zones of meaning

Communication is a process of constructing meanings through shared symbols, both verbal and nonverbal. Communication can only be understood in context. Context may be the social, physical, or situational constraints in which communication occurs or the larger political, societal, and historical environments. Power is pervasive and plays an enormous, though often hidden, role in intercultural communication interactions.

The relationship between communication and culture can be viewed in three complementary ways.

1. Culture influences communication.
2. Culture is enacted through communication.
3. Communication is a way of contesting and resisting dominant culture.

The context, or physical and social setting in which communication occurs affects that communication. Finally, the power relationships—determined largely by social institutions and roles—influence communication.

Now that we have laid the foundation of our approach to intercultural communication, the next step is to examine the role of identity in intercultural communication. We communicate our identity to others and we learn who we are through communication.

REFERENCES

Baldwin, J. R., & Lindsley, S. L. (1994). *Conceptualizations of culture.* Tempe, AZ: Arizona State University Urban Studies Center.

Bellah, R. N., Madsen, R., Sullivan, W. M., Swidler, A., & Tipton, S. M. (1985). *Habits of the heart: Individualism and commitment in American life.* New York: Harper & Row.

Boyd, B. M. (1995). *The redneck way of knowledge.* New York: Vintage.

Carbaugh, D. (1988). Comments on "culture" in communication inquiry. *Communication Reports, 1,* 38–41.

Geertz, L. (1973). *The interpretation of culture.* New York: Basic Books.

Grossberg, L. (1993). Can cultural studies find true happiness in communication? *Journal of Communication, 43* (4), 89–97.

Hall, S. (1992). Cultural studies and its theoretical legacies. In L. Grossberg, C. Nelson, & P. Treichler (Eds.), *Cultural Studies* (pp. 277–294). New York: Routledge.

Harris, M. (1983). *Cultural anthropology.* New York: Harper & Row.

Hofstede, G. (1984). *Culture's consequences.* Beverly Hills: Sage.

———. (1991). *Cultures and organizations: Software of the mind.* New York: McGraw-Hill.

hooks, b. (1991). Black is a woman's color. In H. L. Gates, Jr. (Ed.), *Bearing witness: Selections from African-American autobiography in the twentieth century.* New York: Pantheon, pp. 338–348.

Hymes, D. (1972). Models of the interaction of language and social life. In J. Gumperz & D. Hymes (Eds.), *Directions in sociolinguistics: The ethnography of speaking* (pp. 35–71). New York: Holt, Rinehart & Winston.

Katriel, T. (1990). "Griping" as a verbal ritual in some Israeli discourse. In D. Carbaugh (Ed.), *Cultural communication and intercultural contact* (pp. 99–112). Hillsdale, NJ: Lawrence Erlbaum.

Katriel, T., & Philipsen, G. (1990). What we need is communication: "Communication" as a cultural category in some American speech. In D. Carbaugh (Ed.), *Cultural communication and intercultural contact* (pp. 77–94). Hillsdale, NJ: Lawrence Erlbaum.

Keesing, R. M. (1981). Theories of culture. In R. W. Casson (Ed.), *Language, culture, and cognition* (pp. 42–66). New York: MacMillan.

Kluckhohn, F., & Strodtbeck, F. (1961). *Variations in value orientations.* Chicago: Row, Peterson & Co.

Kroeber, A. L., & Kluckhohn, C. (1952). *Culture: A critical review of concepts and definitions.* New York: Vintage.

Nelson, C., Treichler, P. A., & Grossberg, L. (1992). Cultural studies: An introduction. In L. Grossberg, C. Nelson, & P. Treichler (Eds.), *Cultural Studies* (pp. 1–22). New York: Routledge.

Philipsen, G. (1992). *Speaking culturally: Explorations in social communication.* Albany: State University of New York Press.

Rosaldo, R. (1989). *Culture and truth: The remaking of social analysis.* Boston: Beacon.

Seymour-Smith, C. (1986). *Macmillan dictionary of anthropology.* London: Macmillan.

Turner, G. (1990). *British cultural studies: An introduction.* Cambridge, MA: Unwin Hyman.

Williams, R. (1981). The analysis of culture. In T. Bennett, G. Martin, C. Mercer, & J. Woollacott (Eds.), *Culture, ideology and social process: A reader* (pp. 43–52). London: Open University Press.

———. (1983). *Keywords: A vocabulary of culture and society* (Rev. ed). New York: Oxford University Press.

Winthrop, R. H. (1991). *Dictionary of concepts in cultural anthropology.* New York: Greenwood Press.

IDENTITY

Identity is a bridge between culture and communication. It is important because we communicate our identity to others and we learn who we are through communication. It is through communication with our family, friends, and others that we come to understand ourselves and form our identity. Issues of identity are particularly important in intercultural interactions.

Conflicts may arise between who we think we are versus who others think we are. For example, a female college student living with a family in Mexico on a homestay may be treated protectively and chaperoned when she socializes. This may conflict with her view of herself as an independent person. In this case, the person's identity is not confirmed but is questioned or challenged in the interaction.

This chapter examines the relationship between communication and identity and the role of identity in intercultural communication. In the first section we discuss various approaches to understanding identity, including those from psychology and communication. Everyone has multiple identities that are created and negotiated through communication. We then turn our attention to the development of specific aspects of our social and cultural identity including those related to gender, race or ethnicity, and nationality. Finally, we discuss the role of context in forming our identities and the relationship between identity, language, and communication.

PERSPECTIVES TOWARD UNDERSTANDING IDENTITY

How do we come to understand who we are? What are the characteristics of identity? In this section we discuss three main contemporary perspectives that provide answers to these questions. The social psychological perspective views the self in relation to the community to which a person belongs. The communication perspective recognizes the role of interaction with others as a factor in developing the self. Finally, the critical perspective views identity as the result of contexts quite distant from the individual.

Social Psychological Perspective

The social psychological perspective emphasizes that identity is created in part by the self and in part in relation to group membership. This perspective recognizes that the self is composed of multiple identities, and that these notions of identity are culture bound.

How do we come to understand who we are? One helpful perspective comes from the notion of self-concept. Noted psychoanalyst Erik Erikson has charted the development of ego identity in children and young adolescents. According to Erikson, our identities are self-created, formed through a series of identity conflicts, diffusion, confusion, and crises (Erikson, 1950, 1968).

i am a door . . .
i am caught between two rooms
swinging from one to another.
grasping moments as the wind
sways me from the first to the next.
living, loving, caressing life in each
taking a little from one
and giving to the other, and back.

i hear the strains of my mother's voice
over the aroma of the eggplant curry
wafting over my father's intense study
of the *Indian Express*—his favorite newspaper.
the aunts and uncles came in droves
to my sister's wedding to eat
and gossip during the ceremony,
and through the night.
glimpses of life . . . very Indian.

in the other room, the surround sound
heard Simon and Garfunkel over troubled waters,
while Pink Floyd cried about the walls in our lives.
Simpsons and Butterfinger were definitely in
as Gore and Quayle babbled using innocuous verbiage.
the computer was never shut off
as reams of paper saw term papers
discuss new ways to communicate.
glimpses of life . . . very American.

between these two worlds
i am happy, confused, angry
And in pain—all at the same time.
for i am a door
caught between two rooms.
i see and feel both of them
but i don't seem to belong to either.
    —Nagesh Rao (October, 1992)

We sometimes internalize negative identities as we try to answer the question of who we are. Occasionally we may need a moratorium, a time out, in the process. Identities are not created in one smooth, orderly process. They are created in spurts, with some events providing good insights about who we are and interrupting long periods during which we may not think much about ourselves or our identities.

Writer Sandra Cisneros describes what it's like to live in the borders between many different worlds.

I'm amphibious. I'm a person who doesn't belong to any class. The rich like to have me around because they envy my creativity; they know they can't buy that. The poor don't mind if I live in their neighborhood because they know I'm poor like they are, even if my education and the way I dress keep us worlds apart. I don't belong to any class. Not to the poor, whose neighborhood I share. Not to the rich, who come to my exhibitions and buy my work. Not to the middle class from which my sister Ximena and I fled.

Source: Sandra Cisneros, *Woman Hollering Creek* (1991), pp. 71–72.

The process of identity development involves an exploration of one's abilities, interests, options, and values. These explorations often occur in relation to group membership. They help form:

that part of an individual self concept which derives from knowledge of his (her) membership of a social group(s) together with value and emotional significance attached to that membership. (Tajfel, 1978, p. 63)

We identify with many groups as we are growing up. Groups may be based on gender, race, ethnicity, sexual orientation, religion, and nationality (Tajfel, 1981, 1982). By comparing ourselves and others to such groups, we come to understand who we are. Gender identification seems to occur early (between one and three years of age); racial and ethnic identification occurs later (between seven and nine years of age). Members of minority groups seem to develop a sense of identity earlier than majority group members.

Because we belong to various groups, we develop multiple identities that come into play at different times, depending on the context. In going to church or temple, we may highlight our religious identity. In going to clubs or bars, we may highlight our sexual orientation identity. Women who join social groups exclusive to women (or men who attend social functions just for men) are highlighting their gender identity.

In the United States, young people are often encouraged to develop a strong sense of identity, to "know who they are," to be independent and self-reliant. However, this emphasis on developing identity is not shared by many societies. In many African and Asian societies, the experience of childhood and adolescence revolves around the family experience. In these societies, then, educational, occupational, and even marriage choices are made not only by the individual but with extensive family guidance.

These cultural differences demonstrate that identity development does not occur in the same way in every society. Many African and Asian societies, for example, emphasize dependency and interdependency, particularly with the relationship to the family. In some cultural contexts, it makes more sense to speak of a familial or relational self rather than the self-creation of one's personal identity. (Roland, 1994, p. 16).

A Communication Perspective

The communication perspective builds from the notions identified above. In addition, it emphasizes that identities are not created by the self alone but are co-created through communication with others. A communication perspective recognizes that identities emerge when messages are exchanged between persons. They are negotiated, co-created, reinforced, and challenged through communication (Hecht, Collier, & Ribeau, 1993). This means that presenting our identities is not a simple process. Does everyone see you as you see yourself? Probably not. To understand how these images may conflict, let's explore the processes of avowal and ascription.

Avowal is the process by which an individual portrays him- or herself. In contrast, ascription is the process by which others attribute identities to an individual. Sometimes these are congruent. For example, we, the authors of this book, see ourselves as professors and hope that students also see us as professors. However, we also see ourselves as young. Many students do not concur, and they ascribe an "old person" identity to us. This ascribed identity challenges our avowal identity. These conflicting views influence the communication between us and our students.

Different identities are emphasized depending on the person we are communicating with and the topic of conversation. In a social conversation with someone we are attracted to, our gender or sexual orientation identity is probably more important to us than other identities (ethnicity, nationality). And our communication is probably most successful when the person we are talking with confirms the identity we think is most important at the moment. So, we can think of intercultural communication competence as communication that affirms the identity that is most salient in any conversation (Collier & Thomas, 1988). For example, if you are talking with a professor about a research project, the conversation would be most competent if the interaction confirms the salient identities (professor and student), rather than other identities (for example, those based on gender, religion, or ethnicity).

How do you feel when someone does not recognize the identity you feel is most salient? For example, suppose your parents treat you as a child (ascription) and not as an independent adult (your avowal). How does the conflict affect communication?

Central to the communication perspective is the idea that our identities are expressed communicatively. They are expressed in core symbols, labels, and norms. Core symbols tell us about the fundamental beliefs, the central concepts that define a particular identity. Communication scholar Michael Hecht and his colleagues have identified the contrasting core symbols associated with various ethnic identities. For example, core symbols of African American identity may

I have an experience and interaction in an intercultural situation every day of my life. Both of my parents are German and have lived there the majority of their lives. I, on the other hand, have lived here for most of my life. This is very difficult because my parents still do everything the German ways, such as dress, eating, and the rules of the household and discipline. Almost every day I am challenged with the German ways and how they want me to be, and sometimes how I act and dress isn't German enough and they don't like that and then they even treat me differently— for example, if I dress like an American college girl and curl my hair and wear lipstick. This is culturally unacceptable in their eyes, and they will treat me worse and give me less respect. This is very difficult because I don't want them to hate me or treat me disrespectfully, but I also don't want to dress and act like someone I'm not. This makes me very frustrated sometimes, because inside I am still the same person. Yet, if I dress like an American girl they disrespect me. I try to explain to them that I've gone to school here my whole life and that is how I was brought up, but they still seem to think that I should dress and look like a German girl. A lot of times it is very difficult to talk to them; I try telling them that I am German but that I've been raised among all Americans and that I can't stay looking and acting like a German because, basically, I'm not.

—Carla

be positivity, sharing, uniqueness, realism, and assertiveness. Individualism is often cited as a core symbol of European American identity. Communication styles express these symbols and, conversely, shape and create them. Labels are a category of core symbols. They are the terms we use to refer to particular aspects of our own and others' identities (for example, African American, Latino, White, European American).

Finally, some norms of behavior are associated with particular identities. For example, women may express their gender identity by being more concerned about safety than men. They may take more precautions when they go out at night, such as walking in groups. People might express their religious identity by participating in activities such as going to church or Bible study meetings.

Critical Perspective

Contextual Identity Formation   The driving force behind a critical approach to identity is the attempt to understand identity formation within the contexts of history, economics, politics, and discourse. To grasp this notion, ask yourself: How and why do people identify with particular groups and not others? What choices are available to them?

We are all subject to being pigeonholed into identity categories, or contexts, even before we are born. Many parents ponder a name for their unborn child, who is already part of society through his or her relationship to the parents.

Our identities include ethnicity, gender, age, and sexual orientation. Living in a multicultural society gives us the opportunity to express these various aspects of identity in different ways at different times. Ethnicity is often expressed in community celebrations, such as St. Patrick's Day, Kwanzaa, O-bon, Day of the Dead, or the Korean Day parade shown here. *(© Joel Gordon)*

Some children have a good start at being Jewish or Chicana before they are even born. We cannot ignore the ethnic, socioeconomic, or racial positions from which we start our identity journeys.

French psychoanalyst Jacques Lacan (1977) gives the example of two children on a train that stops at a station. Each looks from the window and identifies the location: One child responds that they are in front of the door for the ladies bathroom; the other says they are in front of the gentlemen's. Both children see and use labels from their seating position. Just as we are never "out" of position, we are never "outside" of language and its system that helps define us.

The identities that others may ascribe to us are socially and politically determined. They are not constructed by the self alone. We must ask ourselves what drives the construction of particular kinds of identities. For example, the invention of the label "heterosexual" is a relatively recent one, less than a hundred years old (Katz, 1995). Today, people do not hesitate to identify themselves as "heterosexuals." A critical perspective insists on the constructive nature of this process and attempts to identify the social forces and social needs that give rise to these identities.

Resisting Ascribed Identities   When we invoke such discourses about identity, we are pulled into the social forces that feed the discourse. We might resist the position it puts us in, and we might try to ascribe other identities to ourselves. However, we must nevertheless begin from that position in carving out a new identity.

French philosopher Louis Althusser uses the term *interpellation* to refer to this process. He notes that we are pushed into this system

> *by that very precise operation which I have called interpellation or hailing, and which can be imagined along the lines of the most commonplace everyday police (or other) hailing: "Hey you there!" . . . Experience shows that the practical telecommunication of hailings is such that they hardly ever miss their man: verbal call or whistle, the one hailed always recognizes that it is really him who is being hailed. And yet it is a strange phenomenon, and one which cannot be explained solely by "guilt feelings." (Althusser, 1971, p. 163)*

This hailing process that Althusser describes operates in intercultural communication interactions. It establishes the foundation from which the interaction occurs. For example, occasionally someone will ask Tom, one of the authors of this book, if he is Japanese. The question puts him in an awkward position. He does not hold Japanese citizenship, nor has he ever lived in Japan. Yet, the question probably doesn't mean to address these issues. What does the person mean to ask? What does it mean to be "Japanese"? How can Tom reconfigure his position in relation to this question?

The Dynamic Nature of Identities   The social forces that give rise to particular identities are never stable but are always changing. Therefore, the critical perspective insists on the dynamic nature of identities. For example, the emergence of the European Economic Community has given new meaning to the notion of being "European" as an identity. The search for stable identities is as futile as the search for stable labels for those identities.

Closer to home, look at the way that identity labels have changed from "colored" to "negro" to "Black" to "Afro-American" to "African American." Although the labels seem to refer to the same group of people, the political and cultural identities of these labels are different. The contexts in which the terms developed and were used varied considerably.

SOCIAL AND CULTURAL IDENTITIES

People can identify with a multitude of groups. This section describes some of the major types of groups.

Gender Identity

We often begin life with gendered identities. When newborns arrive in our culture, they may be greeted with clothes and blankets in either blue or pink. To establish a gender identity for a baby, visitors may ask if the baby is a boy or a girl. But gender is not the same as biological sex. This distinction is important in understanding how our views on biological sex influence gender identities.

What it means to be a man or a woman is heavily influenced by cultural notions. For example, some activities are considered more masculine or more feminine. When people hunt or sew or fight or read poetry, it can transform the ways that others view them. Similarly, the programs that people watch on television—soap operas, football games, and so on—affect how they socialize with others, contributing to gendered contexts.

As culture changes, so does the notion of what we idealize as masculine or feminine. Cultural historian Gail Bederman observes: "Even the popular imagery of a perfect male body changed. In the 1860s, the middle class had seen the ideal male body as lean and wiry. By the 1890s, however, an ideal male body required physical bulk and well-defined muscles" (1995, p. 15). The male body, as well as the female body, can be understood not in its "natural" sense but in relation to idealized notions of masculinity and femininity. To know that this man or that woman is particularly good looking requires an understanding of the gendered notions of attractiveness in a culture.

Our notions of masculinity and femininity change constantly, driven by commercial interests, advertising, and other cultural forces. Our expression of gender not only communicates who we think we are but also constructs a sense of who we want to be. We learn what masculinity and femininity mean in our culture. Through various media, we monitor how these notions shift, and we negotiate how we communicate our gendered selves to others.

Consider, for example, the contemporary trend against body hair on men. The ideal male body is sleek, with little body hair. Many men view their own bodies in relation to this ideal and opt to change themselves accordingly.

> *It seems that vanity's latest conquest is the hairy man: Nature's foliage, once the soul of virility, is an unsightly hedge.*
> *So he reaches for the razor, the foam, the depilatory cream—and yes! the wax! Enter the smooth man.*
> *He is turning up in ads, on runways, in gyms, on billboards, in salons.*
> *"Are we waxing more guys? Definitely," says Gary Walker, co-owner of Ilo in Washington, D.C. "Not your average guy: They're in their late 20s to mid-40s, and coming from gyms and health clubs." (Horyn, 1992, p. H5)*

Of course, at one time a hairy body was considered *more* masculine, not less. The dynamic character of gender reflects its close connection to culture. Society has many images of masculinity and femininity; we do not all seek to look and act according to a single ideal. At the same time, we *do* seek to communicate our gendered identities as part of who we are.

Age Identity

As we age, we also play into cultural notions of how someone our age should act, look, and behave. As we grow older, we sometimes look at clothes in stores and feel that we are either too old or too young for that "look." These feelings stem from an understanding of what age means and how we identify with that age.

Some people feel old at 30; others still feel young at 40. There is nothing inherent in age that tells you that you are young or old. Our notions of age and youth are all based on cultural conventions. These same cultural conventions also suggest that it is inappropriate to engage in a romantic relationship with someone who is too old or too young.

Our notions of age often change as we grow older ourselves. When we are quite young, someone in college seems old. When we are in college, we often do not feel old. Yet, the relative nature of age is only one part of the identity process. Social constructions of age are also part of the process. Different generations often have different philosophies, values, and ways of speaking. For example, the slang expression "going postal" may mean nothing to people in their 40s, but to people in their 20s it may mean becoming uncontrollably angry. These slang ways of speaking create in-groups among generations. Although not all people in any generation are alike, the attempt to find trends across generations reflects our interest in understanding age identity.

Racial and Ethnic Identity

Racial Identity   Race consciousness is largely a modern phenomenon. In the United States today, the issue of race seems to be both sensitive and pervasive. It is the topic of many public discussions, from television talk shows to talk radio. Yet many people feel uncomfortable discussing the topic of race. Many think it should not be an issue in U.S. life. Perhaps we can better understand the contemporary issues if we look at how the notion of race has developed historically in the United States.

I think that my being in college with kids just a little older than my son has helped me "learn the language" of the younger generation. So my college classmates have helped me acculturate into the younger generation at a more rapid speed than others my age. When I sit in class with these young people who have graduated from high school and are going to college, it is very easy to focus on these kids as being representative of the younger generation. Then there are the stereotypical "bad" teenagers—the gang members, the druggies, and so on. It isn't fair to generalize the younger generation with these stereotypes, either.

Are the cultural differences of our two age groups just as approachable as any other intercultural exchange? I believe that they are. By using the skills that I am learning in bridging cultural differences, I am getting better at bridging the generation gap between "old mom" and "18-year-old teenager." Interpersonal skills, flexibility, motivation, attitudes, knowledge, skills, and love are all applicable when communicating interculturally with teenagers.
—Marcia

Current debates about race started when 17th- and 18th-century European explorers encountered people who looked different from themselves. The debates centered on religious questions of whether there was "one family of man." If so, what rights were to be accorded to those who were different? Debates about which groups were "human" and which were "animal" pervaded popular and legal discourse and provided a rationale for slavery. Later, in the 18th and 19th centuries, the scientific community tried to establish a classification system of race, based on genetics and cranial capacity. However, these efforts were largely unsuccessful.

Most scientists have abandoned a strict biological basis for classifying racial groups. They defer instead to a social science approach to understanding race. They recognize that racial categories like White and Black are constructed in social and historical contexts.

Several arguments refute the physiological basis for race. First, racial categories vary widely throughout the world. In general, distinctions between White and Black are fairly rigid in the United States, and many people become uneasy when they are unable to categorize individuals. In contrast, Brazil recognizes a wide variety of intermediate racial categories in addition to White and Black. These variations indicate a cultural, rather than a biological, basis for racial classification (Omi & Winant, 1992). Terms like *mulatto* and *Black Irish* demonstrate cultural classifications; terms like *Caucasoid* and *Australoid* are examples of biological classification.

Second, U.S. law uses a variety of definitions in determining racial categories. The 1982 Susie Phipps case in Louisiana reopened debates about race as socially created rather than biologically determined. Susie Phipps applied for a passport and discovered that under Louisiana law she was Black because she was $\frac{1}{32}$ of African descent. (Her great-grandmother had been a slave.) She then sued to be reclassified as White. Not only did she consider herself White, inasmuch as she grew up among Whites and attended White schools, but she also was married to a White man. Because her children were ⅟₆₄ of African descent, they were legally White. Although she lost her lawsuit, the ensuing political and popular discussions persuaded Louisiana lawmakers to change the way the state classified people racially. It is important that the law was changed, but this legal situation does not hide the fact that social definitions of race continue to exist.

A third example of how racial categories are socially constructed is illustrated by their fluid nature. As more and more southern Europeans came to the United States in the 19th century, the established Anglo and German society tried to classify some of these new immigrants (Irish, Jewish, and southern European) as non-White. However, this attempt was not successful. Instead, the racial line was drawn around Europe, and people outside of Europe (for example, immigrants from China) were then designated as non-White (Omi & Winant, 1992).

Racial categories, then, are based to some extent on physical characteristics, but they are also constructed in fluid social contexts. It probably makes more sense to talk about *racial formation* than racial categories. This term casts race as a complex of social meanings rather than as fixed and objective. How people construct these meanings and think about race influences the ways in which they communicate with others.

Ethnic Identity   Ethnic identity may be seen as a set of ideas about one's own ethnic group membership. It typically includes several dimensions: self-identification, knowledge about the ethnic culture (traditions, customs, values, and behaviors), and feelings about belonging to a particular ethnic group. Ethnic identity often involves a common sense of origin and history, which may link ethnic groups to distant cultures in Asia, Europe, Latin America, or other locations.

Ethnic identity means having a sense of belonging to a particular group and knowing something about the shared experience of the group. One of the authors of this book, Judith, grew up in an ethnic community. She heard her parents and relatives speak German. Her grandparents made several trips back to Germany and talked about their German roots. This experience contributed to the ethnic identity she feels.

For some U.S. residents, ethnicity is a specific and relevant concept. They see themselves as connected to an origin outside the United States—as Mexican American, Japanese American, Welsh American, and so on—or to the region prior to its being the United States—Navajo, Hopi, and so on. For others, ethnicity is a vague concept. They see themselves as "American" and reject the notion of hyphenated Americans. We'll discuss the issues of ethnicity for White people later.

What does *American* mean, though? Who defines it? Is there just one meaning or many different meanings? It is important to determine what definition is being used by those who insist that we should all just be "Americans." If one's identity is "just American," how is this identity formed and how does it influence communication with others who see themselves as "hyphenated Americans" (Alba, 1985, 1990; Carbaugh, 1989)?

Racial Versus Ethnic Identity   Scholars dispute whether racial and ethnic identity are similar or different. Some scholars emphasize ethnic identity to avoid any racism inherent in a race-centered approach. Others reject this interpretation (Spindler & Spindler, 1990). On the one hand, discussions about ethnicity tend to assume a "melting pot" perspective on U.S. society. On the other hand, discussions about race as shaped by U.S. history allow for racism. If we never talk about race but only ethnicity, can we consider the effects and influences of racism?

Bounded Versus Dominant Identities   One way to sort out the relationship between ethnicity and race is to differentiate between bounded and dominant (or normative) identities (Frankenburg, 1993; Trinh, 1986/7). Bounded cultures are those groups that are specific but not dominant.

For most White people, it is easy to comprehend the sense of belonging in a bounded group. Clearly, for example, being Amish means following the *ordnung* (community rules). Growing up in a German American home, Judith's identity included a clear priority on seriousness and not much communicative expressiveness. This identity was different from that of her Italian American friends at college who seemed much more expressive.

However, what it means to belong to the dominant, or normative, White culture is more elusive. Although it is more difficult to define, it is just as real. It is often not easy to see what the cultural practices are that link White people together. For example, we often don't think of Thanksgiving Day or Valentine's Day as White U.S. holidays.

Our sense of racial or ethnic identity develops over time, in stages, and through communication with others. The stages of development seem to reflect phases in the development of understanding who we are. They also depend to some extent on the type of group to which people belong. Many ethnic or racial groups experience the common forces of oppression. As a result, they may generate attitudes and behaviors consistent with a natural internal struggle to develop a strong sense of self- and group-identity in response to this oppression.

National Identity

Among the many identities that we may have, we also have a national identity. This identity is often confused with racial or ethnic identity, but it is different. Nationality, unlike racial or ethnic identity, is one's legal status in relation to a nation. Many U.S. citizens may trace their family history to Latin America, Asia, Europe, or Africa. But their nationality, or citizenship, is with the United States.

Although nationality may seem a clear-cut issue, this is not the case when the nation's status is unclear. For example, bloody conflicts erupted over the attempted separation in the mid-1800s of the Confederate States of America from the United States. Similar conflicts erupted in more recent times when Eritrea tried to separate from Ethiopia, and Chechnya from Russia. Less-bloody conflicts also involving nationhood led to the separation of Slovakia and the Czech Republic.

Contemporary nationhood struggles are being played out as Quebec attempts to separate from Canada, Corsica and Tahiti from France, Scotland from Great Britain, and Oaxaca from Mexico. Sometimes, nations disappear on the political map, persist in the social imagination, and re-emerge later. Examples of such nations include Poland, Ukraine, Latvia, Lithuania, Estonia, and Norway. In all of these instances, people identify with various ways of thinking about nationality.

Regional Identity

Closely related to nationality is the notion of regional identity. Many regions of the world have separate, but vital and important, cultural identities. The Scottish Highlands is a region of northern Scotland that is distinctly different from the Lowlands. Regional identity remains strong in the Highlands.

Here in the United States, regional identities remain important but perhaps less so as the nation moves toward homogeneity. Southerners, for example, often view themselves and are viewed by others as a distinct cultural group. Texas advertises itself as "A Whole Other Country," promoting its regional identity. Although some regional identities can lead to national independence movements, they are often cultural identities that affirm distinctive cuisines, dress, manners, and sometimes language. These identities may become important in intercultural communication situations. For example, suppose you meet someone who is Belgian. Whether the person is Flemish or Walloon may raise important communication issues. Flemish Belgians speak Vlaams, or Flemish, a Dutch dialect. The language of the Walloon region of Belgium is a French dialect known as Walloon.

Personal Identity

Many issues of identity are closely tied to one's notion of self. Each of us has a personal identity, but it may not be unified or coherent. We may see ourselves in one way and feel that many others view us in different ways. Think about your name, for example. Some people cherish their name and want others to learn to pronounce and spell it. Others hate their name and even change it. They may feel that their name does not communicate their personality.

Who we think we are is important to us, and we try to communicate that to others. We are more or less successful depending on how others respond to us. We use the various ways that identity is constructed to portray ourselves as we want others to see us.

IDENTITY DEVELOPMENT ISSUES

Minority Identity Development

As we mentioned earlier, minority group members in the United States tend to develop a sense of racial and ethnic identity much earlier than majority group members. Whites tend to take their culture for granted; although they may develop strong ethnic identity, they often do not really think about their racial identity (Ferguson, 1990). There probably is a hierarchy of salient identities that change over time and place.

This section outlines stages in minority identity that noted social psychologists have discerned. Although these stages center on racial and ethnic identities, they may also apply to other majority/minority identities such as gender or sexual orientation (Ponterotto & Pedersen, 1993).

Stage 1: Unexamined Identity   This stage is characterized by the lack of exploration of ethnicity. Minority members may initially accept the values and attitudes of the majority culture, including negative views of their own group. They may have a strong desire to assimilate into the dominant culture, and they may express positive attitudes toward the dominant group. At this stage, ideas about identity may come from parents or friends. Or the person may generally lack interest or concern with ethnicity. As one woman in the African American community put it, "Why do I need to learn about who was the first black woman to do this or that? I'm just not too interested" (Phinney, 1993, p. 68).

Stage 2: Conformity   This stage is characterized by an internalization of the values and norms of the dominant group and a strong desire to assimilate into the dominant culture. Individuals in this phase may have negative, self-deprecating attitudes toward themselves, as well as toward their group in general. An ethnic Hawaiian stated:

> *I think I waste a lot of time on my own kind, I mean the Hawaiians. . . . I am a Hawaiian myself and I hate to say this, but I don't care much for them. . . . They are not an ambitious people. Their only ambition is to play music. They don't care about anything else. (Jacobs & Landau, 1971, p. 64)*

People who criticize other members of their own group may be given negative labels such as "Uncle Toms" or "oreos" for African Americans, "bananas" for Asian Americans, "apples" for Native Americans, and "Tio Tacos" for Chicanos. Such labels condemn attitudes and behaviors that support the dominant White culture. This stage continues until the person encounters a situation that causes him or her to question pro-dominant culture attitudes, which initiates the movement to the next stage: an ethnic identity search.

Stage 3: Resistance and Separatism   Many kinds of events can trigger the move to the third stage, including negative events, such as encountering discrimination or name calling. A period of dissonance, or a growing awareness that not all dominant group values are beneficial to minorities, may also lead to this stage. Suppose, for example, that someone who has been denying his or her racial heritage meets another person from that racial group who exhibits strong cultural connections. This encounter may result in a concern to clarify the personal implications of heritage. One member of an ethnic group explained about attending ethnic fairs: "Going to festivals and cultural events helps me to learn

Our perceptions may be in error because we put labels on people rather than see them as individuals. When you label somebody, it is a form of stereotyping. For example, in our community in Guadalupe, approximately 40% of the population is Yaqui and 60% are of Spanish Mexican descent. I remember as a young girl when I was growing up and in school, some Mexicans would label Yaquis as dirty. During that time, I felt awful and I didn't want to be Yaqui. I felt embarrassed about being Yaqui.

Then I asked my mom a stupid question. "Why do we have to be Yaqui?" My mom sat down and had a talk with me. She said it didn't matter what race we are; it is what we make of ourselves as people. We have choices in life and we choose what we want to be. You can be a nice person or a bad person. "What do you want to be?" she asked me. I said, "I want to be a good person." So she told me to just try to be a good person and do my best. Then she told me that we were Mexicans, too, because her dad was Mexican and that I was Yaqui because of my dad. I didn't feel as bad afterwards, even though I still felt embarrassed sometimes.

—Felipa

more about my own culture and about myself" (Phinney, 1993, p. 71). Another person explained, "I think people should know what black people had to go through to get to where we are now" (p. 71).

This stage may be characterized by a blanket endorsement of one's group and all the values and attitudes attributed to the group. At the same time, the person may reject the values and norms associated with the dominant group.

Stage 4: Integration The ideal outcome of the identity process is the last stage, an achieved identity. A person who has reached this stage has a strong sense of his or her own group identity (based on gender, race, ethnicity, sexual orientation, and so on) and an appreciation of other cultural groups. In this stage, the individual accepts racism and other forms of oppression as a reality but redirects any anger from the previous stage in more positive ways. The end result is a confident and secure identity, with a desire to eliminate all forms of injustice, not just oppression aimed at one's own group.

Majority Identity Development

Rita Hardiman (1994), educator and pioneer in antiracism training, presents a model of identity development for members of the dominant group that has some similarities to the model for minority members. She outlines five stages.

Stage 1: Unexamined Identity The first stage is the same as for minority individuals. In this case, individuals may be aware of physical and some cultural differences, but they do not fear other racial or ethnic groups or feel a sense of superiority.

Stage 2: Acceptance The second stage represents the internalization, conscious or unconscious, of a racist (or otherwise biased) ideology. This may be a passive acceptance or an active acceptance. The point is that individuals are not aware that they have been programmed to accept this worldview.

In the passive acceptance stage, individuals have no conscious identification with being White. However, some assumptions, based on an acceptance of inequities in the larger society, are subtly racist. Consider the following assumptions:

- Minority groups are culturally deprived and need help to assimilate.
- Affirmative action is reverse discrimination because people of color are being given opportunities that Whites don't have.
- White culture—music, art, and literature—is "classical"; works of art by people of color are folk art or "crafts."
- People of color are culturally different, whereas Whites are individuals with no group identity, culture, or shared experience of racial privilege.

Individuals in this stage usually take one of two positions with respect to racial issues and interactions with minorities: They either avoid contact with minority members or adopt a patronizing stance toward them. Both positions are possible at the same time.

In contrast, Whites in the active acceptance stage are conscious of their Whiteness and may express their feelings of superiority collectively. (For example, they might join the White Student Union.) Some people never move beyond this phase—whether it is characterized by passive or active acceptance. If they do, it is usually a result of a number of cumulative events. One of the authors, Judith, gradually realized that her two nieces, who are sisters—one of whom is African American and one of whom is White—had very different experiences. Both girls lived in a middle-class neighborhood. Both were honor students in high school and went to Ivy League colleges. However, they often had very different experiences. On more than one occasion the African American girl was followed by security while shopping. She also was stopped several times by police while driving her mother's red sports car. Her White sister never had these experiences. Eventually, the realization prodded Judith to the next stage.

Stage 3: Resistance The next stage represents a major paradigm shift. It is a move from blaming minority members for their conditions to one that names and blames their own dominant group as a source of racial or ethnic problems. This resistance may take the form of passive resistance, with little behavioral change, or active resistance—an ownership of racism. Individuals may feel embarrassed, try to distance themselves from other Whites, or gravitate toward being with persons of color.

Stage 4: Redefinition In the fourth stage, people begin to refocus or redirect their energy to redefining Whiteness in nonracist terms. They realize they don't

One of my earliest experiences with a person ethnically diverse from me was when I was in kindergarten. A little girl in my class named Adelia was from Pakistan. I noticed that Adelia was a different color from me, but I didn't think it was a bad thing. I got along with her very well. We played the same games, watched the same cartoons, and enjoyed each other's company. Soon I discovered that my other friends didn't like Adelia as much as I did. They didn't want to hold hands with her, and they claimed that she was different from us. When I told them that Adelia was my friend, they didn't want to hold hands with me either. They started to poke fun at me and excluded me from their games. This hurt me so much that I stopped playing with Adelia, and I joined my friends in avoiding her. As a result, Adelia began to resent me and labeled me prejudiced.

    —Tara

have to accept the definition of White that society placed on them. They can move beyond the connection to racism to see positive aspects of being European American and to feel more comfortable being White. As Hardiman states:

One of the greatest challenges in all this is to identify what White culture is. Because Whiteness is the norm in the United States society, it is difficult to see. Like fish, whose environment is water, we are surrounded by Whiteness and it is easy to think that what we experience is reality rather than recognizing it as the particular culture of a particular group. And like fish who are not aware of water until they are out of it, White people sometimes become aware of their culture only when they get to know, or interact with, the cultures of people of color. Difficult as this process is, it is necessary to "see the water" before it can be possible to identify ways in which the culture of Whites needs to be redefined beyond racism. (Hardiman, 1994, pp. 130–131)

Stage 5: Integration As in the final stage of minority identity development, in this stage individuals are finally able to integrate their Whiteness into all other facets of their identity. They not only recognize their identity as White, but they also appreciate other groups. This integration affects other aspects of social and personal identity, including religion and gender roles.

Characteristics of Whiteness

What does it mean to be White in the United States? What are the characteristics of a White identity? Is there a unique set of characteristics that define Whiteness, just as other racial identities have been described? Let's look at the dialogue between Victor, who is African American, and David, who is White, in the film, *The Color of Fear*, produced in the early 1990s.

Victor: What I hear from White people is, they talk about being human. They don't talk about themselves as White people. What I want to know is what it means to be White.

White culture is difficult to define. White people often don't think of some of their activities as being White cultural practices. Sunbathing, for example, is important to some White people. What are other cultural activities that are important to and practiced by White people? *(© David Epperson/Tony Stone Images, Inc.)*

David: We don't look at ourselves as part of an ethnic group. I think that's what you're looking for and you're not going to find it.

Victor: Do you know that that means something? The fact that you have no answer to that?

It may be difficult for most White people to describe exactly what cultural patterns are uniquely White, but scholars have tried to do so. For example, Ruth Frankenburg says that Whiteness may be defined not only as race or ethnicity, but as a set of linked dimensions that are related: a location of structural advantage of race privilege; a standpoint from which White people look at themselves, others, and society; and a set of cultural practices, unmarked and unnamed.

A Location of Structural Advantage   One could argue that being White in the United States is linked with privilege but that the two are not synonymous. All Whites do not have power and do not have equal access to power. At times during U.S history, some White communities were not privileged and were viewed as separate or different. Examples include the Irish in the early part of the 20th century and German Americans during World War II. Scholars point out that the memory of marginality outlasts the marginality. In addition, the boundaries between Americanness and Whiteness are much more fluid for White ethnic groups than for people of color.

I don't really remember when I realized I was White. As long as I can remember, I knew that I was White. I grew up in Oregon City, a small city that is basically White. I remember one kid in my grade school who was not White. His name was Mark. Then there was an African American in junior high school, but he was not in my grade.

Although I know that I am White, I don't often think about what it means. I think that because I am White, I am accepted more for who I am. White people are not judged as heavily on stereotypes as Blacks, Hispanics, and Asians. People make more of an effort to get to know me as an individual.

—David

There is an emerging perception that being White does not mean privilege, particularly as demographics change in the United States and as some Whites perceive themselves in the minority. Charles A. Gallagher (1994), a sociologist, concluded a study in the early 1990s on what it means to be White in the United States today. He surveyed students at Temple University in Philadelphia, asking them how they felt about being White. He also asked the students to estimate the ratio of Whites to Blacks on campus. Many students reported that they thought the ratio was 30% White, 70% Black; they perceived themselves in the minority. The actual ratio was 70% White and 30% Black. Students' perceptions affected their sense of identity, which can affect intercultural communication.

Gallagher found that many of the students, mostly from working class families, were very aware of their Whiteness. They felt that being White was a liability, that they were being prejudged as racist and blamed for social conditions that they personally did not cause. They also said they were denied opportunities that were unfairly given to minority students. In this case, Whiteness is not invisible; it is a salient feature of the students' identities.

The point is not whether these perceptions are accurate. The point is that identities are negotiated and challenged through communication. People act on their perceptions, not on some external reality.

A Standpoint from Which to View Society   Some viewpoints are shared by many Whites. The frequent opinion polls reveal significant differences in how Whites and Blacks view many issues. For example, according to polls most African Americans doubt O. J. Simpson's guilt or have no faith in the legal system, whereas most Whites think Simpson is guilty.

According to a CBS News poll reported in the *Arizona Republic* in April, 1993, 38% of Whites (as compared to 27% of Blacks) think race relations in the United States are generally good. How can the perception of race relations be so different for Whites and Blacks? Something about being White and something about being African American influences how we view the world and, ulti-

TABLE 4-1 BLACK AND WHITE VIEWPOINTS

Viewpoint	Percent of Black Respondents*	Percent of White Respondents*
"The average African American is just as well off as an average White person, in terms of income."	0%	44%
"Racism is a big problem."	65%	35%
"Discrimination is a major reason for economic and social problems of Blacks."	84%	30%
"I'd rather have the federal government provide more services, even if it costs more in taxes."	63%	39%

*Of the total number of respondents, 112 were Black and 192 were White.

Source: Based on a Washington Post/Kaiser Family Foundation/Harvard University survey of middle-class Blacks and Whites (having incomes between $30,000 and $75,000), as reported in *The Washington Post National Weekly Edition* (1995, October 16–22), p. 8.

mately, how we communicate with others. A national survey conducted by *The Washington Post* in 1995 bears this out (Table 4-1). In the survey, researchers found that

> The sharpest divisions occurred in the way whites and black view the world. Simply put, a majority of whites said they believed that many blacks have achieved equality with whites on the cornerstone issues that gave momentum to the civil rights movement more than 30 years ago. Most blacks, in stark contrast, said they believe that racism and discrimination have been on the rise in the past decade. (Morin, 1995, p. 6)

In a research study, Ruth Frankenburg interviewed a number of White women, some of whom reported that they viewed being White as less than positive—as artificial and dominant, bland, homogeneous, and sterile. These individuals saw White culture as less interesting and less rich than non-White culture. On the other hand, some viewed being White as positive: as representing what was "civilized," as in classical music and fine art.

A Set of Cultural Practices Is there a specific, unique "White" way of viewing the world? As noted earlier, some views held consistently by Whites are not necessarily shared by other groups. And some cultural practices as well as core symbols (for example, individualism), are expressed primarily by Whites and significantly less by members of minority groups. These cultural practices are most clearly visible to those who are not White, to those groups who are excluded (Helms, 1994). For example, the celebration of Snow White's beauty—emphasizing her beautiful pure white skin—is often seen as problematic by people who are not White. Perhaps it is easier to see why Snow White is offensive if one is not White.

These points of view demonstrate the extent to which Whites and Blacks view the world differently and how they have very different ideas about race relations in the United States. Two Whites offered the following views:

> *I just feel as though the white person is being blamed for everything that goes wrong with the African Americans. Nobody owes any of us anything. Let's get on with our lives and make the best of it. . . . Come on. Everything in the world can't be racial."*
>
> —Merle Barone, 64, retired department store clerk

> *The percentage of black people that are middle class and the percentage of white people that are middle class I would say are equal.*
>
> —Gloria Jane Smith, 46, nurse

Three African Americans offered the following points of view:

> *Whites do not want to get it. The reason they don't acknowledge the problems is because then they would have to admit that the system is corrupt and that it's working for their benefit and then they would have to give up something they have and would have to share.*
>
> —Kolima David Williams, 39, chemist

> *You give an opportunity to a black kid in a corporation and he's supposed to hold his head down, but the manager's sons and daughters don't hold their heads down when they walk around the place. . . . Black kids, they're supposed to be saddened by the fact that they got their jobs because the government said so. What difference does it make if the government said so or if daddy said so?*
>
> —Ed Smith, director, Leaders for the 21st Century

> *I can't escape the thought that white America, which stopped short of embracing middle-class blacks at the moment we most wanted inclusion, may have already lost its opportunity. The refusal of the larger society to accept us, on our own terms, combined with our unwillingness to return to the ghetto, is likely to result in even more isolation, frustration, and desperation. And, worst of all, more anger.*
>
> —Sam Fulwood, III, 39, correspondent for the *Los Angeles Times*

Source: R. Morin, "Across the Racial Divide," *The Washington Post National Weekly Edition* (1995, October 16–22), pp. 6–10.

Multiracial and Multicultural People

The United States has an estimated 2 million multiracial people—that is, people whose ancestry includes two or more races. The development of racial identity for biracial children is a fluid process of complex transaction between the child and the broader social environment (Miller & Rotheram-Borus, 1994, p. 150).

Many individuals grow up in biracial or bicultural homes. In addition, many others develop multicultural identities for other reasons. Examples include global nomads, people who grow up in many different cultural contexts because

There are increasing numbers of multiracial individuals and families in the United States. Being multiracial means living in the borders between cultural groups and, sometimes, identifying with more than one racial or ethnic group. Do we have a tendency to want to place people in one specific racial or ethnic category rather than recognizing their multiple identities? *(© Joel Gordon)*

their parents moved around a lot; children of missionaries, international business employees, or military families often are global nomads. People who maintain long-term romantic relationships with members of another ethnic or racial culture also tend to develop multicultural identities.

Although these individuals may develop identities in stages similar to those described, they may have a less clear sense of cultural identity. They may feel as if they live in cultural margins, struggling with two sets of cultural realities: not completely part of the dominant culture but not an outsider either. Not White and not Black, they may be criticized from both cultures: too Black for White folk and too White for the Black community, for example.

Communication scholar Victoria Chen (1992) says that some Chinese American women feel caught between traditional values of their parents' culture and their own desire to be Americanized. From the parents' point of view, the daughters are never Chinese enough. From the perspective of many people within the dominant culture, though, it is difficult to relate to Chinese American women simply as "American women, born and reared in this society" (p. 231).

Social psychologist Peter Adler describes the multicultural person as one who comes to grips with a multiplicity of realities. This identity is defined not by a sense of belonging but is a new psychocultural style of self-consciousness. Multicultural individuals may become "culture brokers" who can facilitate cross-cultural interaction and conflict. However, Adler also identifies the stresses and tensions of being a multicultural person:

> *They may confuse the profound with the insignificant, not sure what is really important.*
> *They may feel multiphrenic, fragmented.*
> *They may suffer a loss of their own authenticity and feel reduced to a variety of roles.*
> *May retreat into existential absurdity. (1974, p. 35)*

Communication scholar Janet Bennett (1993) describes two types of marginal individuals based on her interviews with multicultural individuals. Some people become trapped by their own marginality; Bennett labels these people *encapsulated.* Those who thrive in their marginality Bennett labels *constructive marginals.*

Encapsulated marginal people feel disintegrated in shifting cultures. They have difficulty making decisions, are troubled by ambiguity, and feel pressure from both groups. They try to assimilate but never feel comfortable, never feel "at home."

In contrast, constructive marginal people thrive in their marginal existence. They see themselves (rather than others) as choice makers. They recognize the significance of being "in between," as many multicultural people do. They are able to make commitments within the relativistic framework. Even so, this identity is constantly being negotiated and explored; it is never easy, given society's penchant for easy categories.

IDENTITY AND LANGUAGE

The labels that refer to particular identities are an important part of intercultural communication. These labels do not, of course, exist outside of their relational meanings. It is the relationships—not only interpersonal, but social—that help us understand the importance of the labels.

Communication scholar Dolores Tanno describes her own multiple identities reflected in the various labels (Spanish, Mexican American, Latina, Chicana) applied to her. The label "Spanish" was applied by her family and designates an ancestral origin (Spain). The label "Mexican American" reflects two important cultures that make up her identity. "Latina" reflects cultural and historical connectedness with others of Spanish descent (for example, Puerto Rican and South American), and "Chicana" promotes political and cultural assertiveness in representing her identity. She stresses that she is all of these, that each reveals a different facet of her identity: symbolic, historical, cultural, and political.

In emphasizing the fluidity and relational nature of labels, Stuart Hall notes that:

> At different times in my thirty years in England, I have been "hailed" or interpellated as "coloured," "West-Indian," "Negro," "black," "immigrant." Sometimes in the street; sometimes at street corners; sometimes abusively; sometimes in a friendly manner; sometimes ambiguously. (Hall, 1985, p. 108)

Hall underscores the dynamic nature of identity and the self as he continues:

> In fact I "am" not one or another of these ways of representing me, though I have been all of them at different times and still am some of them to some degree. But, there is no essential, unitary "I"—only the fragmentary, contradictory subject I become. (pp. 108–109)

These and other terms construct relational meanings in communication situations. The interpersonal relationships between Hall and the other speaker are important. But equally important are these terms' social meanings.

IDENTITY AND COMMUNICATION

Identity has a profound influence on intercultural communication processes. This section focuses on one of the communication concerns that arise in intercultural interactions: encounters with people who do not know our identities. In intercultural communication interactions, mistaken identities are often exacerbated and can create communication problems.

Sometimes we assume knowledge about another person's identity. These assumptions guide the ways that we communicate with that person (and conceivably with others). One of the authors of this book, Tom, notes: "The question

Living in the country of France for five years, I've learned that the French are not too keen on the citizens of the country of Belgium.

In America we can assume that everyone has heard at least one Polish joke in his or her life. Well, the same goes for Belgian jokes. As a matter of fact, Belgians are looked down on as being slow, backward, and not very intelligent.

I witnessed this stereotyping all the time, no matter what situation or class of person. When people do something stupid, they risk being asked if they are Belgian.
—Kathleen

here is one of identity: Who am I perceived to be when I communicate with others? . . . My identity is very much tied to the ways in which others speak to me and the ways in which society represents my interests" (Nakayama, 1994, p. 13).

Think about the assumptions that you might make about others based on their physical appearances. What do you "know" about people if you know they are from the South, Mexico, Australia, or Pakistan? Perhaps it is easier to think about the times that people have made erroneous assumptions about you, based on shallow information—assumptions that you became aware of in the process of communication. Knowing about someone's nationality, place of origin, education, religion, and so on can lead to mistaken conclusions about the person's identity.

The problem of erroneous assumptions has increased during the information age, due to our enormous stockpile of information about the world. We are daily bombarded with information from around the world about places and people. This glut of information and intercultural contacts have heightened the importance of understanding identity.

Given the many identities that each of us negotiate for ourselves in our everyday interactions, it is clear how our identities and those of others make intercultural communication problematic. We live in an era of information overload, but we are also furnished with a wide array of communication media that multiply the identities we must negotiate. Consider the relationships that develop by E-mail, for example. Some people even create new identities as a result of online interactions. We change who we are depending on the people we communicate with and the manner of our communication.

SUMMARY

In this chapter, we explored some of the facets of identity and the ways that identities are problematic in intercultural communication. Identities are dynamic and are created by the self and by others in relation to group membership. They may be created for us by existing contexts and structures. When these created identities are incongruent with our sense of our own identity, we need to challenge and renegotiate those identities.

Identities are multiple and reflect gender, ethnicity, sexual orientation, race, nationality, and other aspects of our lives. Identities also develop in relation to minority and majority group membership. The development of such identity may follow several stages for individuals of either group.

Identity is expressed through language and labels. Sometimes communication problems arise when we make faulty assumptions about other people's identities in intercultural interactions. It is important to remind ourselves that identities are complex and subject to negotiation.

REFERENCES

Adler, P. (1974). Beyond cultural identity: Reflections on cultural and multi-cultural man. *Topics in Culture Learning, 2* (pp. 23–40), Honolulu: East-West Center.

Alba, R. D. (1985). The twilight of ethnicity among Americans of European ancestry: The case of Italians. *Ethnic and Racial Studies, 8*, 134–158.

———. (1990). *Ethnic identity: The transformation of white America.* New Haven, CT: Yale University Press.

Althusser, L. (1971). Ideology and ideological state apparatuses (notes towards an investigation). In B. Brewster (Trans.), *Lenin and philosophy and other essays* (pp. 134–165). London: NLB.

Bederman, G. (1995). *Manliness & civilization: A cultural history of gender and race in the United States, 1880–1917.* Chicago: University of Chicago Press.

Bennett, J. M. (1993). Cultural marginality: Identity issues in intercultural training. In R. M. Paige (Ed.), *Education for the intercultural experience* (pp. 109–136). Yarmouth, ME: Intercultural Press.

Bernal, M. E., & Knight, G. (Eds.). (1993). *Ethnic identity.* Albany: State University of New York Press.

Carbaugh, D. (1989). *Talking American: Cultural discourse on* <u>Donahue</u>. Norwood, NJ: Ablex.

Chen, V. (1992). The construction of Chinese American women's identity. In L. F. Rakow (Ed.), *Women making meaning* (pp. 225–243). New York: Routledge.

Cisneros, S. (1991). *Woman hollering creek.* New York: Random House.

Collier, M. J., & Thomas, M. (1988). Cultural identity: An interpretive perspective. In Y. Y. Kim & W. B. Gudykunst (Eds.), *Theories in intercultural communication* (pp. 99–122). Newbury Park, CA: Sage.

Erikson, E. (1950). *Childhood and society.* New York: W. W. Norton.

———. (1968). *Identity: Youth and crisis.* New York: W. W. Norton.

Ferguson, R. (1990). Introduction: Invisible center. In R. Ferguson, M. Gever, T. M. Trinh & C. West (Eds.), *Out there: Marginalization and contemporary cultures* (pp. 9–14). New York and Cambridge: New Museum of Contemporary Art and MIT Press.

Frankenburg, R. (1993). *White women, race matters: The social construction of whiteness.* Minneapolis: University of Minnesota Press.

Gallager, C. A. (1994). White construction in the university. *Socialist Review, 1/2,* 167–187.

Gergen, K. J. (1991). *The saturated self: Dilemmas of identity in contemporary life.* New York: Basic Books.

Hall, S. (1985). Signification, representation, ideology: Althusser and the post-structuralist debates. *Critical Studies in Mass Communication, 2,* 91–114.

Hardiman, R. (1994). White racial identity development in the United States. In E. P. Salett & D. R. Koslow (Eds.), *Race, ethnicity and self: Identity in multicultural perspective* (pp. 117–142). Washington, DC: National MultiCultural Institute.

Hecht, M. L., Collier, M. J., & Ribeau, S. A. (1993). *African American communication: Ethnic identity and cultural interpretation.* Newbury Park, CA: Sage.

Helms, J. (1994). *A race is a nice thing to have: A guide to being a white person.* Topeka, KS: Content Communication.

Horyn, C. (1992, October 4). Salons wax, curls wane as men shed pesky hair. *The Arizona Republic,* pp. H1, H5.

Jacobs, P., & Landau, S. (1971). *Colonials and sojourners: A documentary analysis of America's racial history and why it has been kept hidden* (Vol. 2). New York: Vintage.

Katz, J. (1995). *The invention of heterosexuality.* New York: Dutton.

Lacan, J. (1977). The agency of the letter in the unconscious or reason since Freud. In A. Sheridan (Trans.), *Écrits: A selection* (pp. 146–178). New York: W. W. Norton. (Original work published in 1957)

Miller, R. L., & Rotheram-Borus, M. J. (1994). Growing up biracial in the United States. In E. P. Salett & D. R. Koslow (Eds.), *Race, ethnicity and self: Identity in multicultural perspective* (pp. 143–169). Washington, DC: National MultiCultural Institute.

Morin, R. (1995, October 16–22). Across the racial divide. *The Washington Post National Weekly Edition,* pp. 6–7.

Nakayama, T. K. (1994). Dis/orienting identities: Asian Americans, history, and intercultural communication. In A. González, M. Houston & V. Chen (Eds.), *Our voices: Essays in ethnicity, culture, and communication* (pp. 12–17). Los Angeles: Roxbury.

Omi, M., & Winant, H. (1992). Racial formation. In P. S. Rothenberg (Ed.), *Race, class and gender in the United States* (pp. 26–35). New York: St. Martin's Press.

Ponterotto, J. G., & Pedersen, P. B. (1993). *Preventing prejudice* (Chaps. 4 & 5). Newbury Park, CA: Sage.

Phinney, J. S. (1993). A three-stage model of ethnic identity development in adolescence. In M. E. Bernal & G. Knight (Eds.), *Ethnic identity* (pp. 61–79). Albany: State University of New York Press.

Roland, A. (1994). Identity, self, and individualism in a multicultural perspective. In E. P. Salett & D. R. Koslow (Eds.), *Race, ethnicity and self: Identity in multicultural perspective* (pp. 117–142). Washington, DC: National Multi-Cultural Institute.

Spindler, G., & Spindler, L. (1990). *The American cultural dialogue.* London: Falmer Press.

Tajfel, H. (1978). Social categorization, social identity and social comparison. In H. Tajfel (Ed.), *Differentiation between social groups* (pp. 61–76). London: Academic Press.

———. (1981). *Human categories and social groups.* Cambridge: Cambridge University Press.

———. (1982). *Social identity and intergroup relations.* Cambridge: Cambridge University Press.

Tanno, D. (1994). Names, narratives, and the evolution of ethnic identity. In A. González, M. Houston & V. Chen (Eds.), *Our voices: Essays in ethnicity, culture, and communication* (pp. 30–33). Los Angeles: Roxbury.

Trinh, T. M. (1986/7). Difference: A special third world women issue. *Discourse, 8.*

HISTORY

Americans ignore history, for to them everything has always seemed new under the sun. The national myth is that of creativity and progress, of a steady climbing upward into power and prosperity, both for the individual and for the country as a whole. Americans see history as a straight line and themselves standing at the cutting edge of it as representatives for all mankind. They believe in the future as if it were a religion; they believe that there is nothing they cannot accomplish, that solutions wait somewhere for all problems.
 —Frances Fitzgerald, *Fire in the Lake: Vietnamese and Americans in Vietnam*

In the previous chapter we discussed the stages of identity development that the individual experiences. We also examined how identity is negotiated by the individual in communication. In this chapter we extend our discussion of identity by exploring how cultural group identity is formed and negotiated.

Identity is shaped in part by historical forces, as discussed in Chapter 4. However, people often overlook this set of dynamics in intercultural communication. We typically think of "history" as something contained in history books. We may view history as those events and people, mostly military and political, that played significant roles in making the world what it is today. This chapter examines some of the ways in which history is important in understanding intercultural interaction.

The authors of this book find, in the classes we teach, that European American students often want to de-emphasize history. "Why do we have to dwell on the past? Can't we all move on?" they ask. In contrast, some students say that without history they think it is impossible to understand who they are. How do these different viewpoints affect the communication among such students? What is the possibility for meaningful communication interactions among them?

On a larger scale, we can see how history influences intercultural interaction in many different contexts. For example, the recent conflicts in the former Yugoslavia make little sense outside of an understanding of the historical antagonisms between the different groups that reside in the area. These conflicts predate the communist era of a unified Yugoslavia. It would be erroneous to see these conflicts as solely the outcome of the termination of communism. Historical antagonisms help explain the current-day animosity felt by many Koreans toward Japanese (Japanese imperialism prior to and during World War II left a long-lasting impression). Likewise, historical antagonisms (the Franco-Prussian War as well as both world wars) help explain the current-day animosity felt by many French toward Germans.

How we think about the past very much influences how we think about ourselves and others even here in the United States. One of the authors, Judith, went to college in Southern Virginia after growing up in Delaware and Pennsylvania. She was shocked to encounter the antipathy that her dormitory suite-mates expressed toward northerners. The suite-mates stated emphatically that they had no desire to travel or visit the North; they felt certain that "Yankees" were unfriendly and unpleasant people.

For Judith, the Civil War was a paragraph in a history book; for her suite-mates, the history held a more important meaning. It took a while for friend-

The Civil Rights movement in the United States was an important social movement that changed many of the racial barriers in society. Understanding this history helps us understand how African Americans have experienced life in the United States. This 1963 photo shows demonstrators marching down Constitution Avenue in Washington, D.C. How does history help us understand some of the cultural differences in society today? Do you know how your family experienced and was influenced by U.S. culture before and during the Civil Rights movement? (© UPI/Corbis-Bettmann)

ships to develop between Judith and her suite-mates. Indeed, this exemplifies the central focus of this chapter: that various histories contextualize intercultural communication, positioning people in differing places from which they can communicate and understand the other people's messages.

We first discuss the various histories that provide the contexts in which we communicate: political, intellectual, social, family, national, and cultural group histories. We then describe how these histories are intertwined with our various identities, based on gender, sexual orientation, ethnicity, race, and so on. This chapter introduces two identities that have strong historical bases. They are diasporic and colonial identities, which we will explain later in this chapter. We pay particular attention to the role of narrating our personal histories. Finally, we explore how history influences intercultural communication.

FROM HISTORY TO HISTORIES

Many different kinds of history influence our understanding of who we are—as individuals, as family members, as members of cultural groups, as citizens of a nation. There are many histories that help us understand our different identities. These histories necessarily overlap and influence each other. For example, when Fidel Castro came to power, many Cubans left Cuba to move to the United States. The families that departed have histories about that experience that help them understand their cultural identity. Political histories tell the story of that exodus, but not necessarily the story of every family even though a family's history may be very much influenced by that event. Identifying the various forms of historical contexts is the first step in understanding how history affects communication.

Political, Intellectual, and Social Histories

Some people restrict their notion of history to documented events. Although we cannot read every book written, we do have greater access to written history. When these types of history focus on political events, we call them political histories. Written histories that focus on the development of ideas are often called intellectual histories. Some writers attempt to understand the everyday life experiences of various groups in the past; what they document are called social histories.

Although these types of history seem more manageable than the broad notion of history as "everything that has happened before now," we must also remember that many historical events never make it into books. For example, the very strict laws that forbad teaching slaves in the United States to read kept many of their stories from being documented. Absent history, of course, does not meant that the people did not exist, that their experiences do not matter, or that their history has no bearing on all of us. To consider such absent histories requires that we think in more complex ways about the past and the ways it influences the present and the future.

Family Histories

Family histories occur at the same time as other histories, but on a more personal level. Often, they are not written down but are passed along orally from one generation to the next. Some people do not know which countries or cities their families emigrated from or what tribes they belonged to or where they lived in the United States. Other people place great emphasis on knowing that their ancestors fought in the Revolutionary War, survived the Holocaust, or were forced on the Trail of Tears in which Cherokees were relocated West. Many of these family histories are deeply intertwined with ethnic group histories, but the family histories identify the family's participation in these events.

You might talk to members of your own family to see how they feel about your family's history. Find out, for example, how family history influences the way they think about who they are. Do they wish they knew more about their family? What things has your family continued to do that your forebears proba-

My history is somewhat vague, but I will write what I know.

Father's side: My great-grandfather came to the United States in the late 1800s. He and my great-grandmother came from Yugoslavia. My great-grandfather worked as a coal miner in Hazleton, PA. He died of "black lung." I don't know much about my great-grandmother. My grandfather and grandmother moved to Philadelphia in the 1940s.

Mother's side: My great-grandfather on my mom's side came to the United States in 1908 from Ireland. My great-grandmother is Scottish. As I write this I realize I don't know much about the maternal side of the family. I will definitely find out. I strongly believe it is important to know the history of my family in the United States. It is something to pass on to children and keep the spirit of this country alive!

    —Jennifer

The history of my family on my mother's side dates back to before the American Revolution, when my ancestors came over on the Mayflower. Our extensive family history has been documented through Daughters of the American Revolution and passed on through many generations. All of us know we are descendants of Wyndell Trout. My father's side of the family is more recent to the United States and is not as well documented. They are of German-Czechoslovakian heritage.

I believe it is important to understand one's culture and heritage. It makes me feel proud; the fact that all members of my family, including my brother and sister, know who we are gives us a confidence and respect toward others who find pride in their heritage. I often am disappointed by the lack of interest my peers have in their heritage. Many feel they don't need to know, that it doesn't affect them. In my opinion it provides you with a better understanding of yourself.

    —Heather

bly also did? Do you eat some of the same foods? Practice the same religion? Celebrate birthdays or weddings in the same way? Oftentimes, the continuity between past and present is taken for granted.

National History

The history of any nation is important to the people of that nation. We typically learn national history in school. In the United States, we learn about the Founding Fathers—George Washington, Benjamin Franklin, John Jay, Alexander Hamilton, and so on—and U.S. national history typically begins with the arrival of Europeans to North America.

    U.S. citizens are expected to recognize the great events and the so-called great people (mostly men of European ancestry) who were influential in the development of the country. In history classes, students learn about the Revolutionary War, Thomas Paine, the War of 1812, the Civil War, Abraham Lincoln,

I am the fourth generation of females raised in Philadelphia. My great-grand-mother raised me until she died, when I was 13. Her mother was a slave who had 19 children. Charlotte, North Carolina was the place my great-grandmother said she was born. I care because my grandmother had personal information about why Blacks should be glad slavery is over. She encouraged my family to make use of all of the benefits of freedom. She always said, "Get an education so you can own some-thing, because we couldn't own anything. We couldn't even go to school." So that is why she moved to the city of Philadelphia. She made getting an education a reward instead of a joke.
  —Marlene

I know very little about the history of my family in the United States, although I have bits and pieces of information. For instance, I know that my background is primarily Irish and German on my father's side and Scottish on my mother's side. Both of my parents grew up in the South. I do not know if I am descended from plantation owners. I am not sure about any other parts of my family history because my parents never talked about it. My grandmother is currently gathering infor-mation for me about her mother, but my grandfather will not talk about his past. I care about my history because I feel that I should know about where I came from so I can tell my children if they are interested.
  —Ruth

The history of my family in the United States is a short one. I am the first genera-tion of the Cho line. My parents grew up in Asia (Hong Kong and Taiwan) and became naturalized U.S. citizens. I was born in New Jersey, a citizen by birth. The first to be born here: guess it's special, huh?
  —Mimi

Woodrow Wilson, Franklin D. Roosevelt. They are told stories, verging on myths, that give life to these events and people. For example, students learn about Patrick Henry's "give me liberty or give me death" speech, although the text of the speech was collected by a biographer who "pieced together twelve hundred words from scattered fragments that ear witnesses remembered from twenty years before" (Thonssen, Baird, & Braden, 1970, p. 335). Students also learn about George Washington having chopped down a cherry tree and con-fessing his guilt.

National history gives us a shared notion of who we are and solidifies our sense of nationhood. Although we may not fit into the national narrative, we are expected to know this particular telling of U.S. history so we can understand the many references used in communication. It is one way of constructing cultural discourses. Yet, U.S. students do not often learn in-depth about the histories of other nations and cultures unless they study the languages of those countries. As any student of another language knows, it is part of the curriculum to study not only the grammar and vocabulary of the language, but also the culture and history of the people who speak that language.

The authors of this book, Judith and Tom, both studied French. Because we learned a great deal about French history, we understand references to the *ancien régime* (the political system before the French Revolution in 1789), *les Pieds-noirs* (colonial French who returned to France during the struggle over Algerian independence), *la Bastille*, and other commonly used terms. The French have their own national history, centering on the development of France as a nation. For example, French people know that they live in the *Vème République* (or Fifth Republic) and they know what that means within the grand narrative of French history.

When Judith lived in Algeria, her French friends spoke of *les Événements* (the events), but her Algerian friends spoke of *la Libération*—both referring to the war between France and Algeria that led to Algerian independence. When Tom lived in France, he also heard the expression *la Libération*, but it referred to the end of the German occupation in France during World War II. Historical contexts shape language. We must search for salient features in communicating across cultural differences.

Cultural Group Histories

Although people may share a single national history, each cultural group within the nation may have its own history. The history may be hidden, but it also is related to the national history. Cultural group histories help us understand the identity of the group.

Consider, for example, the expulsion of many Acadians from eastern Canada and their migration and establishment in Louisiana. These historical events are central to understanding the cultural traits of the Cajuns. The forced removal in 1838 of the Cherokees from Georgia to settlements in what eventually became the state of Oklahoma resulted in a 22% loss of the Cherokee population. This event, known as the Trail of Tears, explains much about the Cherokee Nation. The migration in 1846 of 12,000 Mormons from Nauvoo, Illinois, to the Great Basin was prompted by the murder of leader Joseph Smith in 1844. These events explain much about the character of Utah. The northward migration of African Americans in the early part of the 20th century helps us understand the settlement patterns and working conditions in many northern cities such as Cleveland, Detroit, Chicago, and New York. These cultural histories are not typically included in our national history, but they are important in the development of group identity, family histories, and the contemporary lives of individual members of these co-cultures.

We prefer to view history as the many stories we tell about the past, rather than one story on a singular time continuum. Certainly, the events of families, cultural groups, and nations are related. Even world events are related. Ignorance of the histories of other groups makes intercultural communication more difficult and fraught with potential misunderstandings.

The internment of U.S. Americans of Japanese ancestry was a significant historical event that even today continues to emphasize the importance of race in our society. In 1942 the army evacuated this mother and her three children from their home on Bainbridge Island, near Seattle, Washington. Although history helps us to understand how this group of U.S. Americans has experienced life in the United States, it is often not talked about. When did you learn about the internment of Japanese Americans? Do you think that U.S. Americans still assume that racial characteristics can identify a person as a U.S. citizen? (© UPI/Corbis-Bettmann)

HISTORY, POWER, AND INTERCULTURAL COMMUNICATION

Power is a central dynamic in the writing of history. It influences the content of what we know and the way history is delivered. Power dictates what is taught and what is silenced, what is available and what is erased. Let's look at what this means.

The Power of Texts

As we hope you have seen by now, history is extremely important in understanding identity. Yet, as literature professor Frederic Jameson observed, history is not a narrative at all; however, history is accessible to us only in textual, narrative form (1981, p. 35). People do not have equal access to the writing and production of these texts, though.

Political documents, for example, reflect the disparities of access to political participation in various countries at various times in history. Some languages have been forbidden, making the writing of texts difficult or impossible. For example, U.S. government Indian schools forbad children to speak their native languages. Japanese Americans in U.S. concentration camps, or internment camps, were not allowed to have cameras. As a result, few pictures document their experiences, which makes it more difficult for people today to understand what this experience was about.

You might note the difference it makes to you, whether we use the term *internment camps* or *concentration camps*. The U.S. federal government used both terms in the 1940s, but the historical weight of the German concentration camps often casts a shadow over our understanding of the U.S. concentration camps. Denotatively, the use of the term *concentration camp* is correct, but connotatively it invokes quite different responses. You may wish to keep this in mind as you read Chapter 6, which discusses the importance of language and discourse in intercultural communication.

The relative availability of political documents and the ways that they reflect powerful inequities are reinscribed in the process of writing history. History writing requires documentation and texts, and we only have what is available. In writing history, we often ask ourselves, "What was important?" without asking "Important to whom? For what purposes?" Once texts are written, they are available for teaching and learning about the past. The seeming unity of the past, the linear nature of history, is merely the reflection of a modernist identity, grounded in the Western tradition.

The Power of Other Histories

We live in a period of rapid change, and this change causes us to rethink cultural struggles and identities. It may be difficult for you to envision, but at one time a unified story of mankind—that "grand narrative"—dominated how people

The recovery of the history of Native American Indian resistance to the intrusion and decimation of their people is retold by Chief Black Elk. Notice the narrative that this tells, which differs from the narratives of westward expansion and the celebration of the conquering of the frontier.

> *Our party wanted to go out and fight anyway, but Red Cloud made a speech to us something like this: "Brothers, this is a very hard winter. The women and children are starving and freezing. If this were summer, I would say to keep on fighting to the end. But we cannot do this. We must think of the women and children and that it is very bad for them. So we must make peace, and I will see that nobody is hurt by the soldiers."*
>
> *The people agreed to this, for it was true. So we broke camp next day and went down from the O-ona-gazhee to Pine Ridge, and many, many Lakotas were already there. Also, there were many, many soldiers. They stood in two lines with their guns held in front of them as we went through to where we camped.*
>
> *And so it was all over.*
>
> *I did not know then how much was ended. When I look back now from this high hill of my old age, I can still see the butchered women and children lying heaped and scattered all along the crooked gulch as plain as when I saw them with eyes still young. And I can see that something else died there in the bloody mud, and was buried in the blizzard. A people's dream died there. It was a beautiful dream.*
>
> *And I, to whom so great a vision was given in my youth—you see now a pitiful old man who has done nothing, for the nation's hoop is broken and scattered. There is no center any longer, and the sacred tree is dead.*

Source: *Black Elk Speaks, Being the Life Story of a Holy Man of the Oglala Sioux,* as told to John G. Neihardt, 1932, 1959 (pp. 229–230), New York: Washington Square Press.

thought of the past, present, and future. This is no longer the case. French philosopher Jean-François Lyotard writes:

> *In contemporary society and culture—postindustrial society, postmodern culture— the grand narrative has lost its credibility, regardless of what mode of unification it uses, regardless of whether it is a speculative narrative or a narrative of emancipation. (Lyotard, 1984, p. 37)*

In place of the "grand narrative" are revised and restored histories that had been suppressed, hidden, or erased. The cultural movements that are making this shift possible are empowering to the cultural identities. Recovering various histories is necessary to rethinking what some cultural identities mean. It also helps us rethink the dominant cultural identity. For example, the celebrations and protests over the 500th anniversary of Christopher Columbus' arrival in the so-called New World reflects a new way of thinking about the past.

Power in Intercultural Interactions

Power is also the legacy, the remnants of the history that leaves cultural groups in particular positions. We are not equal in our intercultural encounters, nor can we ever be equal. Long histories of imperialism, colonialism, exploitation, wars, genocide campaigns, and more leave cultural groups out of balance when they communicate.

Regardless of whether we choose to recognize the foundations for many of our differences, these inequalities influence how we think about others and how we interact. They also influence how we think about ourselves, our identities. These are important aspects of intercultural communication. It may seem daunting to confront the history of power struggles. Nevertheless, the more you know, the better you will be positioned to engage in successful intercultural interactions.

HISTORY AND IDENTITY

In the last chapter, we saw how individual identities develop. The following section discusses the development of cultural identities, which is influenced largely by history.

Histories as Stories

Faced with these many levels of history, you might wonder how we make sense of them in our everyday lives. Although it might be tempting to ignore them all and just pretend to be "ourselves," this belies the substantial influence that history has on our own identities.

According to communication scholar Walter Fisher (1984, 1985), telling stories is fundamental to the human experience. Instead of referring to humans as *Homo sapiens*, Fisher prefers to call them *Homo narrans* because it underscores the importance of narratives in human life. Histories are stories that we use to make sense of who we are and who we think others are.

It is important to recognize that a strong element in our cultural attitudes encourages us to forget history at times. French writer Jean Baudrillard observes:

> *America was created in the hope of escaping from history, of building a utopia sheltered from history. . . . [It] has in part succeeded in that project, a project it is still pursuing today. The concept of history as the transcending of a social and political rationality, as a dialectical, conflictual vision of societies, is not theirs, just as modernity, conceived precisely as an original break with certain history, will never be ours. (Baudrillard, 1988, p. 80)*

The desire to escape history is significant in what it tells us about the ways that our culture negotiates its relation to the past, as well as the ways we view the relationship of other nations and cultures to their pasts. By ignoring history, we sometimes come to wrongheaded conclusions about others that reinforce particular stereotypes; for example, that Southerners are lazy because they live in one of the poorest regions of the United States belies the history of the region and the many reasons for the economic situation. The paradox is that we really cannot escape history even if we fail to recognize it or try to suppress it.

Ethnic and Racial Histories

People from nonmainstream cultural groups often struggle to retain their histories. Theirs are not the histories that everyone learns about in school; yet, these histories are vital to understanding how others perceive us and why. Mainstream history has neither time nor space to include all ethnic and racial histories. Sometimes the histories of cultural groups seem to question, even undermine, the celebratory nature of a national history.

When the parents of Tom, one of the authors of this book, meet other Japanese Americans of their generation, they are often asked, "What camp were you in?" This question makes little sense outside of its historical context. We can see how this question is embedded in understanding a particular moment in history, a moment that is not widely understood. Most Japanese Americans were interned in concentration camps during World War II. In the aftermath of that experience, the use of that history as a marker has been important in maintaining cultural identity.

For Jewish people, remembering the Holocaust is crucial to their identity. A Jewish colleague recalls growing up in New York City in the 1950s and 1960s and hearing stories of Nazi atrocities. Survivors warned that such atrocities could happen again, that being a victim is always a possibility. Recent attempts by revisionists to deny that the Holocaust happened have been met with fierce opposition and a renewed effort to document that tragedy in unmistakable detail. The Holocaust Museum in Washington, D.C. is a memorial to that history for all of us.

Ethnic and racial histories are never isolated but crisscross other cultural trajectories. We may feel placed in the position of victim or victimizer by distant historical events. We may even feel both of these positions at the same time. Consider, for example, the position of German American Mennonites during World War II. They were punished as pacifists and yet also were seen as aggressors by U.S. Jews. To complicate matters even further, U.S. citizens of German ancestry were not interned in concentration camps, as were U.S. citizens of Japanese ancestry. How we think about being victims and victimizers is quite complex.

French writer Maurice Blanchot, in facing the devastation left by the Holocaust, the dropping of the nuclear bomb, and other human disasters, redefines the notion of responsibility, separating it from fault. In *The Writing of the Disaster*, Blanchot writes:

> *My responsibility is anterior to my birth just as it is exterior to my consent, to my liberty. I am born thanks to a favor which turns out to be a predestination—born unto the grief of the other, which is the grief of all. (Blanchot, 1986, p. 22)*

This perspective is helpful in facing and dealing with the different positions that history finds for us.

The displacement of various populations is embedded in the history of every migrating or colonizing people. Migrations, sometimes caused by natural disasters such as the drought in the Midwest during the Depression and sometimes caused by human decisions, influence how we live today. Native peoples throughout most of the United States were exterminated or removed to settlements in other regions. The state of Iowa, for example, has few Native Americans and only one reservation. The residents of Iowa had nothing to do with the events in their state's history, but they are the beneficiaries through the ownership of farms and other land. So, although contemporary Iowans are not in a position of fault, they are, through these benefits, in a position of responsibility. Like all of us, their lives are entangled in the web of history from which there is no escape, only denial and silence.

Hidden Histories

For people whose histories are hidden from the mainstream, speaking out is an important step in the construction of personal and cultural identities. Telling our personal narratives offers us an important entry into history and to reconciling with the events of history. These stories help us understand how others negotiated the cultural attitudes of the past that have relevance for the present.

Gender Histories   Feminist scholars have long insisted that much of the history of women has been obliterated, marginalized, or erased. Historian Mei Nakano notes:

> *The history of women, told by women, is a recent phenomenon. It has called for a fundamental reevaluation of assumptions and principles that govern traditional history. It challenges us to have a more inclusive view of history, not merely the chronicling of events of the past, not dominated by the record of men marching forward through time, their paths strewn with the detritus of war and politics and industry and labor. (Nakano, 1990, p. xiii)*

Although there is much interest in women's history among contemporary scholars, it is often difficult to write that history due to the restrictions on women's access to public forums, public documents, and public records. Yet, the return to the past to find and recover identities that can be adapted for survival is one theme of writer Gloria Anzaldúa. She takes the crying woman (*la Llorana*) as a cultural and historical image that gives her the power to resist cultural and gender domination. She states:

> *My Chicana identity is grounded in the Indian woman's history of resistance. The Aztec female rites of mourning were rites of defiance protesting the cultural changes which disrupted the equality and balance between female and male, and protesting their demotion to a lesser status, their denigration. Like* la Llorana, *the Indian woman's only means of protest was wailing. (Anzaldúa, 1987, p. 21).*

Anzaldúa's history may seem distant to you, but it is intimately tied to what Chicana identity means to her.

Sexual Orientation Histories   In recounting his experiences as a young man whom the police registered as "homosexual," Pierre Seel recounts how police lists were used by the Nazis to round up homosexuals for internment. The incarceration and extermination of gays, among the various groups deemed "undesirable," is often overlooked by World War II historians. Seel recalls:

> One day at a meeting in the SOS Racisme [an antiracism organization] room, I finished by getting up and recounting my experience of Nazism, my deportation for homosexuality. I remarked as well the ingratitude of history which erases that which is not officially convenient for it.[1] (Seel, 1994, p. 162)

This suppression of history is the effect of attempts to construct a specific understanding of the past. If we do not or cannot listen to the voices of others, we will miss the significance of historical lessons. For example, a recent attempt to force gays and lesbians to register with the police in the state of Montana was finally vetoed by the governor after he learned of the law's similarities to those in Nazi Germany.

The late Guy Hocquenghem, a gay French philosopher, lamented the letting go of the past because it left nothing to sustain and mature his community. He once observed:

> I am struck by the ignorance among gay people about the past—no, more even than ignorance: the "will to forget" the German gay holocaust. . . . But we aren't even the only ones who remember, we don't remember! So we find ourselves beginning at zero in each generation. (Hocquenghem & Blasius, 1980, p. 40)

How we think about the past and what we know about the past contribute to building and maintaining communities and cultural identities. Our relationships with the past are intimately tied to issues of power. A recent book, *"The Pink Swastika: Homosexuality in the Nazi Party,* attempts to blame the Holocaust on German gays and lesbians" ("Under Surveillance," 1995, p. 14), which illustrates our point. This book depicts gays and lesbians as perpetrators, rather than victims, of the Nazis, with the intention of representing gay identity negatively. Stories of the treatment of gays and lesbians during World War II promote a common history. It influences intercultural communication among gays and lesbians in France, Germany, the Netherlands, and other nations.

Racial and Ethnic Histories   The injustices done by any nation are often swept under the carpet. In an attempt to bring attention and renewed understanding of the internment of Japanese Americans during World War II, academician John Tateishi collected the stories of some of the former internees. He notes at the outset of the book that:

> This book makes no attempt to be a definitive academic history of Japanese American internment. Rather it tries to present for the first time in human and personal

terms the experience of the only group of American citizens ever to be confined in concentration camps in the United States. (Tateishi, 1984, p. vii)

Although this collection of oral histories is not an academic history, it offers understanding and insight into the experience of many Japanese Americans. Because this historical event demonstrates the fragility of the constitutional system and its guarantees in the face of prejudice, it is not often discussed as a significant event in U.S. history. For Japanese Americans, however, it has been the most defining event in the development of the community.

Not all histories are so explicitly suppressed. For example, in recounting his personal narrative, French writer René Han tells us:

I was born in France. My parents were both Chinese. I am therefore Chinese because they left on my face the indelible imprint of the race. In life, nationality, when it doesn't match with physical traits, is less important than appearance. But I am French. I have never been anything but French and, for nothing in the world, would I be anything else.[2] (Han, 1992, p. 11)

Disjointedness is a central theme and a problem faced by René Han throughout his life. As he says:

There is my appearance and there is me. Appearance is the way others look at me. For them, I am above all Chinese. For me, it's my own perception that I have of my being. And I never see myself as anything but a Frenchman living in France among other French people.[3] (Han, 1992, p. 12)

The intercultural communication problems that arise from negotiating the complexities of how others view oneself and how one views oneself are neither unique to France nor rare. The desire to view the world in discrete units, as if people never migrate, presents problems for intercultural contact.

As mentioned in Chapter 4, people often confuse "nationality"—a legal status that denotes citizenship in a particular country—with "race" or "ethnicity." Why do you think this confusion occurs? In what ways do we engage in stereotypes when we assume that French citizens must look a particular way? Or that Mexican citizens must look a specific way? We know that we live in a world of transnational and transcontinental migrations. Yet, we often react as if we believed otherwise. What do you think are the ideological and political underpinnings of such thinking?

Diasporic Histories   The international relationships that many racial and ethnic groups have with others who share their heritage and history are often overlooked in intercultural communication. These international ties may have been created by transnational migrations, slavery, religious crusades, or other historical forces. Because most people do not think about the diverse ways that people have connections to other nations and cultures, we consider these histories to be hidden. In his book, *The Black Atlantic*, scholar Paul Gilroy (1993) emphasizes that, to understand the identities, cultures, and experiences of African descendants in Britain and the United States, we must examine the connections between Africa, North America, and Europe.

A massive migration, often caused by war or famine or persecution, that results in the dispersal of a unified group, is called a diaspora. A cultural group (or even an individual) that flees its homeland is likely to bring along some old customs and practices to the new homeland. Diasporic migrations often cause people to cling more strongly to their group's identity. Over the years, though, people become acculturated to some degree in their new homelands.

Consider, for example, the dispersal of eastern European Jews who migrated during or after World War II to the United States, Australia, South America, Israel, and other parts of the world. They brought their Jewish culture and also their eastern European culture. They also adopted new cultural patterns as they became U.S. residents, Argentinians, Israelis, and so on. Imagine the communication differences among these people over time. Imagine the differences between these groups and the dominant culture of their new homelands.

History helps us understand the cultural connections among people affected by diasporas and other transnational migrations. It is important that we recognize these relationships. Yet, we must be careful to distinguish between the ways that these connections are helpful or hurtful to intercultural communication. For example, some cultures tend to regard negatively those who have left the homeland. Many Japanese tend to look down on Japanese Canadians, Japanese Americans, Japanese Brazilians, Japanese Mexicans, and Japanese Peruvians. By contrast, the Irish tend not to look down on Irish Americans or Irish Canadians. Of course, we must remember that there are many other intervening factors that might influence diasporic relationships on an interpersonal level.

During a trip to Paris, Tom, one of the authors of this book, met a sociologist named Helena, who works for the Centre National de la Recherche Scientifique in France. Helena immigrated to France from Brazil. She is a Brazilian of Japanese ancestry. Because there are more people of Japanese descent in Brazil than in the United States, it was not surprising to encounter someone of her ethnic and national groups. Tom was in Paris to discuss popular culture; the interaction between him and Helena was guided by this topic. Despite their shared Japanese heritage, they communicated in French.

Colonial Histories   As you probably know from history, many nations did not stay within their own borders. Due to overpopulation, limited resources, notions of grandeur, or other factors, nations lost some of their people, who left their homelands to colonize territories. It is important to recognize these colonial histories so we can better understand the dynamics of intercultural communication today.

Let's look at the significance of colonialism in determining language. Three of the most important colonizers were Britain, France, and Spain. As a result of colonialism, English is spoken in Canada, Australia, New Zealand, Belize, Nigeria, South Africa, India, Pakistan, Bangladesh, Zimbabwe, Hong Kong, Singapore, and the United States. French is spoken in Canada, Senegal, Tahiti, Haiti, Benin, Côte d'Ivoire, Niger, Rwanda, Mali, Chad, and the Central African Republic. Spanish is spoken in most of the Western Hemisphere, from Mexico to Chile and Argentina, including Cuba, Venezuela, Colombia, and Panama—certainly because of colonization by Spain.

Many foreign language textbooks proudly display maps that show the many places around the world where that language is commonly spoken. It's nice to know that one can speak Spanish or French in so many places. But the maps don't reveal why those languages are widely spoken in those regions, and they don't reveal the legacies of colonialism in those regions. For example, the United Kingdom maintains close relations with many of its former colonies through the Commonwealth. The Queen of England is also the Queen of Canada, Australia, New Zealand, and the Bahamas.

Other languages have been spread through colonialism, including Portuguese in Brazil, Macao, and Angola; Dutch in Angola, Suriname, and Mozambique; and a related Dutch language, Afrikaans, in South Africa. Russian is spoken in Kazakhstan, Azerbaijan, and Tajikistan. Many nations have reclaimed their own languages in an effort to resist the influences of colonialism. For example, Arabic is spoken in Algeria, and Vietnamese is spoken in Vietnam; at one time, French was widely spoken in both of these countries.

The languages that we speak are not freely chosen by us. We must learn the languages of the societies into which we are born. The authors of this book, for example, both speak English, although their ancestors came to the United States from non-English-speaking countries. We did not choose to learn English, among all of the languages of the world. Although we don't resent our native language, we recognize why many individuals might resent a language imposed on them. Think about the historical forces that led you to speak some language(s) and not others. Understanding history is crucial to understanding the linguistic worlds we inhabit. Relations of colonialism are often part of these histories.

The imposition of language is but one aspect of cultural invasion. Much colonial history is a history of oppression and brutality. To cast off the legacy, many people have looked toward postcolonialism—an intellectual, political, and cultural movement that calls for the independence of colonialized states and also liberation from colonialist *mentalités*, or ways of thinking. The legacy of this latter invasion, the cultural invasion, often lasts much longer than the political relationship.

INTERCULTURAL COMMUNICATION AND HISTORY

One way to understand specific relationships between communication and history is to examine the attitudes and notions that individuals bring to an interaction; these are the antecedents of contact. A second method is to look at the specific conditions of the interaction and the role that history plays in these contexts. Finally, we can also examine how various histories are negotiated in intercultural interaction.

In the following passage, Franz Fanon, an anticolonialist writer and activist, describes the process of colonization. Notice how colonialists legitimate their position in relation to the people they are colonizing.

> *The oppressor, in his own sphere, starts the process, a process of domination, of exploitation and of pillage, and in the other sphere the coiled, plundered creature which is the native provides fodder for the process as best he can, the process which moves uninterruptedly from the banks of the colonial territory to the palaces and the docks of the mother country. . . . The settler makes history; his life is an epoch, an Odyssey. He is the absolute beginning: "This land was created by us"; he is the unceasing cause; "If we leave, all is lost, and the country will go back to the Middle Ages." . . .*
>
> *The settler makes history and is conscious of making it. And because he constantly refers to the history of his mother country, he clearly indicates that he himself is the extension of that mother country. Thus the history which he writes is not the history of the country which he plunders but the history of his own nation in regard to all that she skims off, all that she violates and starves.*
>
> *The immobility to which the native is condemned can only be called in question if the native decides to put an end to the history of colonization—the history of pillage—and to bring into existence the history of the nation—the history of decolonization.*

Source: Franz Fanon, *The Wretched of the Earth* (translated by C. Farrington), 1968, p. 51, New York: Grove Press.

Antecedents of Contact

We may be able to negotiate some aspects of history in interaction, but it is important to recognize that we bring our personal histories to each intercultural interaction. These personal histories involve our prior experience and our attitudes. Social psychologist Richard Brislin (1981) identifies four elements of personal histories that influence interaction.

First, childhood experiences are part of the personal histories that people bring to interactions. The authors of this book both grew up hearing negative comments about Catholics. Our first interactions with members of this religion were tinged with some suspicion. This personal history did not affect initial interactions with people of other religions.

Secondly, people may bring historical myths to the interaction. These are myths with which many people are familiar. The Jewish conspiracy myth, that Jewish people are in control of U.S. government and business, is one example.

Thirdly, the languages that people speak influence interactions. Languages may be an attraction or a repellent in seeking intercultural interactions. For example, many people from the United States enjoy traveling in Britain because English is spoken there. These same people may have little desire, or may be afraid to visit Russia, simply because it is not an English-speaking country.

Finally, people tend to be affected by recent, vivid events. For example, after the bombing of the World Trade Center in New York, interactions between Arab Americans and U.S. residents were often strained, characterized by suspicion. The media's treatment of such catastrophic events often creates barriers and reinforces stereotypes. Perhaps recent histories, such as the Los Angeles uprisings, are more influential in our interactions than the hidden or past histories, such as the massacre at Wounded Knee or the women's suffrage movement at the turn of the century.

Conditions of Contact

The contact hypothesis is the notion that better communication between groups of people is facilitated by simply putting them together in the same place and allowing them to interact. Although it seems clear that history does not support this notion, many public policies and programs in the United States and abroad are based on this hypothesis. Examples include desegregation rulings, the prevalence of master-planned communities like Reston, Virginia, and many international student exchange programs. All of these programs are based on the assumption that simply giving people from different groups the opportunities to interact will result in more positive intergroup attitudes and reduced prejudice.

Gordon Allport (1979) and Yehudi Amir (1969), two noted psychologists, have tried to identify the conditions under which the contact hypothesis holds true and the conditions when it won't. The histories of various groups figure prominently in their studies. From theirs and subsequent studies, psychologists outline at least eight conditions that must be met (more or less) in order for positive attitude change to occur and facilitate intergroup communication (Stephan & Stephan, 1985).

1. Group members should be of equal status, both within and outside the contact situation. Communication will occur more easily if there is no disparity between individuals in status characteristics (education, socioeconomic status, and so on). This condition does not include temporary inequality, like student/teacher or patient/doctor roles.

   Consider the implications of this condition for relations among various ethnic groups in the United States. How are we likely to think of individuals from specific ethnic groups if our interactions are characterized by inequality? A good example is the interaction between residents and recent immigrants—for example, in the Southwest, where Mexican Americans often provide housecleaning, gardening, and similar services for Whites. It is easy to see how the history of these two groups within the United States contributes to the lack of equality in the interaction, contributes to stereotyping, and inhibits effective intercultural communication. The history of relations between Mexican Americans and Whites varies within the Southwest. For example, Spanish families have lived in New Mexico longer than other European families; by contrast, Arizona has a higher concentration of recent immigrants from Mexico. Intergroup interactions in New Mexico are characterized less by inequality (Stephan & Stephan, 1989).

2. Strong normative and institutional support for the contact should be provided. This suggests that positive outcomes do not happen by accident when individuals from different groups come together. Rather, institutional encouragement is necessary. An example is university support for contact between U.S. and international students, or for contact between different cultural groups within the university. Other examples include corporate management sponsorship of diversity within businesses, or local community support for integrating elementary and high schools. Finally, institutional support may also mean government and legal support, expressed through court action.

3. Contact between the groups should be voluntary. This seems to contradict the previous condition, but it doesn't. Although support must exist beyond the individual, individuals need to feel that they have a choice in making contact. If individuals feel that they are being forced to interact, as with some diversity programs or affirmative action programs, it is unlikely that the intercultural interaction will have positive outcomes.

4. The contact should have the potential to extend beyond the immediate situation and should occur in a variety of contexts with a variety of individuals from both groups. This suggests that very superficial contact between members of different groups is not likely to have much impact on attitudes (stereotypes, prejudice) or result in productive communication. Just sitting beside someone in a class or sampling food from different countries is not likely to result in really understanding a person from another culture or appreciating his or her cultural background (Stephan & Stephan, 1992). For example, international students who live with host families are much more likely to have positive impressions of the host country and to develop better intercultural communication skills than those who go on "island programs," in which students interact mostly with other foreigners to the host country.

5. Programs should maximize cooperation within groups and minimize competition. For example, bringing a diverse group of students together should not involve pitting the African Americans against the European Americans on a sports team. Instead, it might involve creating diversity within teams to emphasize cooperation. There is a successful summer camp in Maine for Arab and Jewish youth; the camp brings together members of these historically conflicting groups for a summer of cooperation, discussion, and relationship building.

6. Programs should equalize numbers of group members. Positive outcomes and successful communication will be more likely if the groups are represented in numerical equality.

7. Group members should have similar beliefs and values. A great deal of research supports the notion that people are attracted to those whom they *perceive* to be similar to themselves. This means that in bringing diverse groups of people together, we should look for common ground—similarities based on religion, interests, common competencies, and so on. An

In this story, intercultural scholar Parker Johnson describes the way in which history affects his everyday experience in the United States. History, although in the past, continues to affect contemporary cultural experiences.

> *Racism is a lifelong unlearning and relearning process like alcoholism and sexism; it is not a task to be solved and done within a finite moment. It is not solely about "Black-White" relations; there are many other racial, ethnic, and cultural groups. However, our fixation with the "Black-White paradigm" does reveal our passionate and unreconciled history of slavery which is often subtle and piercing in its manifestations. For example, I drive to Harrisburg [PA] and see the Plantation Inn near the junction of route 15 and the Penn turnpike. Would we ever see a "concentration camp inn" or an "internment camp inn"? We are comfortable with the abominable history of slavery and keep it alive with such symbols. The same is true of the Confederate flag which is so proudly displayed in Gettysburg. It is fundamentally racist to display that flag and ask Black folks to get over slavery with the constant reminder displayed throughout the country. We see slavery with the constant reminder displayed throughout the country. We see no Nazi flags prominently displayed in Germany or the U.S. despite [their] importance to German history. Let's challenge these ideas and reclaim our humanity.*

Source: Parker Johnson, "Eliminating Racism as a Social Disease," *Hanover Evening Sun* (1995, October 21), p. 2.

international group of mothers works for peaceful measures in the Middle East. Although they represent different ethnic groups, they come together with a shared goal—to protect their children from military action between the warring factions in the region.

8. Finally, programs should promote individuation of group members. This means that the program should downplay the characteristics that mark the different groups (such as language, physical abilities, or racial characteristics). Instead, group members might focus on the characteristics that are expressions of individual personalities.

This list of conditions can help us understand how domestic and international contexts vary (Gudykunst, 1979). It is easy to see how the history within a nation-state may lead to conditions and attitudes that are more difficult to facilitate. For example, historical conditions between African Americans and White Americans may make it impossible to meet these conditions; interracial interactions in the United States cannot be characterized by equality (Riordan, 1978).

It is important to note that this list of conditions is incomplete. Meeting all of the conditions does not guarantee positive outcomes when diverse groups of people interact. However, the list is a starting place, and it is important to be able to identify which conditions are affected by historical conditions that may be difficult to change, and which can be more easily facilitated by communication professionals.

Negotiating Histories in Interaction

How can we negotiate interactions, given individual attitudes and personal and cultural histories? First, it is important to recognize that each of us brings our histories (some known, some hidden) to interactions. We can try to evaluate the role that history plays for those with whom we interact.

Secondly, we should understand the role that histories play in our identities, in what we bring to the interaction. Communication scholar Marsha Houston (1994) says there are three things that White people who want to be her friends should never say: "I don't notice you're black," "You're not like the others," and "I know how you feel." In her opinion, each of these denies or rejects a part of her identity that is deeply rooted in history.

Sometimes it is unwise to ask people where they are "really from." Such questions assume that they cannot be from where they said they were from, due to racial characteristics or other apparent features. Recognizing a person's history and the link to identity in communication is a first step in establishing intercultural relationships. It is also important to recognize your own historical blinders and assumptions.

SUMMARY

In this chapter, we explored some of the dimensions of history in intercultural communication. Multiple histories are important for empowering different cultural identities. They include political, intellectual, social, family, national, and cultural group histories.

History is constructed through narrative. Our understanding of the events that occur comes to us through our "telling" of the events. Histories that typically are not conveyed in a widespread manner are considered to be hidden. These include histories based on gender, sexual orientation, race, and ethnicity. All kinds of histories contribute to the success or failure of intercultural interaction.

REFERENCES

Allport, G. (1979). *The nature of prejudice.* New York: Addison-Wesley.

Amir, Y. (1969). Contact hypothesis in ethnic relations. *Psychological Bulletin, 71,* 319–343.

Anzaldúa, G. (1987). *Borderlands/La frontera: The new mestiza.* San Francisco: Spinsters/Aunt Lute.

Baudrillard, J. (1988). *America* (C. Turner, Trans.). New York: Verso.

Blanchot, M. (1986). *The Writing of the Disaster* (A. Smock, Trans.). Lincoln: University of Nebraska Press.

Brislin, R. W. (1981). *Cross cultural encounters: Face to face interaction.* New York: Pergamon.

Fanon, F. (1968). *The wretched of the earth* (C. Farrington, Trans.). New York: Grove Press.

Fisher, W. (1984). Narration as a human communication paradigm: The case of public moral argument. *Communication Monographs, 51*, 1–22.

———. (1985). The narrative paradigm: An elaboration. *Communication Monographs, 52*, 347–67.

Fitzgerald, F. (1972). *Fire in the lake: Vietnamese and Americans in Vietnam.* New York: Vintage.

Gilroy, P. (1993). *The Black Atlantic: Modernity and double consciousness.* New York: Verso.

Gudykunst, W. B. (1979). Intercultural contact and attitude change: A review of literature and suggestions for future research. *International and Intercultural Communication Annual, 4*, 1–16.

Han, R. (1992). *Un chinois de Bourgogne, avant-mémoires.* Paris: Librairie Académique Perrin.

Hocquenghem, G., & Blasius, M. (1980, April). Interview. *Christopher Street, 8*(4) 36–45.

Houston, M. (1994). When Black women talk with White women: Why dialogues are difficult. In A. González, M. Houston & V. Chen (Eds.), *Our voices: Essays in ethnicity, culture, and communication* (pp. 133–139). Los Angeles: Roxbury.

Jameson, F. (1981). *The political unconscious: Narrative as a socially symbolic act.* Ithaca, NY: Cornell University Press.

Johnson, P. (1995, October 21). Eliminating racism as a social disease. *Hanover Evening Sun*, p. 2.

Lyotard, J.-F. (1984). *The postmodern condition: A report on knowledge* (G. Bennington & B. Massumi, Trans.). Minneapolis: University of Minnesota Press.

Nakano, M. (1990). *Japanese American women: Three generations, 1890–1900.* Berkeley and San Francisco: Mina Press and National Japanese American Historical Society.

Neihardt, J. G. (1932, 1959). *Black Elk speaks, being the story of a holy man of the Oglala Sioux.* New York: Washington Square Press.

Riordan, C. (1978). Equal-status interracial contact: A review and revision of the concept. *International Journal of Intercultural Relations, 2*, 161–185.

Seel, P. with Bitoux, J. (1994). *Moi, Pierre Seel, déporté homosexuel.* Paris: Calmann-Lévy.

Stephan, C. W., & Stephan, W. G. (1992). Reducing intercultural anxiety through intercultural contact. *International Journal of Intercultural Relations, 16*, 89–106.

———. (1989). Antecedents of intergroup anxiety in Asian Americans and Hispanic Americans. *International Journal of Intercultural Relations, 13*, 203–216.

Stephan, W. G., & Stephan, C. (1985). Intergroup anxiety. *Journal of Social Issues, 41*, 157–176.

Tateishi, J. (1984). *And justice for all: An oral history of the Japanese American detention camps*. New York: Random House.

Thonssen, L., Baird, A. C., & Braden, W. W. (1970). *Speech criticism* (2nd ed.). New York: Ronald Press.

Under surveillance. (1995, December 26). *The Advocate*, p. 14.

NOTES

1. "*Un jour de réunion, dans la salle de SOS Racisme, je finis par me lever et par raconter mon expérience du nazisme, ma déportation pour homosexualité. Je fis également remarquer l'ingratitude de l'histoire qui gomme ce qui ne lui convient pas officiellement*" (Seel, 1994, p. 162)

2. "*Je suis né en France. Mes parents étaient, tous les deux, chinois. Je suis donc chinois parce qu'ils ont laissé, sur mon visage, l'empreinte indélébile de la race. Dans la vie d'un homme la nationalité, quand elle ne concorde pas avec les traits, importe moins que l'apparence. Pourtant, je suis français. Je n'ai jamais été que français et, pour rien au monde, je ne voudrais cesser de l'être.*" (Han, 1992, p. 11)

3. "*Il y a mon apparence et il y a moi. L'apparence, c'est le regard des autres. Pour eux, je suis, d'abord, un Chinois. Moi, c'est la propre perception que j'ai de mon être. Et je ne me suis jamais perçu que comme un Français, un Français vivant en France parmi les autres.*" (Han, 1992, p. 12)

LANGUAGE AND INTERCULTURAL COMMUNICATION

As we hope you are seeing in this book, intercultural communication is far more than language, but language clearly cannot be overlooked as a central element in communication. This chapter focuses on verbal aspects of intercultural communication; the next chapter focuses on the nonverbal elements.

The contributions of the social science approach generally focus on language and its relation to intercultural communication. The interpretive approach focuses on contextual uses of linguistic codes, whereas the critical approach emphasizes the relations between discourse and power. This chapter unravels the contributions and limitations of each of these approaches. In the first section, we begin with the distinction between language and discourse. We then identify the components of language and explore the relationship between language, meaning, and perception. In the second section, we explore cultural variations of language. In the third section, we discuss the relationship between language and power, and examine multilingualism and translation.

THE STUDY OF LANGUAGE

Language Versus Discourse

French theorists who laid the early foundations for the structural study of language distinguished what they called *la langue*, "language," and *la parole*, or "discourse." *La langue* refers to the entire system of language: its theoretical conceptualization. For example, when we consider what is English, should we include the various forms of English spoken around the world, in South Africa, Ireland, Zimbabwe, Australia, New Zealand, Singapore, Hong Kong, Nigeria, and Kenya? Do we include the different kinds of English that have been spoken in the past, such as Old English and Middle English? How about the various forms of pidgin or creole? As you can see, thinking about English is very complex indeed.

In contrast, *la parole* is language in use. We think about discourse by focusing on how language is actually used by particular communities of people, in particular contexts, for particular purposes. Because there are so many different ways of expressing the same idea, the selection of one approach over another is critical to the study of communication. The discursive practices of physicians and lawyers, for example, often makes it difficult for those without medical or legal backgrounds to understand what professionals in the field are saying among themselves. One of the authors of this book, Tom, has a sister who is a physician. When she and her husband, who is also a physician, speak to each other about work-related issues, they invoke a discourse that they understand but that Tom does not. One time they were talking about a heart attack and referred to it as an *M.I.* Tom jokingly asked, "Why not *H.A.?*" "That term," they explained, "was for 'headache.'" It was obvious to them but not to Tom.

Sometimes the use of specific words and phrases is embedded with a specific history that listeners may find problematic. Consider the expressions, "I'm not your slave," and "Boy, this job is like slave labor." The experience of slavery—or the Holocaust or other horrific histories—is not always taken so metaphorically.

The Components of Language

Linguistics is just one of many ways to think about language. Linguists generally divide up the study of language into four parts: semantics, syntactics, pragmatics, and phonetics. Each part highlights a different aspect of the way that language works.

Semantics   Semantics is the study of meaning—that is, how words communicate the meaning we intend to get across in our communication. The emphasis in semantics is on the generation of meaning, focusing on a single word. For example, what is a chair? Do we define *chair* by its shape? Does a throne count as a chair? Do we define it by its function? If I sit on a table, does that make it a chair?

Syntactics   Syntactics is the study of the structure, or grammar, of a language—the rules for combining words into meaningful sentences. One way to think of syntactics is to consider how the order of the words in a sentence creates a particular meaning. Word order in the sentence "The red car smashed into the blue car" makes a big difference in the meaning of the sentence. "The blue car smashed into the red car" means something else entirely.

In French, there is a difference between *Qu'est-ce que c'est?* and *Qu'est-ce que c'est que ca?* and *C'est quoi, ca?* Although all three questions mean, "What is that?" they each emphasize something different. (Roughly translated, they mean: What's that? What's *that?* and That is *what?*) This illustrates that in French, meaning often depends more on syntax than on the emphasis of single words in a sentence, which is often the case for English as well.

Pragmatics   Pragmatics is the study of how meaning is constructed in relation to receivers, how language is actually used in particular contexts in language communities. For example, if someone said, "That's a lovely outfit," you might interpret it variously depending upon the intonation, your relationship with the speaker, and so on. The person might be mocking the outfit or flirting with you. Or the comment could simply be a compliment. The meaning does not come from the words or the word order alone.

Phonetics   Phonetics is the study of the sound system of language, how words are pronounced, which units of sounds (phonemes) are meaningful for a specific language, and which sounds are universal. Because different languages use different sounds, it is often difficult for non-native speakers to learn how to pronounce some sounds.

French, for example, has no equivalent for the voiced "th" sound (as in *mother*) or the unvoiced "th" sound (as in *think*) in English. French speakers often substitute similar sounds to pronounce English words with "th." In contrast, English speakers often have a difficult time pronouncing the French "r" (as in *la fourrure*), which is produced further back in the mouth than in English.

The Japanese language has a sound that is between the English "r" and "l." This makes it difficult for Japanese speakers to pronounce some English words,

There have been a few different times when an accent has affected my perception of a person. Usually when the person with the accent is a male, I find it to be attractive. This may seem funny, but I think a lot of people feel this way. At first, I want to ask a whole bunch of questions: where the person is from, what it's like there, and so on. Then I realize I may be sticking my nose where it doesn't belong. So then I try to back down and not be so forward.
  —Lyssa

especially those in which the "r" and "l" sounds are both used—for example, the word *gorilla*. It also is difficult for English speakers to pronounce Japanese words that contain the "r" / "l" sound—including the words *ramen* and *karaoke*.

The International Phonetic Alphabet (IPA) helps linguists transcribe the pronunciation of words in different languages. The IPA was developed in 1889 by linguists who realized that it was impossible to transcribe unfamiliar languages without a common notation system. It is based primarily on the Latin alphabet but has been modified over the years to accommodate sounds that weren't easily represented by the Latin alphabet. Most languages have from 15 to 50 meaningful sound units, but the total number of all sound units for all languages is in the hundreds (West, 1975).

Language and Meaning

Universal Dimensions of Meaning Intercultural communication scholars are interested in many issues concerning the universality of language. They may look for aspects of structure or meaning that are the same in all languages. They may explore the rules of speaking and using language. The study of comparative linguistics helps us see the diversity of communication systems.

Intercultural communication scholars are also concerned with the role of translation and interpretation—that is, how people understand each other when they speak different languages. Because we cannot learn every language in the world, spoken now or in the past, we often rely on translators and interpreters to help us cross linguistic differences. What are the parameters of this mode of communication? How do we understand how this communication process works?

Finally, scholars are concerned with the power of language and the ways in which discourse may be used to oppress or hurt individuals or groups of people. Language is based on a system of differences. *Cat* and *hat*, for example, sound different, and it is this difference that communicates the meaning. Many differences are arbitrary or cultural. For example, when you learned the mnemonic device "Roy G. Biv" to remember the colors of the rainbow (*r*ed, *o*range, *y*ellow, *g*reen, *b*lue, *i*ndigo, *v*iolet) were you aware that different languages classify colors in different ways? The system of difference in any language influences how we classify the entire world, including peoples and cultures. In short, language becomes a way of regulating societies through how we view the world.

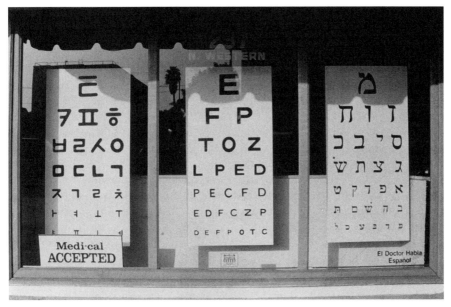

Language is an important aspect of intercultural communication. The particular symbols used in any language are arbitrary and have no meaning in and of themselves, as these multilanguage optometrist charts illustrate. Language symbols communicate meaning only when used in particular contexts. (© Bill Aron/Tony Stone Images, Inc.)

Charles Osgood, a noted psychologist, spent many years investigating the cross-cultural universals of meanings. He found that there are similar dimensions of meaning in many language groups; people everywhere can reflect on a word and characterize meaning for that word according to its value, potency, and activity. On the basis of these three dimensions, Osgood developed the semantic differential—a way of measuring attitudes or affective meaning.

For example, we can measure the evaluative dimension of meaning for the word *abortion*. (In other words, we can determine whether the word has a good or bad meaning for us.) We can also identify the potency of the word—whether it evokes a strong or weak reaction. Finally, we can also determine the activity associations of a word. The activity dimension of *abortion*, for example, might be "fast" or "slow." For women who have experienced abortion, it may seem a long, drawn-out experience.

These dimensions are probably related to core perceptions and survival reactions; confronting unknown stimuli triggers these dimensions of meaning. The most powerful is the evaluative dimension; it is important to find out if something is good or bad. But we also need to know if it is strong or weak, fast or slow.

Cross-Cultural Comparisons of Meaning   It is useful to understand these dimensions in making cross-cultural comparisons. For example, people in the United States tend to have a negative evaluation of *Monday*, the first day of the work week, and a positive evaluation of *Friday*, whereas many Arabic speakers who are Muslims have a negative evaluation of *Saturday*, their first day of the week, after the holy day, Friday. By using this etic conceptual framework, we can measure people's affective responses to words such as *leisure* or *work*. Comparing the responses would help us understand cultural variations. It would also help us understand cultural expressions such as "Monday morning blues" or "T.G.I.F.," which may not communicate the same meanings in other cultures.

Language and Perception

How much of our perception is shaped by the particular language we speak? Do English speakers see the world differently from Arabic speakers? Is there anything about the particular language we speak that constrains or shapes our perception of the world? These questions are at the heart of the "political correctness" debate today. We can answer these questions from two different points of view: the nominalist position and the relativist position.

The Nominalist Position   This position assumes that perception is not shaped by the particular language we speak. Language is simply an arbitrary "outer form of thought." Everyone has the same range of thoughts, which we express in different ways with different languages. According to this position, any thought can be expressed in any language, although some may take more or fewer words. Different languages do not mean that people have different thought processes or inhabit different perceptual worlds. A tree is an *arbre* in French and an *arbol* in Spanish, but we all perceive the tree in the same way.

The Relativist Position   This second position assumes that the particular language we speak, especially the structure of that language, determines our thinking and our perception of reality and, ultimately, important cultural patterns. This position is best represented by the Sapir-Whorf hypothesis. As you may recall from Chapter 2, the hypothesis was proposed by Edward Sapir, a linguist, and his student, Benjamin Whorf. This hypothesis is based on linguistic research they conducted in the 1930s and 1940s on Native American languages. They proposed that language is not just an "instrument for voicing ideas but is itself the shaper of ideas, the guide for the individual's mental activity" (Hoijer, 1994, p. 194). According to the Sapir-Whorf hypothesis, language defines our experience. For example, there are no possessives (his/her/our/your) in the Navajo language; we might conclude, therefore, that Navajos think in a particular way about the concept of possession. Another example is the variation in verb forms with English, Spanish, and French. In English and Spanish, the present continuous verb form is used often. A student might say, "I am studying," or *"Estoy estudiando."* A French speaker would use the simple present form, *"J'étudie."* The Sapir-Whorf hypothesis suggests that, because there is variation in this verb form, French, English, and Spanish speakers may think differently about movement or action.

Another frequently cited example is variation in color vocabulary. Navajos use one word for blue and green, two words for two different colors of black, and one word for red; these four words form the vocabulary for primary colors in Navajo culture. The Sapir-Whorf hypothesis suggests that English and Navajo speakers "see" colors differently. Other examples of variations in syntax and semantics reflect differences in perception. The Sapir-Whorf hypothesis has had tremendous influence on scholarly thinking about language and its impact on everyday communication. It questions the basic assumption that we all inhabit the same perceptual world, the same social reality.

The qualified relativist position takes a moderate, more reasonable view of the relationship between language and perception. This position recognizes the power of language but sees language as a tool, rather than a prison. This view allows for more freedom than the Sapir-Whorf hypothesis allows. As you read the research findings that follow, you may see the wisdom of the qualified relativist position.

Recent Research Findings

Communication scholar Thomas M. Steinfatt (1989) summarizes three areas of research that investigate the Sapir-Whorf hypothesis. These three areas are children's language acquisition, cross-cultural differences in language, and cognitive development of children who are deaf. As you will see, most of the research in these areas does not support a strict interpretation of the Sapir-Whorf hypothesis.

Language Acquisition in Children   If language structures thought, then language must precede and subsequently influence thought. Do you remember thinking before you could speak? Is it possible to think without language? B. F. Skinner, Jean Piaget, and Lev Vygotsky, and other psychologists have wrestled with this question. As their works indicate, these psychologists seem to conclude that language and thought are so closely related that it is difficult to speak of one as initiating influence over the other. Their work does not provide evidence for a strong relativist position.

Cross-Cultural Differences in Language   Do groups with different language labels perceive the world in different ways? One study compared perception of color variations in U.S. English speakers and the Dani of western New Guinea, who classify colors into roughly two groups, light and dark (Heider & Oliver, 1972). The researcher showed a paint chip to an individual, removed the paint chip, and then showed the person the same chip along with others, asking the individual to identify the original paint chip. There was little difference in the responses of the U.S. English speakers and the Dani, who were able to identify the original paint chip even though their language may not contain a word for that color.

Consider a more familiar example. Many men in the United States might identify someone's shirt as "blue," whereas women viewing the same shirt might call it "aqua" or "turquoise" or "teal." Men and women in the United States both *see* the color distinctions, but men tend to use fewer words than women to distinguish colors.

Another example of cross-cultural research involves variations in verb forms. The Chinese language has no counterfactual verb form (illustrated by "If I had known, I *would have gone*, but I did not"). Researchers constructed stories using the counterfactual form and found that the Chinese respondents understood the concept of counterfactual and could answer questions appropriately even though this structure is not present in Chinese (Au 1983, 1984, 1985; Bloom 1981, 1984). There is no evidence that Chinese speakers are unable to think in terms of counterfactuals but rather that they do not normally express thoughts using such constructions. Although these research examples do not support the nominalist position, they do not provide strong evidence for the relativist position either.

Cognition of Children Who Are Deaf   Researchers tried to determine if children who are deaf or who have limited language use have diminished ability in perception or logical thinking. Their studies indicated that the children with disabilities had the same semantic or categorizing competence as the hearing and the same level of cognitive skills. The children were deficient in purely linguistic skills and short-term memory storage. The researchers concluded that children who are deaf do not seem to have a different worldview (Rhodda & Grove, 1987).

CULTURAL VARIATIONS IN LANGUAGE

Language is powerful and can have tremendous implications. Uttering the words *I do* can influence lives dramatically. Being called names can be hurtful and painful, despite the old adage "sticks and stones can break my bones, but words will never hurt me."

The particular language we use predisposes us to think in particular ways and not in others. For example, as we mentioned in Chapter 2, the fact that English speakers do not distinguish between a formal and informal *you* (as in German, with *du* and *Sie* and in Spanish, *tu* and *usted*) may mean that English speakers think about formality and informality differently than German or Spanish speakers. In Japanese, formality is not simply noted when saying *you*. It is part of the entire language system: nouns take the honorific "o" before them, and verbs take more formal and polite forms. *Doitsu-go ga dekimasen* ("I—or you, he, she, we, they—don't speak German") is more polite and formal than *Doitsu-go ga dekinai*.

Variations in Communication Style

Communication style combines both language and nonverbal communication. It is the "tonal coloring," the metamessage that contextualizes how listeners

A new Russian dictionary translates Russian idioms into English. Idiomatic expressions reveal a lot about what people think is important. According to Michael Specter, Russian seems to have abundant idioms about God, food, and the soul.

> *"Without this type of idiomatic expression people simply could not communicate,"* said Yevgeny N. Shiryaev, deputy director of the Russian Academy of Sciences Institute of Russian Language and an expert on the development of common speech. *"Words would not add up properly. And of course the type of idioms we often rely on—earthy, physical phrases—tell a lot about our culture."*
>
> *A Russian could pretty much convey the entire range of human emotion with reference only to kasha, the grain dish. Nobody round here would argue with this notion, for example:* "Kashu maslom ne isportish," *which means, literally, you cannot spoil kasha with too much butter. What it really means, of course, is you can't have too much of a good thing—and in Russia a good thing is usually, well, food, soaked in butter.*
>
> *God's name is invoked in every imaginable way. If somebody is a complete loser he is* "ni bogu svechka ni chyortu kocherga"—*neither a candle to God nor a rod to the devil, i.e., useless. But not even God can compare with the soul. No word has more significance in the Russian language than* dusha, *or soul. . . . Russian souls are also always being engraved upon, trampled upon, put aside, unburdened, and burdened.*
>
> *The Russian people are so practical. After all,* "Snyavshi golovu, po volosam ne plachut"—*or, once your head has been cut off, there's no use crying about your hair. Now doesn't that make "there's no use crying over spilled milk" seem a little pathetic?*

Source: Michael Specter, "The Rich Idioms of Russian: Verbal Soul Food of a Culture," *New York Times* (1995, August 20), p. E3.

are expected to accept and interpret verbal messages. William Gudykunst and Stella Ting-Toomey (1988) identify four major dimensions of communication styles: direct/indirect, elaborate/exact/succinct, personal/contextual, and instrumental/affective.

Direct/Indirect Styles The direct/indirect dimension refers to the extent to which speakers reveal their intentions through explicit verbal communication; this dimension of communication styles relates to the speaker's level of silence. A direct communication style is one in which verbal messages reveal the speaker's true intentions, needs, wants, and desires. An indirect style is one in which the verbal message is often designed to camouflage the speaker's true intentions, needs, wants, and desires. Most of the time, individuals and groups are more or less direct depending on the context.

Many English speakers in the United States hold the direct speech style as the most appropriate in most contexts. This is revealed in sayings like "don't

My wife and I have experienced various situations in which we misunderstood each other because I did not verbally express what I meant. I would assume that she had understood my point without my verbally telling her. In the early stage of our relationship this seemed to be a tremendous challenge that we would not be able to handle in the long run. We did not know how we would live our lives and where we would spend our future together, since we came from two different cultures.

I decided to stop our relationship since it was still in an early stage of development, before marriage. So, I wrote a poem so as not to offend her or cause an uncomfortable situation. With this poem, I meant to tell her that we had to stop our relationship, with the implication that we would no longer see each other. I was completely puzzled when I found that she came to my house more frequently than usual. Almost every morning before she went to work, she stopped by my house and tried to make a plan of what we would do later in the day. I didn't have the courage to start a discussion about the poem. I assumed she understood it, since I wrote it in English. Yet, her behavior did not reflect that she understood. Our relationship went on and after a few years I found out that she thought the poem was a romantic one, encouraging the development of our relationship.

—Api

beat around the bush," "get to the point," "what exactly are you trying to say?" Although "white lies" may be permitted in some contexts, a direct style emphasizes honesty, openness, individualism, and forthrightness.

In contrast, some cultural groups prefer a more indirect style. Preserving the harmony of the relationship has a higher priority than being totally honest. A speaker might look for a "soft" way to communicate that there is a problem in the relationship, perhaps providing contextual cues (Ueda, 1974). Some languages have many words and gestures that convey "maybe." For example, three Indonesian students living in the United States were invited by their advisor to participate in a cross-cultural training workshop. They did not want to participate, nor did they have the time. But they did not want to offend their professor, whom they held in high regard. Rather than tell the professor they couldn't attend, they just didn't return his calls and didn't show up to the workshop.

An international student from Tunisia told the authors of this book that he had been in the United States for several months before he realized that if one was asked directions and didn't know the location of the place, one should tell the truth instead of devising a response. He explained that he had been taught that it was better to engage in conversation, to give a person some response, than to disappoint the person by revealing that he didn't know.

Differing communication styles are responsible for many problems that arise between men and women and between persons from different ethnic groups. Many problems are caused by different priorities for truth, honesty, harmony, and conflict avoidance in relationships.

Elaborate/Exact/Succinct Styles   This dimension of communication styles refers to the quantity of talk that people value. The elaborate style is the use of rich, expressive language in everyday talk. For example, the Arabic language has many metaphorical expressions used in everyday speech. In this style, a simple assertive statement means little; the listener will believe the opposite.

In contrast, the succinct style values understatement, simple assertions, and silence. Amish people often use this style of communication. A common refrain is "if you can't say anything good, don't say anything at all." Free self-expression is not encouraged. Silence is especially appropriate in ambiguous situations; if one is unsure of what is going on, it is better to remain silent. The exact style falls between elaborate and succinct, as expressed in the maxim, "verbal contributions should be no more or less information than is required" (Grice, 1975). The exact style emphasizes cooperative communication and sincerity as a basis for interaction.

In international negotiations, there is often a visible difference in style that can contribute to misperceptions and misunderstandings. For example, when Saddam Hussein and George Bush agreed to prepare speeches to give to the other's people just prior to the Gulf War, George Bush talked for 20 minutes and Saddam Hussein for two hours. In another speech, George Bush revealed directness and succinctness:

> *Kuwait is liberated. Iraq's army is defeated. Our military objectives are met. Kuwait is once more in the hands of the Kuwaitis in control of their own destiny. We share in their joy, a joy tempered only by our compassion for their ordeal. To-night, the Kuwaiti flag once again flies above the capital of a free and sovereign nation, and the American flag flies above our embassy. (George Bush, address from Oval Office, 1991, February 27)*

Bush's speech stands in stark contrast to Saddam Hussein's speech:

> *O glorious Iraqis, O holy warrior Iraqis, O Arabs, O believers wherever you are, we and our steadfastness are holding. Here are the great Iraqi people, your brothers and sons of your Arab nation and the great faithful part of the human family. We are all well. They are fighting with unparalleled heroism, unmatched except by the heroism of the believers who fight similar adversaries. And here is the infidel tyrant whose planes and missiles are falling out of the skies at the blows of the brave men. He is wondering how the Iraqis can confront his fading dreams with such de-termination and firmness. (Saddam Hussein, broadcast on Baghdad Radio, trans. by Reuters, 1991, January 20)*

These different uses of language communicate different things to their culturally disparate audiences. It is not easy to interpret language use from other people's perspectives.

Personal/Contextual Styles   This dimension refers to the extent to which the speaker emphasizes the self, as opposed to his or her role. The personal style is characterized by the use of linguistic devices to enhance the sense of *I*. Language emphasizes personhood, informality, and symmetrical power relationships. For example, as noted earlier, English has no formal/informal pronouns and honorifics. It lends itself well to the personal style. Although the language enables us to distinguish between formal and informal speaking, these distinctions are minor, compared with many other languages.

The Japanese language, for example, lends itself better to the contextual style, in which language emphasizes prescribed roles, status, and formality. The Japanese language offers distinctly different structures to be used by males and females. Similarly, speakers of Korean distinguish among the following three different groups:

1. People who have the same background and who are known

2. People who have a known background but who themselves are not known

3. People who are not known

Instrumental/Affective Styles This dimension of communication styles is closely related to the dimension of direct/indirect styles. An instrumental style is characterized as sender-oriented and goal-oriented, whereas the affective style is receiver-oriented and process-oriented. In the instrumental style, used by many English speakers, the burden is on the sender to make the message clear. Assertiveness is valued, and persuasion is an important skill.

In contrast, the affective style encourages the listener to sense the message before the speaker actually expresses him- or herself verbally. The burden is on the receiver. Again, Japanese are often characterized as valuing this style, trying to sense what others mean by reading contextual cues. People who use an affective style see information as complex indicators of fluid human relationships.

The point is not to stereotype specific groups (such as Japanese or English speakers). We should not expect any group to use a particular communication style all the time. On the contrary, language use can vary in many different ways beyond just linguistically. Furthermore, we might consider how tolerant we are when we encounter others who communicate in very different ways, and how willing or able we are to alter our style to communicate better.

Variations in Contextual Rules

Understanding some of the cultural variations in communication style is useful, but it is also important to realize that the particular style we use may vary from context to context. Think of the contexts in which you communicate during the day: classroom, family, work, and so on. Think about how you alter your communication to suit these contexts. You may be more direct in your family contexts and less direct in classroom settings. Similarly, you may be more instrumental in task situations and more affective when socializing with your friends.

Many research studies examine the rules for the use of socially situated language in particular contexts. They attempt to identify contexts and then "discover" the rules that apply in these contexts for a given speech community.

Researchers Jack Daniel and Geneva Smitherman (1990) studied the communication dynamics in Black churches. They first identified the priorities among community members: unity between the spiritual and the material; the centrality of religion; the harmony of nature and the universe; and the participatory, interrelatedness of life. They then described a basic communication format, the call-response, in both the traditional religious context as well as in secular life contexts. In church, the speaker and audience interact back and forth, alternating with sermon and music. In secular life, call-response takes the form of banter between the rapper (rhetor) and others in the social group.

Daniel and Smitherman discuss in their text problems that can occur in Black-White communication:

> When the Black person is speaking, the white person, because call-response is not in his cultural heritage, obviously does not engage in the response process, remaining relatively passive, perhaps voicing an occasional, subdued, "mmmmmmhm." Judging from the white individual's seeming lack of involvement in the communication, the Black communicator gets the feeling that the white isn't listening to him . . . and the white person gets the feeling that the Black person isn't listening because he keeps interrupting. (1990, p. 39)

People communicate differently in different speech communities. Thus, the context in which the communication occurs is a significant part of the meaning. Although we might communicate in one way in one speech community, we might change our communication style for another speech community. Understanding the dynamics of various speech communities helps us see the range of communication styles.

DISCOURSE: LANGUAGE AND POWER

Discourse refers to language in use. By this we mean that all discourse is social. The language that is used, the words and the meanings that are communicated, depend not only on the context but also on the social relations that are part of that interaction. For example, bosses and workers may use the same words, but the meanings that are communicated are not always the same. A boss and a worker may both refer to the company personnel as a "family." To the boss, this term may mean "one big happy family." To a disgruntled employee, it may mean a "dysfunctional family." To some extent, the disparity is due to the inequality between boss and worker, to the power differential.

Discourse and Social Structure

Just as organizations have particular structures and specific job positions within them, societies are structured so that individuals occupy social positions. Differences in social positions are central to understanding communication. For one thing, not all positions within the structure are equivalent. Everyone is not the

The particular language and speaking style we use varies from context to context. The language used in an informal social context would be different from language used in more formal contexts, such as classrooms, courtrooms, or churches. *(© Elena Rooraid/PhotoEdit)*

same. When men whistle at a woman walking by, it has a different force and meaning than if women were to whistle at a man walking by.

Power is a central element, by extension, of this focus on social position. When a judge in court says what he or she thinks *freedom of speech* means, it carries much greater force than when your neighbor who is not a judge gives an opinion about what this phrase means. When we communicate, we tend to note (however consciously) the group membership and positions of communication participants. Take the examples above. We understand how communication functions, based on the group membership of the judge (as a member of the judicial system) and of the women and men (as members of their gendered groups); we need know nothing about their individual identities.

Groups also hold different positions of power in the social structure. Because intercultural contact happens between members of different groups, the positions of the groups affects communication. Group differences lend meaning to intercultural communication because, as we noted earlier, the concept of differences is key to language.

The "Power" Effects of Labels

We often use labels to refer to other people and to ourselves. Labels acknowledge particular aspects of our social identity. For example, we might label ourselves or others as "male" or "female," indicating one's sexual identity. Or we might say we are "Canadian" or "midwesterner," indicating a national or regional identity. The context in which a label is used may determine how strongly we feel about the label. On St. Patrick's Day, for example, someone may feel more strongly about being an Irish American than about being a woman or a student or a midwesterner.

Sometimes people feel trapped or misrepresented by labels. They might complain, "Why do we have to have labels? Why can't I just be me?" These complaints belie the reality of the function of discourse. It would be nearly impossible to communicate without labels. People rarely have trouble when labeled with terms that they agree with—for example, "man," "student," "Tennessean," or "Venezuelan." Trouble arises, however, from the use of labels that we don't like or that we feel inaccurately describe us. Think about how you feel when someone describes you by terms that you do not like.

Labels communicate many levels of meaning and establish particular kinds of relationships between the speaker and listener. Sometimes people use labels to communicate closeness and affection for another. Labels like "friend," "lover," and "partner" communicate equality. Sometimes people intentionally invoke labels to establish a hostile relationship. Labels like "dumb bitch," "gook," and "camel jockey" intentionally communicate inequality. Sometimes people use labels that are unintentionally offensive to others. When this happens, it demonstrates the speaker's ignorance, lack of cultural sensitivity, and real connection to the other group. The use of terms such as "Oriental" and "homosexual" communicates negative characteristics about the speaker and establishes distance between the speaker and the listener.

Discourse is tied closely to social structure, so the messages communicated through the use of labels depend greatly on the social position of the speaker. If the speaker and listener are close friends, then the use of particular labels may not cause a distancing in the relationship or be offensive. But if the speaker and listener are strangers, then these same labels might invoke anger or close the lines of communication.

Furthermore, if the speaker has a powerful social position, then he or she risks even greater influence and impact. For example, when Edith Cresson was the prime minister of France, she made several statements that created considerable controversy. Her claims that the "Japanese are like ants" and that "25% of all English and Americans are homosexual" did not establish the kinds of relations with Japan, the United Kingdom, or the United States that France desired. Because of Mme. Cresson's powerful position in the social structure, her discursive practices created international and domestic controversies. This would not have been the case had her position been greatly different.

The authors of this book conducted a study about reactions to labeling. We asked White students which of the following ethnic terms they preferred to be called: White, Caucasian, White American, Euro-American, European American, Anglo, or WASP. They did not prefer such specific labels as WASP and European American. They seemed to prefer being called a more general label like White. We concluded that they probably had never thought about what labels they preferred to be called: As we noted in Chapter 4, the more powerful aspects of identity seem to go unnoticed; for many people, whiteness just "is," and the preferred label is one that is general and does not specify origin or history. Individuals from the powerful groups do the labeling of others; they themselves do not get labeled (Martin, Krizek, Nakayama, & Bradford, 1996). For example, when men are asked to describe their identities they often forget to identify gender as part of their identity. Women, on the other hand, often include gender as a key element in their identity. This may mean that men are the defining norm and that women exist in relation to this norm. We can see this in the labels we use for men and women and for people of color. We rarely refer to a "male physician" or a "White physician," but we do refer to a "female doctor" or a "Black doctor."

This "invisibility" of being White may be changing. It seems that Whites are becoming increasingly more conscious of their White identity, which may change the practice of labeling. Perhaps as the norm (being White) is challenged by changing demographics, by increased interaction in a more diverse United States, and by racial politics, more Whites may think about the meaning of labels for their own group.

MOVING BETWEEN LANGUAGES

Multilingualism

People who speak two languages often are called bilinguals; people who speak more than two languages are considered multilingual. Rarely do bilinguals speak both languages with the same level of fluency. It is more common that they prefer to use one language over another, depending on the context and the topic.

Sometimes entire nations are bilingual or multilingual. Belgium, for example, has two national languages, Flemish and French. Switzerland is a multilingual nation that has four official languages—French, German, Italian, and Romansh.

On either the individual level or the national level, multilinguals must engage in language negotiation. That is, they need to work out, whether explicitly or implicitly, which language to use in any given situation. These decisions are sometimes clearly embedded in power relations. For example, French was the court language during the reign of Catherine the Great, in 18th-century Russia. French was considered the language of culture, the language of the elite, whereas Russian was considered a vulgar language, the language of the uneducated. Special-interest groups in many U.S. states, specifically Arizona and California, have attempted to pass laws declaring English the official language. These attempts reflect a power bid to determine which language will be privileged.

Sometimes, a language is chosen as a courtesy to others. One of the authors of this book joined a small group going to see the fireworks display at the Eiffel Tower on Bastille Day one year. (Bastille Day is a French national holiday, celebrated on July 14, to commemorate the storming of the Bastille prison and the

A SACRED LANGUAGE (ON CONTEMPLATING THE ENGLISH-ONLY MOVEMENT IN ARIZONA)

I speak to you
because I like you.
You, the man.
But, do not ask me to
replace my language.
My language is sacred.
Do not tear down the
bridges to my Spanish
island.
No one will see its
beauty.
Do not banish my
language.
Because you, the man, will
begin generations of
ignorance.
Do not attempt to destroy
my language.
Yours is not superior.
I say, learn my beautiful
language as
I have learned yours.
My language, the language of
a many people, cannot banish.
For we are a strong many.
　　—Laura Laguna (Guadalupe, Arizona)

beginning of the French Revolution.) One woman in the group asked, *"Alors, on parle français ou anglais?* ["Are we speaking French or English?"] Because one man felt quite weak at English, French was chosen as the language of the evening.

The reasons that people become bilingual reflect the trends we identified in Chapter 1—changes that drive the need for intercultural communication. Bilingualism results from these imperatives, as people move from one country to another, as businesses want to expand into international markets, and so on. More personal imperatives also drive people to become bilingual. Alice Kaplan, a French professor at Duke University, notes, "Speaking a foreign language is, for me and my students, a chance for growth, for freedom, a liberation from the ugliness of our received ideas and mentalities" (1993, p. 211). Many people use foreign languages to escape from the history of oppression in their own languages.

Perhaps it is easier to think of language as a "prisonhouse," to borrow

Someone with what one considers a southern accent has always given me the per-
ception of ignorance.

I know this is not fair, nor is it a correct assumption. It is just that: an assump-
tion and ignorance on my part.

In my thinking, I imagine the true south to be slow and laid back. I imagine
the people to have an "I'll get there when I get there" type of mentality.

Unfortunately, if I am to be placed in a situation in which I should have to
choose someone to represent me in court, I certainly would not choose someone with
a southern accent.

I know, shame on me!
—Kathleen

Fredric Jameson's metaphor (1972). All of the semantic, syntactic, pragmatic, and phonetic systems are enmeshed in a social system from which there is no escape, except through the learning of another language. Consider the case of Sam Sue, a Chinese American born and raised in Mississippi, who explains his own need to negotiate these social systems—often riddled by stigmatizing stereotypes—by changing the way he speaks:

Northerners see a Southern accent as a signal that you're a racist, you're stupid,
or you're a hick. Regardless of what your real situation is. So I reacted to that by
adapting the way I speak. If you talked to my brother, you would definitely know he
was from the South. But as for myself, I remember customers telling my dad, "Your
son sounds like a Yankee." (Sue, 1992, p. 4)

Among the variations in U.S. English, the southern accent unwittingly communicates many negative stereotypes. Escaping into another accent is, for some, the only way to escape the stereotypes.

Learning another language is never easy, but the rewards of knowing another language are immense. Language acquisition studies have shown that it is nearly impossible for someone to learn the language of a group of people they dislike. Tom, one of the authors of this book, was talking to a student about meeting the program's foreign language requirement. The student said, "I can't take Spanish. I'm from California." Tom did not understand what she meant, so she bluntly explained that she hated Mexicans and wouldn't take Spanish to meet her foreign language requirement. Her well-guarded racism was irritating, but it revealed that she would indeed never learn Spanish.

Translation and Interpretation

Because no one can learn all of the languages in the world, we must rely on translation and interpretation—two distinct but important means of communicating across language differences. Translation generally refers to the process of

People react negatively to being stereotyped by their speech, in this case a southern accent.

> *"Just because we talk slow doesn't mean we think slow," others point out. On the East Coast they seem to think there's something funny about riding around in a pickup truck. Well in the Deep South, we don't think it's all that natural to hurtle through the dark in a crowded subway.*
>
> *It's the women of the South who feel the greatest need to look at all this with a sense of humor, but it doesn't help when these belles have to keep explaining that the size of one's hairdo has never been directly disproportionate to the size of one's IQ.*
> —Marilyn Schwartz

> *I loved Georgia. I took up for Georgia. I had a Georgia public school education. I had a Georgia accent, and it burned me when someone from the North would run down the South, and Georgia in particular. I hated it when New Yorkers would ask, upon hearing me speak, "Where are you from? Texas?"*
>
> *"No," I'd say. "Georgia."*
>
> *And then they would say, with a laugh, "Well, shut yo' mouth, you-all."*
>
> *That wasn't funny. In the first place, nobody had said "Shut yo' mouth" in the South in a hundred years, and Yankees were always screwing up "you-all."*
>
> *"You-all" was never used in singular sense. If I were addressing one person, I would never ask "Would 'you-all' like something to drink?" I would just use "you." And if I were addressing two or more persons, I wouldn't say, "Would you-all like something to drink?" I would use the contraction, "y'all."*
> —Lewis Grizzard

Sources: Marilyn Schwartz, *New Times in the Old South, or Why Scarlett's in Therapy and Tara's Going Condo*, 1993 (p. 12), New York: Crown. Lewis Grizzard, *If I Ever Get Back to Georgia, I'm Gonna Nail My Feet to the Ground*, 1990 (p. 312), New York: Ballantine Books.

producing a written text that refers to something said or written in another language. The original language text of a translation is called the source text. The text into which it is translated is called the target text.

Interpretation refers to the process of verbally expressing what is said or written in another language. Interpretation can either be simultaneous, with the interpreter speaking at the same time as the original speaker, or consecutive, with the interpreter speaking only during the breaks provided by the original speaker.

As we know from language theories, languages are entire systems of meaning and consciousness that are not easily rendered into another language through a word-for-word equivalence. The ways in which different languages convey views of the world are not equivalent, as we noted earlier. Remember the dilemma regarding color? The English word *brown* might be translated as any of these French words, depending on how the word is used: *roux, brun, bistre, bis, marron, jaune,* and *gris* (Vinay & Darbelnet, 1977, p. 261).

Issues of Equivalency and Accuracy   Some languages have tremendous flexibility in expression; others have a limited range of words. The reverse may be true, however, for some topics. This slippage between languages is both aggravating and thrilling for translators and interpreters. The tradition of translation studies has tended to emphasize issues of equivalence and accuracy. That is, the focus, largely from linguistics, has been on comparing the translated meaning to the original meaning. For those interested in the intercultural communication process, the emphasis is not so much on equivalence, but rather on the bridges that people construct to cross from one language to another.

Once when Tom was in Normandy (in northern France) a French policeman asked him to tell an English-speaking woman to get down from a wall that was high above the street. Tom called out to her that the policeman wanted her to get down. She refused. The police officer became angry and began speaking louder and louder, faster and faster, repeating his request. Tom, too, began speaking louder and louder, faster and faster, giving the same request in English. The situation escalated until the woman responded, "Tell him to go to hell!" At this point, Tom felt trapped, so he turned to the police officer and said "*Je ne comprends pas. Je ne parle pas français.* ["I don't understand. I don't speak French."]

Tom tried to apologize, to back out of the situation. But the police officer interrupted him immediately and retorted, "*Mais oui, tu peux parler français!*" ["Oh yes, you can speak French!"] and continued barking angry commands at the woman. Throughout this situation, Tom never really expressed the nuances of the expressions on either side. The police officer, unless he understood English and refused to speak it, did not know the obscenities that were being hurled his way. Nor did the woman understand the demeaning familiar forms of language used by the police officer, or the significance of his demands as a police officer, a position of much more authority than in the United States.

The Role of the Translator or Interpreter   We often assume that translators and interpreters are "invisible," that they simply render into the target language whatever they hear. The roles that they play as intermediaries, however, often regulate how they render what is said. Consider the above example again. Because of the French police officer's position, it was nearly impossible, aside from the linguistic difficulties of translating profanity, for Tom to tell him what the woman was saying.

We often assume that anyone who knows two languages can be a translator or an interpreter. Research shows, however, that high levels of fluency in two languages do not necessarily make someone a good translator or interpreter. The task obviously requires the knowledge of two languages. But that's not enough. Think about all of the people you know who are native English speakers. What might explain why some of them are better writers than others?

Knowing English, for example, is a necessity for writing in English, but this knowledge does not necessarily make a person a good writer. Because of the complex relationships between people, particularly in intercultural situations, translation and interpretation involve far more than linguistic equivalence, which traditionally has been the focus.

In his book, *Contemporary Translation Theories*, linguist Edwin Gentzler speculates that the 1990s "might be characterized as experiencing a boom in translation theory" (1993, p. 181). In part, this "boom" is fueled by a recognition that the traditional focus in translation studies is too limiting to explain the wide variety of ways that meanings might be communicated. Gentzler concludes: "With such insight, perhaps we will be less likely to dismiss that which does not fit into or measure up to our standards, and instead open our selves to alternative ways of perceiving—in other words, to invite real intra- and intercultural communication" (1993, p. 199).

The field of translation studies is rapidly becoming more central to academic inquiry, as it moves from being a marginalized area of inquiry to an area with far-reaching consequences for many disciplines in the university. As these developments proceed, we will see a tremendous impact on how academics approach intercultural communication. Perhaps intercultural communication scholars will begin to play a greater role in the developments of translation studies.

SUMMARY

In this chapter, we have explored many dimensions of language and discourse in intercultural communication. Discourse, or language in use, always has a social context. Linguists study four basic components of language as they investigate how language works: semantics is the study of meaning, syntax is the study of structure, pragmatics studies context, and phonetics studies the sound system of the language.

Some dimensions of meaning are universal, at least to many language groups. People in different cultures can characterize the meaning of a phrase according to three criteria: the phrase's value, its potency, and its level of activity. The particular language we speak influences our perception, but it does not totally determine our perception.

Languages exhibit many cultural variations, both in communication style and in the rules of context. Four types of communication styles are indirect/direct, exact/succinct/elaborated, personal/contextual, and instrumental/affective. The context in which the communication occurs is a significant part of the meaning.

Understanding the role of power in language use is important. The effects of power are revealed in the use of labels, with the more powerful people in a society labeling the less powerful. Individuals who occupy powerful positions in a society often don't think about the way their positions are revealed in their communication.

Another language issue is that of multilingualism. Individuals learn languages for different reasons and the process is often a rewarding one. The complexities of moving between languages is facilitated by interpretation and translation, in which issues of equivalency and accuracy are crucial. Being a good translator or interpreter requires more than just fluency in two languages.

REFERENCES

Au, T. K. (1983). Chinese and English counterfactuals: The Sapir-Whorf hypothesis revisited. *Cognition, 15,* 155–187.

———. (1984). Counterfactuals: In reply to Alfred Bloom. *Cognition, 17,* 239–302.

———. (1985). Language and cognition. In L. L. Lloyd, & R. L. Schiefelbusch (Eds.), *Language perspectives II.* Baltimore: University Park Press.

Bloom, A. (1981). *The linguistic shaping of thought: A study in the impact of language on thinking in China and the West.* Hillsdale, NJ: Lawrence Erlbaum.

———. (1984). Caution—the words you use may affect what you say: A response to Terry Kitfong Au's "Chinese and English counterfactuals: The Sapir-Whorf hypothesis revisited." *Cognition, 17,* 275–287.

Daniel, J. L., & Smitherman, G. (1990). How I got over: Communication dynamics in the Black community. In D. Carbaugh (Ed.), *Cultural communication and intercultural contact* (pp. 27–40). Hillsdale, NJ: Lawrence Erlbaum.

Gentzler, E. (1993). *Contemporary translation theories.* New York: Routledge.

Grice, H. (1975). Logic and conversation. In P. Cole & J. Morgan (Eds.), *Syntax and semantics: Vol. 3. Speech acts.* New York: Academic Press.

Grizzard, L. (1990). *If I ever get back to Georgia, I'm gonna nail my feet to the ground.* New York: Ballantine Books.

Gudykunst, W. B., & Ting-Toomey, S. (1988). *Culture and interpersonal communication.* Newbury Park, CA: Sage.

Heider, E. R., & Oliver, D. C. (1972). The structure of the color space in naming and memory for two languages. *Cognitive Psychology, 8,* 337–354.

Hoijer, H. (1994). The Sapir-Whorf hypothesis. In L. Samovar & R. E. Porter (Eds.), *Intercultural communication: A reader* (pp. 194–200). Belmont, CA: Wadsworth.

Jameson, F. (1972). *The prisonhouse of language.* Princeton, NJ: Princeton University Press.

Kaplan, A. (1993). *French lessons: A memoir.* Chicago: University of Chicago Press.

Martin, J. N., Krizek, R. L., Nakayama, T. K., & Bradford, L. (1996). Exploring whiteness: A study of self-labels for White Americans. *Communication Quarterly, 44,* 125–144.

Osgood, C. E., May, W. H., & Miron, M. S. (1975). *Cross-cultural universals of meaning.* Urbana: University of Illinois Press.

Rhodda, M., & Grove, C. (1987). *Language, cognition, and deafness.* Hillsdale, NJ: Lawrence Erlbaum.

Sapir, E. (Ed.). (1921a). *Language: An introduction to the study of speech.* New York: Harcourt, Brace & World.

———. (1921b). Language, race, and culture. In E. Sapir (Ed.), *Language: An introduction to the study of speech.* New York: Harcourt, Brace & World.

Specter, M. (1995, August 20). The rich idioms of Russian: Verbal soul food of a culture. *New York Times*, p. E3.

Steinfatt, T. M. (1989). Linguistic relativity: Toward a broader view. In S. Ting-Toomey & F. Korzenny (Eds.), *Language, communication and culture* (pp. 35–78). Newbury Park, CA: Sage.

Sue, S. (1992). Growing up in Mississippi. In J. F. J. Lee (Ed.), *Asian Americans* (pp. 3–9). New York: New Press.

Swartz, M. (1993). *New Times in the Old South, or why Scarlett's in therapy and Tara's going condo.* New York: Crown.

Ueda, K. (1974). Sixteen ways to avoid saying "No" in Japan. In J. C. Condon & M. Saito (Eds.), *Intercultural encounters with Japan* (pp. 185–192). Tokyo: The Simul Press.

Vinay, J. P., & Darbelnet, J. (1977). *Stylistique comparée du français et de l'anglais: Méthode de traduction.* Paris: Marcel Didier.

West, F. (1975). *The way of language: An introduction.* New York: Harcourt Brace Jovanovich.

Whorf, B. L. (1956). *Language, thought and reality.* Cambridge: MIT Press.

NONVERBAL CODES AND CULTURAL SPACE

It's your first day with your FTO (Field Training Officer). He drives the squad. You're too nervous to drive. You don't know where you're going anyway. And all this stuff is coming at you. The police radio's on; you can't make sense out of it; your FTO's talking to you constantly; you're hearing all these sounds from the street, languages you've never heard. You're seeing things you've never seen before. You're confused as hell.

Suddenly, your FTO stops the squad and says, "Okay, let's get out, kid." He jumps out and flings somebody against the wall and takes a gun off of him.

You're looking at him in total disbelief. How'd he know that? This guy must be the Great Carnac. Ten years later you've got a kid driving with you and you see something and you fling somebody against a wall. And the kid's looking at you like how did he know? And you know it's not magic.

—Police officer, quoted in C. Fletcher's "The Semiotics of Survival: Street Cops Read the Street" (1992), pp. 137–139

Nonverbal elements of cultural communication play an important role in understanding intercultural communication. Reading nonverbal communication within various cultural spaces can be a key to survival, depending upon the situation. Fletcher, a communication scholar, notes "Urban police officers are one group for whom taking 'everyday life' for granted by screening out the discomfiting or confusing elements can have tragic consequences for both cops and citizens" (1992, p. 135).

You may never become a police officer, but you certainly will find yourself in many intercultural communication situations and cultural spaces. Your own nonverbal communication may create additional problems in some cases and, if the behaviors are inappropriate for the particular cultural space, may exacerbate existing tensions. In other cases, your use of nonverbals might reduce tension and confusion.

The first part of this chapter discusses the importance of understanding nonverbal aspects of intercultural communication. The second section explores cultural patterns of specific nonverbal communication codes (personal space, gestures, facial expressions, and so on) and how these nonverbal codes express power in intercultural contexts. The third section investigates the concept of cultural space and how cultural identity is shaped and negotiated by the cultural spaces (home, neighborhood, and so on) that people occupy.

As urban police officers know, there can never be a guidebook to "reading the streets." The nonverbals of the street change constantly. For the same reason, we believe it is useless to list nonverbals to memorize. Instead, it will be more beneficial for you to learn the framework of nonverbal communication and cultural spaces, so that you can unpack and learn the nonverbal systems of whatever cultural groups become relevant to your life. Understanding communication is a matter of understanding how to figure out *systems* of meaning, rather than discrete elements. Nonverbal intercultural communication is no exception.

DEFINING NONVERBAL COMMUNICATION

In this chapter we discuss two forms of communication beyond speech. The first includes facial expression, personal space, eye contact, use of time, and conversational silence. (What is not said is often as important as what is spoken.)

A second aspect of nonverbal behavior includes the cultural spaces that we occupy and negotiate. Cultural spaces are the social and cultural contexts that form our identity—where we grow up and where we live (not necessarily the physical homes and neighborhoods, but the cultural meanings created in these places).

Comparing Verbal and Nonverbal Communication

Both verbal and nonverbal communication are symbolic, communicate meaning, and are patterned; that is, they are governed by rules that are contextually determined. Societies have different nonverbal languages, just as they have different spoken languages. However, some differences between nonverbal and verbal communication codes have important implications for intercultural interaction.

Let's look at some examples of these differences. The following incident occurred to Judith, one of the authors of this book, when she was new to Algeria, where she lived for a while. One day she stood at her balcony and waved to one of the young Algerian teachers, who was walking across the school yard. Two minutes later, the young teacher knocked on the door, looking expectantly at Judith, as if summoned. Because Judith knew that it was uncommon in Algeria for men to visit women they didn't know well, she was confused. Why had he come to her door? Was it because she was foreign? After a few awkward moments, he left. A few weeks later, Judith figured it out. In Algeria (as in many other places), the U.S. "wave" is the nonverbal signal for "come here." The young teacher had assumed that Judith had summoned him to her apartment. As this example illustrates, rules for nonverbal communication vary among cultures and contexts.

Let's consider another example. Two U.S. students attending school in France were hitchhiking to the university in Grenoble for the first day of classes. A French motorist picked them up and immediately started speaking English to them. They wondered how he knew they spoke English. Later, they took a train to Germany. The conductor walked into their compartment and berated them in English for putting their feet on the opposite seat. How had he known that they spoke English? As this example shows, nonverbal communication entails more than gestures. Even our appearance can communicate loudly. (The students' very appearance probably was a sufficient clue to their national identity.) As this example also shows, nonverbal behavior operates at a subconscious level. We rarely think about the way we stand, the hand gestures we use, and so on. Occasionally, someone points out such behaviors which brings them to a conscious level.

Many people learn nonverbal communication through enculturation. We often think that many postures, including standing and sitting, are "natural" rather than "cultural" stances. The way this man is sitting is seen in the United States as a masculine posture. However, in other cultures, it would be considered rude for him to sit in a way that shows the bottom of his foot to others. How aware are you that many of your gestures are not simply natural but are cultural and may communicate unintended messages? (© Alán Gallegos/AG Photographs)

When misunderstandings arise, we are more likely to question our verbal communication than our nonverbal communication. We can search for a different way to explain verbally what we mean. We can look up words in a dictionary or ask someone to explain unfamiliar words. By contrast, it is more difficult to identify nonverbal miscommunications or misperceptions.

Learning Nonverbal Behavior   Whereas we learn rules and meanings for language behavior in grammar and spelling lessons, we learn nonverbal meanings and behaviors by more implicit socialization. No one explains, "When you talk with someone you like, lean forward, smile, and touch the person frequently, because that will communicate that you really care about him or her." In many contexts in the United States, these behaviors communicate immediacy and positive meanings. How is it interpreted if one does not display these behaviors?

Sometimes we learn strategies for nonverbal communication. Have you ever been told to shake hands firmly when you meet someone? You may have learned that a limp handshake indicates a weak person. Likewise, many young women learn to cross their legs at the ankles and keep their legs together when they sit. These strategies combine socialization and the teaching of nonverbal codes.

Researchers in the 1960s conducted microanalyses of nonverbal interactions in therapy sessions. They found that when things were going well, the therapist and patient mirrored each other's behavior, almost like a dance. When one person leaned back, so did the other. When one crossed his or her legs, so did the other. More recent research seems to support these early studies, showing that when people feel positively or warmly toward each other in conversations, they tend to mimic each other's nonverbal behavior.

Coordinating Nonverbal and Verbal Behaviors   Nonverbal behaviors can reinforce, substitute for, or contradict verbal behaviors. When we shake our heads and say "no," we are reinforcing verbal behavior. When we point instead of saying "over there," our nonverbal behavior is substituting for our verbal communication. If we tell a friend, "I can't wait to see you," and then don't show up at the friend's house, the nonverbal behavior is contradicting the verbal behavior.

What would you think if someone told you that your outfit was wonderful but then rolled his or her eyes? The nonverbal behavior contradicts the verbal message. Which message would you believe, and why? Generally, people believe the nonverbal behavior. Because nonverbal communication operates at a more unconscious level, we tend to think that people have less control over their nonverbal behavior. Therefore, we often think of nonverbal behaviors as the "real" message.

What Nonverbal Behavior Communicates

Relational Messages   Although language is effective and efficient at communicating explicit information and the content of messages, nonverbal communication often communicates the metamessage, or the relational aspect of messages:

how we really feel about the person, and so on. Nonverbal behavior often forms the basis of our judgments about people we meet for the first time. In addition, we usually communicate how we feel about others nonverbally—by facial expression, eye contact, posture, and so on. Nonverbal communication plays a significant role in establishing the relations we have with others.

Status   Nonverbal behavior also communicates status and power. For example, a supervisor may be able to touch subordinates, but usually it is unacceptable for subordinates to touch a supervisor. Large expansive gestures are associated with status; conversely, holding the body in a tight, closed position communicates low status. In general, the more space a person controls in the office or home, the greater that person's status. Similarly, the presence or quantity of office windows communicates employees' relative power in an organization: the more power an employee has, the more windows in his or her office.

Deception   Nonverbal behavior also communicates deception. Early research studies concentrated on leakage in nonverbal communication. Researchers tried to identify which parts of the body people were least able to control and, therefore, which parts communicated "true" feelings. They believed that some nonverbal behaviors (avoiding eye contact, touching or rubbing the face, and so on) indicated lying.

Research shows that deception is communicated by fairly idiosyncratic behaviors and probably as much by verbal communication. Each individual may have his or her own unique way of communicating deception depending on personality, motivation, planning, and age. Only a few nonverbal behaviors (such as pupil dilation, blinking, and higher pitch) are consistently related to deception (Burgoon, Buller, & Woodall, 1989; Zuckerman, DePaulo, & Rosenthal, 1981).

Most nonverbal communication about affect, status, and deception happens at an unconscious level. For this reason, it plays an important role in intercultural interactions. It is pervasive and unconscious. It communicates how we feel about each other and about our cultural groups.

THE UNIVERSALITY OF NONVERBAL BEHAVIOR

Most traditional research in intercultural communication focuses on identifying cross-cultural differences in nonverbal behavior. How do culture, ethnicity, and gender influence nonverbal communication patterns? How universal is most nonverbal communication? Traditional research seeks to answer these questions.

As we have observed in earlier chapters, it is neither beneficial nor accurate to try to reduce an individual to one element of his or her identity (gender, ethnicity, or nationality). Attempts to classify people in discrete categories tend to reduce their complexities and create enormous communication misunderstandings. However, we often classify people according to various categories to help us find universalities. For example, although we may know that not all Germans are alike, we may seek information that helps us communicate better with Germans. In this section, we explore the extent to which nonverbal communication codes are universally shared. We also look for possible cultural variations in these codes that may serve as tentative guidelines to help us communicate better with others.

Recent Research Findings

Research investigating the universality of nonverbal communication has focused on three areas:

1. The relationship of human behavior to that of primates (particularly chimpanzees)
2. Nonverbal communication of sensory-deprived children who are blind or deaf
3. Cross-cultural studies on facial expression

Chimpanzees and humans share many nonverbal behaviors. Both, for example, exhibit the eyebrow flash—a slight raising of the eyebrow that communicates a recognition. This is one of the most primitive and universal animal behaviors. Humans do it when they see someone they know. Primates and humans also share some facial expressions. However, animal communication appears to be less complex, with fewer facial blends.

Researcher Eibl-Eibesfeldt (1974) conducted studies that compared the facial expressions of children who were blind with those of sighted children and found many similarities. Even though the children who were blind couldn't see the facial expressions of others to mimic them, they still made the same expressions. This seems to suggest some innate, genetic basis for these behaviors. However, the blind children's facial expressions were less complex, with fewer facial blends, than sighted children's expressions. The face of a blind child might show a blank expression and then a smile, whereas the face of a sighted child might show subtle changes from a smile to a frown, for example. Or the sighted child's expression might combine a smile and a frown.

Many cross-cultural studies support the notion that facial expressions are universal, to some extent. Six basic emotions are communicated by facial expressions. They include happiness, sadness, disgust, fear, anger, and surprise. Expressions for these emotions are recognized by most cultural groups as having the same meaning (Ekman, 1973; Ekman & Friesen, 1987; Ekman, Friesen, & Ellsworth, 1972).

These research findings may support universalities in nonverbal communication. However, some variations also exist. The evoking stimuli (that is, what causes the nonverbal behavior) may vary from one culture to another. Smiling, for example, is universal. But what prompts a person to smile may be culture-specific.

There are variations in the rules for the nonverbal behavior and in what contexts the nonverbal communication takes place. Whereas people kiss in most cultures, there is variation in who kisses whom and in what contexts. For example, when French friends greet, they often kiss on both cheeks but never on the mouth. Friends in the United States usually kiss on greeting only after long absence and then usually accompanied by a hug. The rules for kissing also vary along gender lines.

Finally, it is important to look for larger cultural patterns to the nonverbal behavior, rather than trying to identify and memorize all of the cultural differences. Researcher David Matsumoto (1990) suggests that, although cultural differences in nonverbal patterns are interesting, noting these differences is not sufficient. Studying every variation in every aspect of nonverbal behavior would be an overwhelming task. Instead, he suggests studying nonverbal communication patterns that vary with other cultural patterns, such as values.

For example, Matsumoto links cultural patterns in facial expressions with cultural values of power distance and individualism and collectivism. Hypothetically, cultural groups that emphasize status differences most likely would express emotions that preserve these status differences. Matsumoto also suggests that within individualistic cultures the degree of difference in emotional display between ingroups and outgroups is greater than the degree of difference between the same groups in collectivist societies. If these theoretical relationships hold true, we could generalize about the nonverbal behavior of many different cultural groups.

Nonverbal Codes

Proxemics   Proxemics is the study of how people use personal space, or the "bubble" that is around us that marks the territory between ourselves and others. O. M. Watson (1970), a proxemics specialist, investigated nonverbal communication between Arab and U.S. students after hearing many complaints from each group about the other. The Arab students complained that the U.S. students were distant and rude. The U.S. students characterized the Arab students as pushy, arrogant, and rude. His investigations showed that the two groups operated with different rules concerning personal space. Watson's research supported Edward Hall's observations about the cultural variations in how much distance individuals placed between themselves and others.

You may recall from Chapter 2 that Hall made a distinction between *contact cultures* and *noncontact cultures*. He described contact cultures as those societies in which people stood closer together while talking, engaged in more direct eye contact, used face-to-face body orientations more often while talking, touched more frequently, and spoke in louder voices. He suggested that societies in South America and Southern Europe were contact cultures, whereas those in Northern Europe, the United States, East Asia, and the Far East were noncontact cultures—in which people tend to stand farther apart when conversing, maintain less eye contact, and touch less often.

THE FIRST TRIP BACK HOME

The first time I came to the United States I stayed for over two years without returning home. My first trip home was really hard because I had forgotten a lot of my native language and I spent most of my time translating everything in my head first before I could express it in proper French. I also had a lot of problems re-adapting to French society and the way of doing things. One of my worst episodes was going to a post office and being very angry at the people around me because I perceived them as not knowing how to properly behave in a public space: They didn't form a waiting line but seemed to be packed in front of the teller, and they were also very close to each other without respecting the personal space that I had been accustomed to while living in the United States.
— Denis

Of course, many other factors besides national culture determine how far we stand from someone. Gender, age, ethnicity, the context of the interaction, and the topic of discussion all influence the use of personal space. In fact, some studies show that national culture is perhaps the least important factor. For example, in Algeria, gender might be the overriding factor. Unmarried young women and men would rarely stand close together, touch each other, or maintain direct eye contact.

Eye Contact   Eye contact often is included in proxemics because it regulates interpersonal distance. Direct eye contact shortens the distance between two people, whereas less eye contact increases the distance. Eye contact communicates meanings about respect and status and often regulates turn-taking.

Patterns of eye contact vary from culture to culture. In many societies, avoiding eye contact communicates respect and deference, although this may vary from context to context. For many U.S. Americans, maintaining eye contact communicates that one is paying attention, showing respect.

When they speak with others, most U.S. Americans look away from their listeners most of the time. They might look at their listeners every 10 to 15 seconds. When a speaker is finished taking a turn, he or she looks directly at the listener to signal completion. However, some cultural groups within the United States use even less eye contact while they speak. For example, some Native Americans tend to avert eye gaze during conversation.

Facial Expression   As noted earlier in this chapter, there have been many investigations of the universality of facial expression. Psychologists Ekman and Friesen (1987) conducted extensive and systematic work in nonverbal communication. They first took pictures of U.S. Americans' facial expressions reflecting six emotions thought to be universal. They then showed these photographs to people in various cultural groups.

However, Ekman and Friesen's studies have been criticized for a few reasons. First, the studies don't tap into universality; people may be able to recognize and identify the six emotions because of exposure to media. Also, the researchers presented a limited number of responses (multiple choice answers) when they asked respondents to identify emotions expressed.

Later studies improved on this research. Researchers took many photographs, not always posed, of facial expressions of members from many different cultural groups; then they asked the subjects to identify the emotion expressed by the facial expression. Researchers then showed these photographs to many different individuals in many different countries, including some without exposure to media. The conclusion supports the notion of universality of facial expression. Some basic human emotions are expressed in a fairly finite number of facial expressions and these expressions can be recognized and identified universally (Boucher & Carlson, 1980; Ekman & Friesen, 1987).

Chronemics Chronemics concerns concepts of time and the rules that govern its use. There are many cultural variations regarding how people understand and use time. Edward Hall distinguished between monochronic and polychronic time orientation. People who have a monochronic concept of time regard it as a commodity: Time can be gained, lost, spent, wasted, or saved. In this orientation, time is linear, with one event happening at a time. In general, monochronic cultures value highly punctuality, completing tasks, and keeping to schedules. Most university staff and faculty in the United States maintain a monochronic orientation to time. Classes, meetings, and office appointments start when scheduled. Faculty members see one student at a time, hold one meeting at a time, and keep appointments almost regardless of any relational emergency. Family problems are considered poor reasons for not fulfilling academic obligations—for both faculty and students.

In contrast, a polychronic orientation conceptualizes time as more holistic, perhaps more circular: Many events can happen at once. U.S. business people often complain that meetings in the Middle East do not start "on time," that people socialize during meetings, and that meetings may be canceled because of personal obligations. Often, tasks are accomplished *because* of personal relationships, not in spite of them.

Many international business negotiations and technical assistance projects fail because of differences in time orientation. International students and business personnel often complain that U.S. Americans seem too busy, too tied to their schedules; they complain that U.S. Americans do not care enough about relationships and about the personal aspects of living.

Silence Cultural groups may vary in the relative emphasis placed on speaking and silence. Silence can be as meaningful as language. In most U.S. American contexts, silence is not highly valued. Particularly in developing relationships, silence communicates awkwardness and sometimes causes people to be uncomfortable. According to scholar William G. Gudykunst's uncertainty reduction theory, the major reason for communicating verbally in initial interactions with people is to reduce uncertainty. In U.S. American contexts, people employ active uncertainty reduction strategies (such as asking questions). However, in many other cultural contexts, one reduces uncertainty by more passive strategies, by being silent, observing, perhaps asking a third party about someone's behavior.

In a classic study on the rules for silence among the Western Apache in Arizona, researcher Keith Basso identified five contexts in which silence was appropriate: meeting strangers, courtship, seeing friends after a long absence, being with people who are grieving, and getting cussed out. Verbal reticence with strangers is directly related to the conviction that the establishment of social relationships is a serious matter that calls for caution, careful judgment and plenty of time.

In courting, individuals can go without speaking for a very long time. Similarly, encounters between individuals who have been apart for a long time may call for silence. For example, parents and children may remain silent for a while after the children have returned from boarding school. The time of silence is to see if the returnee has changed adversely.

The Western Apache also believe that silence is an appropriate response to an individual who becomes enraged and starts shouting insults and criticism. The silence acknowledges that the angry person is not really him or herself—that the person has temporarily taken leave of his or her senses, is not responsible, and therefore may be dangerous. In this instance, silence is a safe way to deal with the person.

Being with people who are sad or bereaved also calls for silence. Basso gives several reasons for this silence. First, talking is unnecessary because everyone knows how it feels to be sad. Secondly, the Western Apache believe that intense grief, like intense rage, produces personality changes and personal instability.

Basso hypothesizes that the underlying commonality in these social situations is that participants perceive their relationships vis-à-vis one another to be ambiguous and/or unpredictable, and silence is an appropriate response to uncertainty and unpredictability. He also hypothesizes that this same contextual rule may apply to other cultural groups.

Communication scholar C. Braithwaite (1990) tried to find out if Basso's rule applied to other communities. He compiled ethnographic accounts from 13 speech communities in which silence seemed to play a similar role. His research included groups of Warm Springs Indians, Japanese Hawaiians, and 17th-century Quakers. Braithwaite extended Basso's rule when he determined that in many communities silence was not just associated with uncertainty. Silence was also associated with social situations in which a known and unequal distribution of power existed among participants.

Cultural Variation or Stereotype?

As noted earlier, one of the problems with identifying cultural variations in nonverbal codes is that it is tempting to overgeneralize these variations and stereotype people. For example, we may think that *all* Amish are silent in all contexts or that *all* Arabs stand close to one another in all contexts. Rather, cultural variations are tentative guidelines that we can use in intercultural interaction. They should serve as examples, to help us understand that there is a great deal of variation in nonverbal behavior. Even if we can't anticipate how someone's behavior may be different from our own, we can be flexible when we do encounter differences in how close a person stands, uses eye contact, or conceptualizes time.

Prejudice is often based on nonverbal aspects of behavior. That is, the negative prejudgment is triggered by physical appearances or physical behavior. The following excerpt from a news article underscores the importance of physical appearances in prejudice:

> *In December, an Asian American male was hit with a glass bottle at his business in San Francisco by an inebriated European American male. The assailant's threats included "I'm not gonna leave, you f——ing gook or Jap or whatever you are. I'm gonna smash your windows and smash you. Go back to wherever you came from."* (Cacas, 1995, p. 8)

As in many other instances of hate crimes, the victim's appearance is more significant than the victim's specific cultural heritage.

Semiotics

The study of semiotics, or semiology, offers a useful approach to understanding how many nonverbal codes and signs communicate meaning. The process of producing meaning is called semiosis. A particularly useful framework for understanding semiosis comes from literary critic Roland Barthes (1964). In his system, meaning is constructed through the interpretation of signs—combinations of *signifiers* and *signifieds*. Signifiers are the culturally constructed, arbitrary words or symbols we use to refer to something else, the signified. Think about this example: The word *man* is a signifier that refers to some signified, an adult male human being.

Obviously, *man* is a general signifier that does not refer to any particular man. The relationship between this signifier and the sign (the meaning) depends on how the signifier is used (for example, as in the sentence, "There is a man sitting in the first chair on the left") or on our general sense of what *man* means. The difference between the signifier *man* and the sign rests on the difference between the word *man* and the meaning of that word. At its most basic level, *man* means an adult human, but the semiotic process does not end there. *Man* carries many other layers of meaning. Roland Barthes calls these layers *myths*. The expression, "Man is the measure of all things," for example, is loaded with many levels of meaning, including the centering of male experience as the norm. *Man* may or may not refer to any particular adult male, but it provides a concept that you can use to construct particular meanings based on the way the sign *man* functions.

What do you have in mind when you think of the term *man?* How do you know when to use this signifier (and when not to use it) to communicate to others? Think of all of the adult males you know: How do they "fit" under this sign?

WATCH YOUR FEET

Almost anyone who has been to Thailand will tell you that the feet are regarded [in value] as the lowest part of the body and the head the highest. Therefore, people should take steps to ensure that their feet do not end up pointing directly at someone, and they should not pat others on the head. With this in mind, I'm sure you can understand my shock when the following incident was related to me by a Thai man who worked for an American multinational in Bangkok. He was in the sales department and was responsible for showing a new expatriot around. The expat was an expert in a new technology the company wished to introduce into the Thai market, so the Thai man figured he would take the guy around to some of the customers who might be interested in the new product. During the first meeting with a customer, the Thai man sat horrified as the expat reclined back in his chair and put his feet on the customer's desk—with the soles of his feet pointing directly at the customer. This is the ultimate insult. "I could not believe it!" the Thai man said. "I mean, this guy is from the company headquarters. He should know better! If some average American made this mistake, I would understand—just as an average Thai might make a mistake in the United States. But this guy was from a big multinational whose business depends on successfully dealing with another culture. I couldn't believe it."
—Chris

In what ways does this sign reign over their behaviors, both verbal and nonverbal, to communicate particular ideas about them?

Intercultural communication is not concerned simply with the cultural differences in nonverbal systems, although that is certainly a central interest. Semiotics can be useful in unpacking the ways that the *cultural codes* regulate nonverbal communication systems. That is, semiotics allows us one way to "crack the codes" of another cultural framework. The goal is to establish entire systems of semiosis and the ways that those systems create meaning. We are not so much interested in the discrete, individual signifiers, but rather the ways that signifiers are combined and configured.

The use of these semiotic systems relies on many codes taken from a variety of places: economic institutions, history, politics, religion, and so on. For example, when Nazi swastikas were spray-painted on Jewish graves in Lyon, France in 1992, the message they communicated relied on semiotic systems from the past. The history of the Nazi persecution of Jews during World War II is well known: the power behind the signifier, the swastika, comes from that historical knowledge and the codes of antisemitism that it invokes to communicate its message. Relations from the past influence the construction and maintenance of intercultural relations in the present.

Because we seek the larger semiotic systems, we need to be aware of the cultural contexts that regulate the semiotic frameworks. When we are in different cultural contexts, the semiotic systems transform the communication situations.

When I first started attending Arizona State University, I moved into one of the coed residence halls on campus. One of the first people I met was an Arab American student named Ray. Ray lived on the same floor as me, and we attended some of the same classes together. We ended up spending a lot of time together studying and playing tennis on weekends. One Saturday after our weekly tennis match, I walked up to Ray after the game to give him a friendly pat on the back. I was startled when he immediately flinched and stared at me in astonishment. As we headed back to our dorm, Ray walked a few steps in front of me and didn't speak a word. After that day, Ray stopped coming over to my room and kept his distance from me. I was extremely confused, and I began to resent his avoiding me. Finally, I confronted Ray and asked him to explain his actions. Ray accused me of belittling him and of treating him as inferior. After telling him that I was just trying to be friendly, he accepted my explanation. But he told me that his family members aren't physical with each other because such behavior is perceived as belittlement. Ray remained wary of me from then on.

When I look back on this incident, I think that my message was encoded by my friendly face, but the channel in which I had sent it—the pat on the back—was perceived by Ray as noise, which disturbed his receiving my message. Ray decoded my message by converting it into something that made sense to him. Unfortunately, the message was decoded in a different way than I intended. Instead of asking me what I meant by such a gesture, Ray assigned meaning to it in his head. Apparently, our cultures and our backgrounds have taught us different things. We were both new in college and, thus, just starting to develop a new culture at the university. It is obvious that Ray and I needed to communicate more clearly and state our intentions. It is also obvious that people everywhere in the world need to encode and decode their messages with more patience and with clear responses.

Based on my experiences and on what I learned, I believe that it is becoming more and more important to research other cultures. Many different people are around us every day. Without being open to different cultures, communication is going to remain difficult.
—Tara

Consider the following example, an observation by writer Edmundo Desnoes, who discusses the work of photographer Susan Meiselas on her trip to Nicaragua. Desnoes comments that Meiselas: "discovered one of the keys to understanding Latin America: a different context creates a different discourse. What she saw and what she shot in Nicaragua could not be plucked away and packaged in New York" (1985, p. 39). That is, the photographs that Meiselas took could not communicate what she saw and experienced and wanted to communicate through the photos. The U.S. context would be regulated by a different semiotic system that would construct different signs and different meanings for the images.

It is wise to be sensitive to the many levels of cultural context that are regulated by different semiotic systems. In other words, it's a good idea to avoid framing cultural context as simply a "nation." Nation-states have other cultural contexts within their borders—for example, commercial and financial districts, residential areas, and bars, which are all regulated by their own semiotic systems. Consider, for example, the clothes that people might wear to a bar. Wearing the same clothes to a business setting would not communicate the same message.

Yet, cultural contexts are not fixed and rigid. Rather, they are dynamic and fleeting, as Marcel Proust noted in *Remembrance of Things Past:*

> *The reality that I had known no longer existed. It sufficed that Mme Swann did not appear, in the same attire and at the same moment, for the whole avenue to be altered. The places we have known do not belong only to the world of space on which we map them for our own convenience. None of them was ever more than a thin slice, held between the contiguous impressions that composed our life at that time; the memory of a particular image is but regret for a particular moment; and houses, roads, avenues are as fugitive, alas, as the years. (1981, p. 462)*

DEFINING CULTURAL SPACE

At the beginning of this book, both authors provided some background information about where we grew up. Our individual histories are important in understanding our identities. As writer John Preston explains, "Where we come from is important to who we are" (1991, p. xi). There is nothing in the rolling hills of Delaware and Pennsylvania or the red clay of Georgia that has biologically determined who Judith and Tom are. However, our identities are constructed, in part, in relation to the cultural milieu of the Mid-Atlantic region or the South. Each region has its own histories and ways of life that help us understand who we are. Our decision to tell you where we are from was meant to communicate something about who we think we are. So, although we can identify precisely the borders that mark out these spaces and make them real, or material, the spaces also are cultural in the ways that we imagine them to be.

The discourses that construct the meanings of cultural spaces are dynamic, ever-changing. (Therefore, the Delaware that Judith left behind, and the Georgia that Tom left behind, are not the same discourses that construct those places now.) In addition, the relations between those cultural spaces and our identities are negotiated in complex ways. (For example, both Judith and Tom participated in other, overlapping cultural spaces that have influenced how we think about who we are.) Thus, because someone is from India does not mean that his or her identity and communication practices are reducible to the history of that cultural space.

What is the communicative (discursive) relationship between cultural spaces and intercultural communication? We define cultural space as the particular

Many cities abound with multiple cultural spaces. In this photo, several different cultural contexts are adjacent and emphasize the increasing significance of multiculturalism. How would people in this urban place experience cultural spaces differently from people who live in less diverse cultural spaces? How might it influence their intercultural communication patterns? *(© Robert Brenner/PhotoEdit)*

configuration of the communication (discourse) that constructs meanings of various places. This may seem like an unwieldy definition, but it underscores the complexity of cultural spaces.

A cultural space is not simply a particular location that has culturally constructed meanings. It can also be a metaphorical place from which we communicate. We can speak from a number of social locations, marked on the map of society, that give added meaning to our communication. Sometimes we speak as parents, sometimes as children, sometimes as colleagues, siblings, customers, Nebraskans, and a myriad of other "places." All of these are cultural spaces.

Cultural Identity and Cultural Space

Home   Cultural spaces are important influences in the ways that we think about ourselves and others. One of the earliest cultural spaces we experience is our home. Although it is not always the case, home can be a place of safety and security. African American writer bell hooks remembers:

> *When I was a young girl the journey across town to my grandmother's house was one of the most intriguing experiences. . . . I remember this journey not just because of the stories I would hear. It was a movement away from the segregated blackness*

of our community into a poor white neighborhood [where] we would have to pass that terrifying whiteness—those white faces on porches staring down on us with hate. . . . Oh! that feeling of safety, of arrival, of homecoming when we finally reached the edges of her yard. (1990, p. 41)

Home, of course, is not the same as the physical location it occupies, nor the building (the house) on that location. Home is variously defined as specific addresses, cities, states, regions, even nations. Although we might have historical ties to a particular place, not everyone feels the same relationship between those places and their own identities.

The relationship between place and cultural identity varies. Writer Steven Saylor explains:

Texas is a long way, on the map and otherwise, from San Francisco. "Steven," said my mother once, "you live in another country out there." She was right, and what I feel when I fly from California to Texas must be what an expatriate from any country feels returning to his childhood home. . . . Texas is home, but Texas is also a country whose citizenship I voluntarily renounced. (1991, p. 119)

The discourses surrounding Texas and giving meaning to Texas no longer "fit" Saylor's sense of who he is or who he wants to be. We all negotiate various relationships to the cultural meanings attached to particular places or spaces we inhabit. Consider writer Harlan Greene's relationship to his hometown in South Carolina. Greene writes:

Now that I no longer live there, I often think longingly of my hometown of Charleston. My heart beats faster and color rushes to my cheek whenever I hear someone mentioning her; I lean over and listen, for even hearing the name casts a spell. Mirages rise up, and I am as overcome and drenched in images as a runner just come from running. I see the steeples, the streets, the lush setting. (1991, p. 55)

Despite his own attachment to Charleston, compared to Saylor's rejection of Texas, Greene does not believe that Charleston feels the same way toward him. He explains, "But I still think of Charleston; I return to her often and always will. I think of her warmly. I claim her now; even though I know she will never claim me" (p. 67).

The complex relationships we have between various places and our identities resist simplistic reduction. These three writers (hooks, Saylor, and Greene) have negotiated different sentiments toward "home."

Neighborhood   One significant type of cultural space that emerged in U.S. cities in the latter part of the 19th century and the early 20th century was the ethnic or racial neighborhood. By law and custom, some cities developed segregated neighborhoods under different political pressures. Malcolm X, in his autobiography, tells of the strict laws that governed where his family could live after their house burned down:

My father prevailed on some friends to clothe and house us temporarily; then he moved us into another house on the outskirts of East Lansing. In those days Negroes weren't allowed after dark in East Lansing proper. There's where Michigan State University is located; I related all of this to an audience of students when I spoke there in January, 1963. . . . I told them how East Lansing harassed us so much that we had to move again, this time two miles out of town, into the country. (1964, pp. 3–4)

The history of "White-only" areas pervades the history of the United States and the development of its cultural geography. Neighborhoods exemplify how power influences intercultural contact. Some cultural groups define who gets to live where and dictate the rules by which other groups must live. These rules were enforced through legal means and by harassment. For bell hooks and Malcolm X, the lines of segregation were clear and unmistakable.

In San Francisco, different racial politics constructed and isolated Chinatown. The boundaries that demarcated the acceptable place for Chinese and Chinese Americans were clear and were carefully guarded through violence:

The sense of being physically sealed within the boundaries of Chinatown was impressed on the few immigrants coming into the settlement by frequent stonings which occurred as they came up Washington or Clay Street from the piers. It was perpetuated by attacks of white toughs in the adjacent North Beach area and downtown around Union Square, who amused themselves by beating Chinese who came into these areas. "In those days, the boundaries were from Kearny to Powell, and from California to Broadway. If you ever passed them and went out there, the white kids would throw stones at you," Wei Bat Liu told us. (Nee and Nee, 1974, p. 60)

In contrast to Malcolm X's exclusion from East Lansing, Michigan, the Chinese of San Francisco were forced to live in a marked-off territory. Yet, we must be careful not to confuse the experience of Chinese in San Francisco with the experiences of all Chinese in the U.S. For example, a different system developed in Savannah, Georgia, around 1900:

Robert Chung Chan advised his kinsmen and the other newly arrived Chinese to live apart from each other. He understood the distrust of Chinatowns that Caucasians felt in San Francisco and New York. . . . Robert Chung Chan, probably more than anyone else, prevented a Chinatown from developing in Savannah. (Pruden, 1990, p. 25)

Nor should we assume that vast migrations of Chinese have led to the development of Chinatowns in other cities outside of China. The settlement of Chinese immigrants in the 13th Arrondissement of Paris, for example, reflects a completely different intersection between cultures. As two sociologists noted, "There is no American-style Chinatown" in Paris [*"Il n'y a pas de Chinatown à la américaine."*] (Costa-Lascoux & Yu-Sion, 1995, p. 197).

Within the context of different power relations and historical forces, settlement patterns of other cultural groups created various kinds of ethnic enclaves across the U.S. landscape. Many small towns across the Midwest were settled by particular European groups—Germans in Amana, Iowa; Dutch in Pella, Iowa;

and so on. Cities, too, have their neighborhoods, based on settlement patterns. South Philadelphia is largely Italian American; South Boston is largely Irish American; Overtown in Miami is largely African American. Although it is no longer legal to mandate that people live in particular districts or neighborhoods based on their racial or ethnic backgrounds, the continued existence of such neighborhoods underscores their historical development and ongoing function. Economics, family ties, social needs, and education are some factors in the perpetuation of these cultural spaces.

The relationships between identity, power, and cultural space are quite complex. Power relations influence who (or what) gets to claim who (or what), and under what conditions. Some subcultures are accepted and promoted within a particular cultural space. Some are tolerated, but others may be unacceptable. Identifying with various cultural spaces is a negotiated process that is difficult (sometimes impossible) to predict and control.

Regionalism   The rise of regional conflict, nationalism, ethnic revival, and religious conflict point to the continuing struggles over who gets to define whom. Such conflicts are not new, though. In fact, some cultural spaces (such as Jerusalem) have been ongoing sites of struggle for a very long time.

Although regions may not always be clearly marked on maps of the world, many people identify quite strongly with particular regions. Regionalism can take many different forms of expression, from symbolic expressions of identification to armed conflict. Within the United States, people may identify themselves or others as Southerners or Midwesterners. People from Montreal might identify more strongly with the province of Quebec than their country, Canada. Similarly, some Corsicans might feel a need to negotiate their identity with France. Sometimes people fly regional flags, wear particular kinds of clothes, celebrate regional holidays, and participate in other cultural activities to communicate their regional identification.

National borders may appear simple, but they often conceal conflicting regional identities. To understand how intercultural communications may be affected by national borders, we must consider how history, power, identity, culture, and context come into play. Understanding these issues will enable you to approach the complex process of human communication.

Changing Cultural Space

Chapter 8 discusses in greater detail the intercultural experiences of those who traverse cultural spaces and their attempts to renegotiate these changes. In this chapter, however, we want to focus on some of the driving needs of those who change cultural spaces.

Traveling   We often change cultural spaces when we travel. Traveling is frequently viewed as an unimportant leisure activity, but it is more than that. In terms of intercultural communication, traveling changes cultural spaces in a way that often transforms the traveler. Changing cultural spaces means changing who you are and how you interact with others. Perhaps the old saying, "When in Rome, do as the Romans do," holds true today as we cross cultural spaces with more frequency than ever.

Do you alter your communication style when you encounter travelers who are not in their traditional cultural space? Do you assume that they should interact in the ways prescribed by your cultural space? These are some of the issues that travel raises.

Migration   People also change cultural spaces when they relocate. Moving, of course, involves a different kind of change in cultural spaces than traveling. In traveling, the change is fleeting, temporary, and usually desirable. It is something that we seek out. People who migrate do not always seek out this change. For example, many people were forced from their homelands of Rwanda and Bosnia and settled elsewhere. Many immigrants leave their homelands and move so they can survive. They often find it difficult to adjust to the change, especially if the language and customs of the new cultural space are unfamiliar.

Even within the United States, people often find it difficult to adapt to new surroundings when they move. Tom, one of this book's authors, remembers that when Yankees moved to the South they often were unfamiliar with the custom of banks closing early on Wednesday, or with the traditional New Year's Day foods in the South. Ridiculing customs of their new cultural space simply led to further intercultural communication problems.

Postmodern Cultural Spaces

When one of the authors, Tom, spent a summer in New York City, a small group of his friends met with him at least once a week to have dinner at a restaurant. They followed a few rules: First, they went to a different restaurant each time; second, they spoke French exclusively (except when they spoke with waiters); and third, they were allowed to invite others who would follow the rules. The group fluctuated but included academics and business people, Europeans, and people from the United States who had traveled or lived abroad.

The group highlighted the dynamic nature of cultural space. Indeed, while group members ate, they not only spoke French, but they also used European table manners. They created a cultural space that was fluid in place and time. It was a moving space that was not quite French but not exactly New York, either. The group traveled throughout lower and mid-Manhattan, taking its cultural space with it. Unmarked by boundaries or ethnic ties, the cultural space the group created remained fluid—a postmodern cultural space.

The fluidity and fleeting nature of this cultural space stand in sharp contrast to the 18th-century notions of space, which promoted land ownership, surveys, borders, colonies, territories. No passport is needed to travel in the postmodern cultural space, because there is no border guarding. The dynamic nature of postmodern cultural spaces underscores its response to changing cultural needs. The space exists only as long as it is needed in its present form.

Postmodern cultural spaces are tenuous and dynamic. They are created within existing places, without following any particular guide: there is no marking off of territory, no sense of permanence or official recognition. The postmodern cultural space exists only while it is used.

The ideology of fixed spaces and categories is currently being challenged by postmodernist notions of space and location. Phoenix, for example, which became a city only in the past few decades, has no Chinatown, no Japantown, no Koreatown, no Irish district, no Polish neighborhood, no Italian area. Instead, people of Polish descent, for example, might live anywhere in the metropolitan area, but might congregate for special occasions or for specific reasons. On Sundays, the Polish Catholic service draws many people from throughout Phoenix. When people want to buy Polish breads and pastries, they can go to the Polish bakery and also speak Polish there. Ethnic identity is only one of several identities that these people negotiate. When they desire recognition and interaction based on their Polish heritage, they may do so. When they seek other forms of identification, they may go to places where they can be Phoenix Suns fans, and so on. Ethnic identity is neither the sole factor nor necessarily the most important factor at all times in their lives.

The markers of ethnic life in Phoenix are the urban sites where people congregate when they desire ethnic cultural contact. At other times, they may frequent other locations in expressing other aspects of their identities. In this sense, the postmodern urban space is dynamic and allows people to participate in the communication of identity in new ways (Nakayama & Drzewiecka, 1996).

SUMMARY

This chapter has examined both nonverbal communication principles and cultural spaces. Nonverbal communication compares to verbal communication and operates at a subconscious level. It is learned implicitly and can reinforce, substitute for, or contradict verbal behaviors.

Nonverbal behaviors can communicate relational meaning, status, and deception. Nonverbal codes are influenced by culture, although many cultures share some nonverbal behaviors. Nonverbal codes include proxemics, eye contact, facial expressions, chronemics, and silence. Sometimes cultural differences in nonverbal behaviors can lead to stereotyping of other cultures.

Semiotics is one approach to studying nonverbal communication. Signs, cultural codes, and myths are discussed as they relate to semiotics.

Cultural space influences cultural identity. Cultural spaces relate to issues of power and intercultural communication. Homes, neighborhoods, regions, and nations are all examples of cultural spaces. Two ways of changing cultural spaces are travel and migration. Postmodern cultural spaces are tenuous and dynamic, accommodating people of different cultural identities who coexist.

REFERENCES

Barthes, R. (1980). *Elements of semiology* (A. Lavers & C. Smith, Trans.). New York: Hill and Wang. (Original work published in 1968)

Basso, K. (1970). "To give up on words": Silence in Western Apache culture. *Southwestern Journal of Anthropology, 26,* 213–320.

Boucher, J. D., & Carlson, G. E. (1980). Recognition of facial expression in three cultures. *Journal of Cross Cultural Psychology, 11,* 263–280.

Braithwaite, C. A. (1990). Communicative silence: A cross-cultural study of Basso's hypothesis. In D. Carbaugh (Ed.), *Cultural communication and intercultural contact* (pp. 321–327). Hillsdale, NJ: Lawrence Erlbaum.

Burgoon, J. K., Buller, D. B., & Woodall, W. G. (1989). *Nonverbal communication: The unspoken dialogue.* New York: Harper & Row.

Cacas, S. (1995, August 4). Violence against APAs on the rise. *Asian Week,* pp. 1, 8.

Costa-Lascoux, J., & Yu-Sion, L. (1995). *Paris-XIIIe, lumières d'Asie.* Paris: Éditions Autrement.

Desnoes, E. (1985). The death system. In M. Blonsky (Ed.), *On signs* (pp. 39–42). Baltimore: Johns Hopkins University Press.

Eibl-Eibesfeldt, I. (1974). Similarities and differences between cultures in expressive movements. In S. Weitz (Ed.), *Nonverbal communication: Readings with commentary* (pp. 20–33). New York: Oxford University Press.

Ekman, P. (1973). Cross-cultural studies of emotion. In P. Ekman (Ed.), *Darwin and facial expression: A century of research in review* (pp. 169–222). New York: Academic Press.

Ekman, P., & Friesen, W. V. (1987). Universals and cultural differences in the judgments of facial expressions of emotion. *Journal of Personality and Social Psychology, 53,* 712–717.

Ekman, P., Friesen, W. V., & Ellsworth, P. (1972). *Emotion in the human face: Guidelines for research and an integration of findings.* New York: Pergamon Press.

Fletcher, C. (1992). The semiotics of survival: Street cops read the street. *Howard Journal of Communications, 4* (1, 2), 133–142.

Greene, H. (1991). Charleston, South Carolina. In J. Preston (Ed.), *Hometowns: Gay men write about where they belong* (pp. 55–67). New York: Dutton.

Hall, E. T. (1959). *The silent language.* New York: Doubleday.

————. (1966). *The hidden dimension.* New York: Doubleday.

————. (1976). *Beyond culture.* New York: Doubleday.

Hawkes, T. (1977). *Structuralism and semiotics.* Berkeley: University of California Press.

hooks, b. (1990). *Yearning: Race, gender, and cultural politics.* Boston: South End.

Matsumoto, D. (1990). Cultural influences on facial expressions of emotion. *Southern Communication Journal, 56,* 128–137.

Nakayama, T. K., & Drzewiecka, J. A. (1996, May). City sites: Postmodern urban space and the communication of identity. Paper presented at the International Communication Association convention, Chicago.

Nee, V. G., and Nee, B. d. B. (1974). *Longtime Californ': A documentary study of an American Chinatown.* Boston: Houghton Mifflin.

Preston, J. (1991). Introduction. In J. Preston (Ed.), *Hometowns: Gay men write about where they belong* (pp. xi–xiv). New York: Dutton.

Proust, M. (1981). *Swann in love: Remembrance of things past* (C. K. S. Moncrieff & T. Kilmartin, Trans.). New York: Vintage.

Pruden, G. B., Jr. (1990). History of the Chinese in Savannah, Georgia. In J. Goldstein (Ed.), *Georgia's East Asian connection: Into the twenty-first century: Vol. 27. West Georgia College Studies in the Social Sciences* (pp. 17–34). Carrollton: West Georgia College.

Saylor, S. (1991). Amethyst, Texas. In J. Preston (Ed.), *Hometowns: Gay men write about where they belong* (pp. 119–135). New York: Dutton.

Watson, O. M. (1970). *Proxemic behavior: A cross cultural study.* The Hague: Mouton.

X, Malcolm, and Haley, A. (1964). *The autobiography of Malcolm X.* New York: Grove Press.

Zuckerman, M., DePaulo, B. M., & Rosenthal, R. (1981). Verbal and nonverbal communication of deception. In L. Berkowitz (Ed.), *Advances in experimental social psychology* (Vol. 14, pp. 1–59). New York: Academic Press.

UNDERSTANDING INTERCULTURAL TRANSITIONS

When I moved to Arizona from San Francisco to go to school, it was a big shock. I was used to seeing many different kinds of people—Asian Americans, African Americans. At my new university in Phoenix, almost everyone is White. And I was treated differently in Phoenix than I was at home. I often got passed by at the supermarket while the clerk waited on someone who was White. Some of the children who lived in my apartment complex followed me one day, yelling, "Chink, Chink, Chinaman."

—Lois

Chapter 7 discusses how we define and move through various cultural spaces. In this chapter, we look more specifically at how we move between cultural contexts. People travel across cultural boundaries for many different reasons: for work, study, or adventure, or because they are forced by political or other events. For example, Trinh Minh, a student at Arizona State University, came to the United States when her family (including her grandparents) was relocated by the U.S. government from Vietnam around 1980. She doesn't remember very much about the move. Her grandparents, though, had a really tough time adjusting, and her grandfather died shortly after arriving in the United States.

Her friend Mei Lin came to Arizona State University from San Francisco. She is homesick and misses the cultural diversity and the opportunities of living in a big city. Another student, Mario, whose parents moved to the United States from Mexico, spent a year in Marburg, Germany, as an exchange student. He studied German, didn't seem to experience culture shock, and had a great time.

What can we learn about cultural transitions from these particular intercultural experiences? Why do people travel across cultural boundaries? Why are some transitions easy for some people and more difficult for others? What can we learn about culture and communication from these experiences?

We begin this chapter by discussing characteristics of three groups of travelers (migrants). We then turn our attention to the individual experience of dealing with cultural transitions and the feelings of culture shock. We identify four models of individual adaptation: the anxiety and uncertainty management model, the U-curve model, the transition model, and the communication-system model. We then explore the relationship between identity, context, and adaptation. We also examine the contexts of intercultural transitions.

TYPES OF MIGRANT GROUPS

We can examine intercultural transitions on both an individual and a contextual level (Berry, 1992). On the individual level, we can look at personal experiences of adapting to new cultural contexts. But we also can examine the larger social, historical, economic, and political contexts in which these individual transitions

People travel to new areas for various reasons. Some migrate for adventure, some to escape oppression, others to improve their economic situation. Do you know why your family came to the United States? What kinds of challenges and experiences did they have in getting here? *(© A. Ramey/Woodfin Camp and Associates)*

occur. To view how these two levels intersect, we will look more closely at individual migrant groups and the contexts in which they travel.

Migration may be long-term or short-term and voluntary or involuntary. The term *migrant* refers to an individual who leaves the primary cultural contexts in which he or she was raised and moves to a new cultural context for an extended period of time. Mei-Lin and Mario's study sojourns were relatively short-term and voluntary. These transitions occurred within a structured sociopolitical context (that is, within Phoenix, Arizona and Marburg, Germany). Trinh's sojourn is long-term one, an experience of being forced to relocate in an unstable social and political context. Cultural transitions may vary in length and in degree of voluntariness. We can identify four types of migrant groups based on these criteria.

There are two groups of voluntary travelers: sojourners and immigrants. *Sojourners* are those travelers who move into new cultural contexts for a limited period of time and for a specific purpose. This includes international students who go abroad to study and technical assistance workers, corporate personnel, and missionaries who go abroad to work for a specific period of time. Some domestic sojourners move from one region to another within their own country for a limited period of time to attend school or work (for example, Native Americans who leave their reservations).

When I go back and forth between my university in Albuquerque and my home on the reservation, I feel like I'm being torn in two. When I'm at school, I'm expected to work by myself, concentrate only on myself. When I go home, my relatives tell me that I've changed, that I need to be more considerate and not to think only of myself. I'm expected to take things slower. Sometimes during exam periods I don't even go home because it is too difficult to change back and forth.

—Rebecca

Another type of voluntary traveler is the *immigrant*. Mario's family, who voluntarily settled in the new culture, exemplify this type of migrant. Although many U.S. Americans believe that most immigrants come to the United States in search of freedom, the truth is that many come for economic reasons. There is tremendous international migration of peoples, but most does not occur from developing countries to industrialized countries. Rather, most movement occurs from developing country to developing country. According to a 1993 United Nations Fund Report, of the 100 million people living outside the country in which they were born, 20 to 30 million moved to the United States or Western Europe.

The voluntariness of immigration is more variable than absolute. Some immigrants feel that they have a choice in moving, whereas others feel that they have less choice. The decision to migrate usually is made while other factors intervene.

There are two types of migrants who move involuntarily: long-term refugees and short-term refugees. According to some sources, there are more refugees than ever before. One estimate is that 13 million people have left their home countries since 1979 because of super-power struggles (refugees from Afghanistan, Angola, and Cambodia count among them) and more recently because of internal ethnic strife (for example, in the former Yugoslavia). Long-term refugees are those like Trinh's family who are often forced to relocate permanently because of war, famine, and oppression. Long-term refugees include those who left Rwanda during the war in 1993, and the Hmong, who were taken from Vietnam by the United States after the Vietnam war and relocated in the United States. In Trinh's case, her family became immigrants when they decided to settle permanently in the United States.

There are also cases of domestic refugees who are forced for short or indefinite periods of time to move within a country. For example, many Japanese Americans were sent to internment camps during World War II. Other examples include those who relocate temporarily because of natural disasters, such as hurricanes and floods. This mass migration of refugees presents complex issues for intercultural communication, pointing to the importance of context. A 1994 newsmagazine describes:

From the prisonlike camps of Hong Kong to the sprawling encampments in the horn of Africa, from the slums of south Beirut to the refugee cities on the Afghan borders, some 17.4 million people are waiting to see whether they can ever go home again, waiting to see whether any nation will open its doors to them. (U.S. News & World Report, 1994, p. 22)

How do we start to unravel the complex communication issues here?

CULTURE SHOCK AND CULTURAL ADAPTATION

We now turn to a discussion of the challenges of adaptation that individuals experience in new cultural contexts. Culture shock is a relatively short-term feeling of disorientation, of discomfort due to the unfamiliarity of surroundings, the lack of familiar cues in the environment. Culture adaptation refers to the longer term process of adjusting and finally feeling more comfortable in the new environment (Kim & Gudykunst, 1988). Kalvero Oberg, an anthropologist who coined the term *culture shock*, suggested that it was like a disease, complete with symptoms (excessive washing of hands, irritability, and so on). If it is treated properly (that is, if the migrant learns the language, makes friends, and so on), the migrant can "recover," or adapt to the new cultural situation and feel at home (Oberg, 1960).

Models of Cultural Adaptation

The Anxiety and Uncertainty Management Model   Communication theorist William Gudykunst (1995) stresses that the primary characteristic of relationships in intercultural adaptation is ambiguity. The goal of effective intercultural communication can be reached by reducing anxiety and seeking information (uncertainty reduction). One kind of uncertainty is predictive, the inability to predict what someone will say or do. We all know how important this is, that we can be relatively sure how people will respond to us. Another kind of uncertainty is explanatory, the inability to explain why people behave as they do. In any interaction, it is important to predict how someone will behave but also to explain why the person behaves in a particular way. How do we do this? Usually we have prior knowledge about someone, or we gather more information about the person.

Migrants also need to reduce the anxiety that is often present in intercultural contexts. Some level of anxiety is optimal during an interaction. Too little anxiety may convey that we really don't care about the person. Too much anxiety causes us to focus only on the anxiety and not on the interaction.

This model assumes that to communicate effectively we will gather information to help us reduce uncertainty and anxiety. How do we do this? The theory is complicated, with 48 theorems and axioms; however, some general suggestions for increasing effectiveness are useful. The theory predicts that the most effective communicators (those who are best able to manage anxiety and predict and explain others' behaviors with confidence) are people who:

I remember my first night in Algiers. We stayed at a monastery high in the hills in a suburb of Algiers. In the middle of the night, sleeping on a cot in a sparsely furnished room, I awoke to an eerie wailing sound—the Muslim call to prayer—"Aaaaaalaaaaaah, Aaaaaaakbaaaaar." I knew this was going to be an exciting experience—teaching high school English for two years in a small town in Algeria. Six months later, I was having difficulty, though. My students were mostly boys, many of whom were older than me. Our social customs were very different. The boys were not used to seeing unveiled women other than their sisters, let alone taking orders from them. Discipline in Algerian schools was the complete responsibility of the teacher; teachers were expected to be very stern and autocratic. Discipline was not self-internalized, as in the U.S. educational system. I couldn't sleep at night; I cried a lot and finally went to a psychologist because I thought I was having a nervous breakdown.

    —Jan

- Have a solid self-concept and self-esteem
- Have flexible attitudes (a tolerance for ambiguity, empathy) and behaviors
- Are complex and flexible in their categorization of others (for example, able to identify similarities and differences, avoid stereotypes)

The situation in which communication occurs is important in this model. The most conducive environments are those that are informal, where there is support and equal representation of different groups. Finally, this model requires that we are open to new information and recognize alternative ways to interpret information.

Of course, these principles may operate differently according to the cultural context; the theory predicts cultural variability. For example, people with more individualistic orientations may stress independence in self-concepts and communities; self-esteem may become more important in interactions. Individualists also may seek similarities more in categorizing. (See also Witte, 1993).

The U-Curve Model   Many theories describe how people adapt to new cultural environments. The pattern of adaptation depends on the circumstances and the migrant, but some commonalities exist. The most common theory is the U-curve theory of adaptation. This theory is based on research conducted by a Norwegian sociologist, Sverre Lysgaard, who interviewed Norwegian students studying in the United States. This model has been applied to many different migrant groups.

The main idea is that migrants go through fairly predictable phases in adapting to a new cultural situation. They first experience excitement and anticipation, followed by a period of shock and disorientation (the bottom of the U-curve); then they gradually adapt to the new cultural contexts. Although this framework is simplistic and does not represent every migrant's experience, most migrants experience these general phases at one time or another.

When my family and I first moved to Arizona from New York, I didn't know a single person and I was eager to meet people. I was ecstatic when I was offered a sales job in which I would be meeting a lot of new people every day. When I first started this new job, I immediately introduced myself to all of my co-workers. Once I began speaking and my thick accent came out, I found that people would stop listening to what I was saying and would stare at me in amazement. They would ask me where I was from and would make statements like, "You must be one of those tough girls, huh?" or "Don't you miss being around other loud Italians?" or "Have you ever gotten into a fight?" I found that my family was experiencing the same thing. I was shocked, but what had amazed me the most was that these people had never been to New York in their lives. If they had been to where I lived, they would have seen my reference group. They would have seen the suburbs where I had lived, and they would have met my family and friends who are all very shy and gentle people.

Being labeled a "loud Italian" hurt, whether they meant it or not. After being categorized like that, I started to wonder what these people were thinking about me all the time. I wondered if they felt hostile to my kind of people. I began to talk less, and I stayed by myself more often because I felt like an outcast to these people. It seemed to me that they were always going to classify me as part of an in-group that I really wasn't a part of.
—Tara

The first phase is the anticipation or excitement phase. When a migrant first enters a new cultural context, he or she may be excited to be in the new situation, and somewhat apprehensive. For example, someone adapting to a new job in a new city in a new region of the country may experience more apprehension than excitement during the first part of the transition. The same would be true for an international student from East Africa who experiences prejudice in the first months at a U.S. college, or for refugees who are forced to migrate into new cultural contexts.

The second phase, culture shock, happens to almost everyone in intercultural transitions. However, migrants who remain isolated from the new cultural context may experience culture shock minimally. For example, U.S. military personnel or diplomatic personnel often live in compounds overseas where they see mostly other U.S. Americans and have little contact with the indigenous cultures. Spouses of international students in the United States sometimes have little contact with U.S. Americans. On the other hand, corporate spouses may experience more culture shock, because they often have more contact with the host culture: placing children in schools, setting up a household, shopping, and so on.

During the culture shock phase, migrants experience disorientation and often a crisis of identity. Because identities are shaped and maintained by our cultural contexts, experiences in new cultural contexts often raise questions about identities. For example, Judy, an exchange teacher in Zaire, thought of herself as a nice person. Being nice was part of her identity. When she experienced a lot of discipline problems with her students, she began to question the authenticity of her identity. When change occurs to the cultural context of an identity, the conditions of that identity also change.

The third phase is adaptation. Gradually, migrants learn the rules and customs of the new cultural context. They may learn a new language, and they figure out how much of themselves to change in response to the new context. A migrant may decide to change some aspects of his or her behavior and not others. Individuals may want to retain a sense of their previous cultural identities; each sojourner has to decide to what degree he or she wants to adapt. However, this phase may be experienced very differently if the sociopolitical context is not conducive to individual adaptation.

Although the U-curve seems to represent the experiences of many short-term sojourners, it may be too simplistic for other types of migrants (Berry, 1992). A more accurate model represents long-term adaptation as a series of U-curves. Migrants alternate between feeling relatively adjusted and experiencing culture shock; over the long term, the feeling of culture shock diminishes.

The Transition Model   Recently, culture shock and adaptation have been viewed as a normal part of human experience, as a subcategory of transition shock. Janet Bennett (1977), a communication scholar, says that culture shock and adaptation are just like any other adult transition. Adult transitions include going away to college for the first time, getting married, or moving from one part of the country to another. All of these transition experiences share common characteristics and provoke the same kinds of responses.

All transition experiences involve *loss* and *change* for the individual. For example, when people marry, they may lose some independence, but they gain companionship and intimacy. When international students come to the United States to study, they leave their friends and customs but gain new friends and new ways of doing things.

Cultural adaptation depends in part on the individual. Each individual has a preferred way of dealing with new situations. Psychologists have found that most individuals prefer either a "flight" or "fight" approach to unfamiliar situations. Each of these approaches may be more or less productive depending on the context. The migrant who prefers a "flight" approach when faced with new situations tends to hang back, get the lay of the land, and see how things work before taking the plunge and joining in. Migrants who take this approach may hesitate to speak a language until they feel they can get it right; they may watch others before they participate. This is not necessarily bad. Taking time out from the stresses of intercultural interaction (to speaking and reading in one's native language, socializing with friends of similar background, and so on) may be appropriate. Small periods of "flight" allow the migrant some needed rest from the challenges of cultural adaptation. However, getting stuck in the "flight" mode can be unproductive. For example, some U.S. students abroad spend all of their time with other American students and have little opportunity for intercultural learning.

I spent my early childhood growing up in a small town in southeast Iowa. In this area there were no other races or cultures that I was aware of. I can remember when I moved from my small secluded home to a large city in California. I had gone from Donnellson, which is not on many maps, to San Diego; almost everyone knows where this city is located.

I must admit I went into a small form of shock. I had never known anyone from another race or background than my own. I was still young and was quite intimidated by these new people, which in my mind is what they were. Once I got past the newness of everything and discovered that everyone was the same, my attitude changed and I didn't notice any difference between me or any of the other kids.

I also recall the first time I met someone of another religion, and that was an experience. As I said, I grew up in a small town that had one church, and the whole town attended church there. It was called the United Church of Christ and it was a Christian church. I had gone to visit my aunt and uncle in Rock Springs, Wyoming, and met some girls my age. I had stayed the night at one of the girls' homes and when we awoke her parents informed us that we were going to church. This was not a problem for me, but I was surprised when we got there. The church was unique in design and structure. That was the first time I was exposed to the Mormon religion. I thought that just about everyone was Christian like me. I didn't look at my new friend any differently, though, because to me everyone has their own beliefs and ways of life—and if we all didn't, the world would be a boring place.
—Heather

A second preference is to "fight," to get in there and participate. Migrants who take this approach use the trial-and-error method. They try to speak the new language, don't mind if they make mistakes, jump on a bus even when they aren't sure it's the right one, and often make cultural gaffes. Bill, a U.S. exchange teacher in France, took this approach. His French was terrible, but he would speak with anyone who would talk to him. When he and his wife first arrived in their town late at night, he went to the Hôtel de Ville (City Hall) and asked for a room! His wife, Jan, was more hesitant. She would speak French only when she knew she could get the grammar right, and would study bus schedules for hours rather than risk getting on the wrong bus or asking a stranger. Getting stuck in the "fight" mode can also be unproductive. Migrants who take this approach to the extreme tend to act on their surroundings with little flexibility. They are likely to criticize the way things are done in the new culture.

Neither of these preferences for dealing with new situations is right or wrong. Individual preference is a result of family, social, and cultural influences. For example, some parents encourage their children to be assertive, and others encourage their children to wait and watch in new situations. Society may encourage individuals toward one preference or the other. An alternative to fight or flight is the "flex" approach, in which the migrant uses a combination of productive fight or flight behaviors. The overall approach is to "go with the flow" while keeping in mind the contextual elements. Hostile contexts (such as racism or prejudice) may encourage extreme flight or fight responses. On the other hand, a supportive environment (tolerance) may encourage more productive responses from the migrant.

The Communication-System Model The three approaches discussed so far concentrate on the psychological feelings of the migrants, on how comfortable the individual feels. What role does communication play in the adaptation process? For an answer, we turn to a model of adaptation developed by communication scholar Young Yun Kim (1977, 1995). Kim suggests that adaptation is a process of stress, adjustment, and growth. As individuals experience the stress of not fitting in with the environment, the response is to adjust. This process of adjusting is really a psychic breakdown of previously held attitudes and behaviors—ones that worked in original cultural contexts.

Adaptation occurs through communication. The migrant communicates with individuals in the new environment and gradually develops new ways of thinking and behaving and, in the process, grows to a new level of functioning. The migrant develops an intercultural identity. Of course, not everyone grows in the migrant experience. Some individuals experience difficulty adapting to new ways. The cognitive dissonance theorists of the 1950s found that individuals typically have three options when confronting ideas or behaviors that do not fit with previously held attitudes: They can reject the new idea, they can try to fit it into their existing framework, or they can change their framework (Festinger, 1957).

It is likely that communication has a double edge in adaptation: Migrants who communicate frequently in their new culture adapt better but also experience more culture shock. Beulah Rohrlich and Judith Martin conducted a series of studies in which they surveyed U.S. American students living abroad in various places in Europe. They discovered that those students who communicated the most with host culture members experienced the most culture shock. These were students who spent lots of time with their host family and friends in many different communication situations (having meals together, working on projects together, socializing, and so on). However, these same students also adapted better and felt more satisfied with their overseas experience than the students who communicated less (Rohrlich & Martin, 1991).

Dan Kealey, who worked for many years with the Canadian International Development Agency, conducted studies of overseas technical assistance workers in many different countries. Kealey and his colleagues tried to understand what characterized effective workers and less effective workers. They interviewed the Canadian workers, their spouses, and their host country coworkers. They discovered that the most important characteristics in adaptation were the interpersonal communication competencies of the workers—how effective they were in their communication skills (Hawes & Kealey, 1981; Ruben & Kealey, 1979).

In a later study, Kealey (1989) also found that those who communicated more in the host country experienced a greater degree of culture shock and had more initial difficulty in adapting to the new country. These people also were

I understand that one of the main ways people make sense of new things is by comparing them with something more familiar. There is the old but vivid example of a child who learns what a cat is, then proceeds to call every other animal it encounters by the name of cat, until the child learns to differentiate between animal types and adds dog, pig, and horse to its categories of reference. As we encounter people who are different from ourselves, or lands that are foreign due to distance or geography, I wonder why we can't just add these to our categories of reference and accept them for what they are. You do not have to like them, embrace them, or agree with them, but just accept that they are different. Three examples that are fresh in my mind should illustrate my point.

First, I am from Nebraska—the land of "Go Big Red," Cornhusker football. I now live in Arizona, a state that has not one but two of its own college football teams. Many Nebraskans have migrated to Arizona for a variety of reasons. Therefore, during the college football season I often hear fellow Nebraskans say things like, "I can't believe the lack of coverage the Huskers receive around here. They blocked the game on TV with another program, and they barely discussed it in the newspaper!" This is Arizona. Why would they do more than mention the score of the game or provide a few details if the game was relevant to the year-end rankings? This is Arizona. They have two of their own college teams, plus a professional team! Of course they aren't going to cover the Huskers the way they do in Nebraska! If you want full coverage, return to Nebraska or subscribe to a Nebraska newspaper. The situation is different here.

Second, I am amazed by folks who will compare the desert with the lush river areas of the central plains or the dense growth of the northwest. When attending conventions in other parts of the country with colleagues from Arizona, I often hear, "Oh look, trees! This is so beautiful and Arizona is so barren and ugly." Of course Arizona is barren, or at least the southern part of it is. It is a desert! It was not meant to be compared with the tree-lined streets of the Midwest or the rolling green hills of any other part of the country. The Valley of the Sun is a desert— period. Accept the different landscape for what it is. You don't have to like it or prefer it over another part of the country. It's just different, not ugly.

Third, I have spent this past year living and teaching in Thailand, a place where the people are very different from most European Americans. And I am amazed by the number of folks (European Americans, thus far)—many of whom have been here much longer than I have, and some of whom intend to live here permanently—who complain and compare the Thais with people back home. This is Thailand, it's not wherever you are from. It's different. The people have their own customs, values, and norms. The food is different, the architecture is different, the main religion is different from Christianity, and the language is Thai. It's a different place, it's just different. It's not better or worse than what you are familiar with, just different. Why do I write about this? Because I am concerned about our seeming lack of ability to accept difference and get on with it. We dwell on difference, debate difference, and often make pronouncements on which thing is better or should be the "norm." Why can't we just accept difference for what it is?

—Chris

rated by their host country coworkers as more successful. As with the student sojourners, communication and adaptation seems to be a case of no pain, no gain. Intercultural interaction may be difficult and stressful, but in the end it can be rewarding.

Specifically, how does communication help migrants adapt? There seem to be three stages in this process of adaptation. The stages are:

1. Taking things for granted, and surprise
2. Making sense of new patterns
3. Coming to understand new information

Scholar Ling Chen (1994) interviewed Chinese international students and described how they experienced these three phases.

In the first phase, the migrant realizes that his or her assumptions are wrong and need to be altered. Chen describes the experiences of one of the students she interviewed, Mr. An. He was arriving in the middle of the night at his new U.S. university, but he wasn't worried. In China, university housing is always taken care of by the university officials. However, in conversations on the plane with a friendly seat mate named Alice, he began to realize that his expectations of having a place to stay were probably a mistake. He was grateful when Alice offered her home. Mr. An explained, "Alice said she could put me up for the night, that I could live in her house until I found a place. . . . I was surprised but also very grateful" (Chen, p. 126).

In the second stage, the migrant slowly begins to make sense of new patterns, through communication experiences. The first step in making sense for Mr. An was the next day when he went to the International Students Office. A clerk handed him a map and told him to find his own housing. Although he had heard that the people in the United States were individualistic and independent, this cultural pattern was now a living experience for him. The dorms were full, but Mr. An learned how to seek alternatives. He explained how he began to make sense of the experience:

> I started to better understand the meaning of independence. I felt I really understood America and was overjoyed [to find] there was a Chinese Student Association on campus. This meant that maybe I could get help from them. (p. 129)

As migrants understand and make sense of their experiences and interactions in new cultural contexts, they come to understand in a more holistic way. Then they can fit the new information into a pattern of cultural understanding. Again, this happens through communication with members of the host country and others who implicitly or explicitly explain the new cultural patterns. Mr. An stayed in touch with Alice for a while and then less and less. He explained:

> One day I realized I had not called Alice in a long time, then it occurred to me that she rarely called me; I was the one who usually made the calls. . . . I just didn't get around to calling her again, but now I don't feel guilty about it. She didn't seem to mind one way or the other. I've learned that many Americans are ready to help others, but never see them again afterwards. (p. 131)

Moving into a new society may mean adapting to the patterns of the host society, as these children are doing as they learn about Thanksgiving. Some of the society's customs may seem strange to newcomers. What are other U.S. customs or activities that newcomers might have difficulty understanding? (© Tony Freeman/PhotoEdit)

At that point, Mr. An understood the U.S. cultural emphasis on helpful intervention, and he was able to make sense of his friendship with Alice, a momentary helping relationship. As Chen says, "Coming to a tentative understanding is the last stage in a cycle of sense-making. . . . In the long run, however, this new perspective will never be completely fulfilled by one's accumulation of knowledge" (p. 131). As Chen points out, there are always more sense-making cycles.

Mass media also plays a role in helping sojourners and immigrants adapt. Radio, television, movies, and so on are powerful transmitters of cultural values. They are available sources of socialization for newcomers. It is possible that mass media play an especially important role in the beginning stages of adaptation. When sojourners or immigrants first arrive, they may have limited language ability and limited social networks. Listening to radio or watching TV may be the primary source of contact at this stage, one that avoids negative consequences of not knowing the language (Nwanko & Onwumechili, 1991).

Individual Influences on Adaptation

Many individual characteristics—including age, gender, preparation, expectations—can influence how well a person adapts (Searle & Ward, 1990; Ward & Searle, 1991; Ward & Kennedy, 1992). There is contradictory evidence

When I first arrived in Belgium, I watched a lot of TV. I always liked to watch TV before I left the United States, so it was a good way for me to learn French. And it was certainly a lot easier and less painful than trying to talk with Belgians. I always hated that pained look they got on their faces when I would screw up the language in my halting speech.
　　—Jesse

concerning age and adaptation. On the one hand, younger people may have an easier time adapting because they are less fixed in their ideas, beliefs, and identities. Because they adapt more completely, though, they may have more trouble when they return home. Older people may have more trouble adapting because they are less flexible, but for that reason they may not change as much and may have less trouble when they move back home (Gullahorn & Gullahorn, 1963; Kim, 1988).

Preparation for the experience may influence how one adapts and is related to expectations. Many U.S. sojourners experience more culture shock in England than in other European countries, because they expect little difference between life there and here in the United States (Weissman & Furnham, 1987). On the other hand, sojourners traveling to cultures that are very different expect to experience culture shock. The research seems to show that overly positive and overly negative expectations lead to more difficulty in adaptation; it seems that positive but realistic or slightly negative expectations prior to the sojourn are best (Martin, Bradford, & Rohrlich, 1995).

Context and Adaptation

Cultural adaptation depends on the context. Some contexts are easier to adapt to than others. Some environments are more accepting. Young Yun Kim (1988) writes about the receptivity of the host environment and the degree to which the environment welcomes newcomers. She maintains that in a country like Japan, which emphasizes homogeneity, people may be less welcoming than in less homogeneous settings, as in many contexts in the United States. Algeria and many Muslim societies tend to be fairly closed to outsiders. In these societies, the distinction between in-group (family and close friends) and out-group (everyone else) is very strong.

Relative status and power between the sojourner and the host group also influence adaptation. African students often find it more difficult to adapt to U.S. colleges because of racism. It is more difficult for women to adapt in many contexts because of the relative lower status of women in many countries. A University of Minnesota study found that international students came to see themselves as their group was perceived; those students who thought their group was perceived positively (for example, Scandinavians) adapted more easily, whereas those who felt discrimination against their group (for example, many Africans) experienced more difficulty (Morris, 1960).

Think about which groups you feel would have a more positive image in the United States and which ones would have more negative images. Which groups of international students do you think U.S. students would want to meet and socialize with? Which groups would students not want to meet? The stereotypes of various cultural groups should make it easy for you to sense which groups would face resistance from U.S. Americans in trying to adapt to U.S. culture.

Outcomes of Adaptation

Much of the early research on cultural adaptation concentrated on a single dimension. More recent research emphasizes a multidimensional view of adaptation. There are at least three aspects, or dimensions, of adaptation: psychological health, functional fitness, and intercultural identity (Kim 1988).

Part of adaptation is feeling comfortable in new cultural contexts. This is the most common definition of adaptation, one that concentrates on the emotional feeling of the individual migrant (Berry, Kim, Minde, & Mok, 1987). Feeling comfortable and psychologically healthy generally occurs more quickly than the second outcome, functional fitness (Ward, 1966).

Functional fitness involves being able to function in daily life in many different contexts. Psychologists Adrian Furnham and Steven Bochner (1986) see adaptation mainly as the process of learning new ways of living and behaving. That is, they emphasize the acquisition of skills as being more important than psychological well-being. They have tried to identify areas of skills that are most important for newly arrived members of a society to acquire. Specifically, newcomers to a society should learn the local rules for politeness (for example, being honest), the rules of verbal communication style (for example, direct/indirect), and typical use of nonverbal communication (proxemic behavior, gestures, eye gaze, facial expressions, and so on). Obviously, this outcome is a much longer proposition. It takes most migrants a long time to function at optimal level in the new society.

Another potential outcome of adaptation is the development of an intercultural identity. The intercultural identity is complex. Social psychologist Peter Adler (1975) writes that the multicultural individual is significantly different from the person who is more culturally restricted. The multicultural person is neither a part of nor apart from culture, but someone who acts situationally. Adler discusses the pitfalls and difficulty of the multicultural life, the risk of not knowing what to believe or how to develop ethics or values. Multicultural people face life with little grounding and lack the basic personal, social, and cultural guidelines that cultural identities provide.

IDENTITY AND ADAPTATION

How individual migrants (or groups) relate to the society they visit depends on three issues. One issue is the degree to which migrants want to maintain their own identity, language, and way of life compared to how much they want to

The question of identity has been very interesting to me because people have the notion, now that I have lived in the United States for so many years, that I am an American: People in my neighborhood in France gave me the nickname "l'américain," the American. People say "your president" (while talking to me about the U.S. president), and I always have to remind them that he is not my president; my president lives in Paris. At the same time, people here in the United States perceive me as being French. People also are really interested in knowing if I feel American or French and which country I prefer. All I can answer to these people is that I have learned more about what it feels like to be French because I am here in the United States—more than if I had stayed home. I have been put in the position of having to look in a "cultural mirror" that taught me a great deal about France. On the other hand, I never feel American because I am not sure that I understand this society all that well, all the time.
—Denis

become part of the larger new society. Immigrants who come to the United States often are encouraged to "become American," which often entails relinquishing their former cultural identity. At the beginning of this chapter, you read about Mario, who studied in Marburg, Germany, for a year. Mario and his siblings have taken different paths with respect to their relationship to Mexican culture. Mario, the oldest child, has tried to keep some Mexican traditions. His brother was very young when he came to the United States. He did not learn to speak Spanish at home but is now trying to learn it in college.

Another issue is the extent to which migrants want to have day-to-day interactions with others in the new society. Some migrants find it painful to deal with the everyday prejudices that they experience and retreat to their own cultural groups. Another issue that affects how migrants relate to their new society is the ownership of political power. In some societies, the dominant group virtually dictates the way in which the nondominant groups may act, whereas in other societies nondominant groups are largely free to select their own course. One of the authors, Tom, learned that when his mother first went to grammar school, she had to pick an "American name" because her own name "was too hard to pronounce." As a first-grader, she chose the name "Kathy" because she thought it sounded pretty. This kind of forced assimilation reflects the power of dominant groups over nondominant groups. In this case, *American* was defined as "English" or "British." Looking at how migrants deal with these identity issues in "host" culture contexts can help us understand different patterns of contact (Berry, 1992).

Modes of Adaptation

There are four basic ways in which people adapt to new cultures. They can assimilate, remain separate, integrate, or become marginalized. These four modes are described below.

Some people may integrate in some areas of life and assimilate in others. One may desire economic assimilation in work, linguistic integration (bilingualism), and social separation (marrying someone from the same group and socializing only with members of one's own group). In some families, individual members choose different paths of relating to the larger culture.

Cultural contexts shift, requiring adaptation to new cultural contexts. Cultural adaptation is a process: It occurs in context, varies with each individual, and is circumscribed by relations of dominance and power in so-called "host" cultures.

Although most individuals experience culture shock during cultural transitions, it would be most prevalent for those who assimilate or integrate and, to some degree, for those who are marginalized. In contrast, individuals who maintain separateness are less likely to experience culture shock, because culture shock presumes cultural contact. Military personnel who live abroad on U.S. bases and have very little contact with members of the host society often experience little culture shock. The very set-up and structure of military bases and military housing is designed to insulate them from such shock.

Assimilation   In an assimilation mode, the individual does not want to maintain an isolated cultural identity but wants to maintain relationships with other groups. When this course is freely chosen by everyone, it creates the archetypal "melting pot." When the dominant group forces this mode, it is a "pressure cooker." Many immigrant groups follow this mode of transitioning. It often entails giving up or losing many aspects of the original culture, including language. The central focus in assimilation is on not retaining one's cultural heritage.

Separation   There are two forms of separation. The first is when migrants willingly choose to retain their original culture and at the same time avoid interaction with other groups. This is the mode followed by groups like the Amish or Hutterites, who settled in the United States from Europe, and who maintain their own way of life and identity and tend to avoid prolonged contact with other groups. These groups chose separation, and the dominant society respected their choice.

However, if such separation is initiated and enforced by the dominant society, the condition constitutes segregation. Many cities in the United States had quite restrictive codes that dictated where members of various racial and ethnic groups could and could not live. You may recall the excerpts in Chapter 7 from Malcolm X's autobiography in which he notes that his family could not live in East Lansing, Michigan, because it was for Whites only. An example of defacto segregation is the practice of redlining, in which banks refuse loans to people of particular ethnic groups. This practice perpetuates ethnic segregation.

Integration   Integration occurs when the migrants have an interest in maintaining their original culture and also in maintaining daily interactions with other groups. This differs from assimilation in that it involves a greater degree of interest in maintaining one's own cultural identity. However, integration depends on the openness and willingness of those in the dominant society to accept the cultures of others.

Marginalization Marginalization occurs when the individual or group expresses little interest in maintaining cultural ties with either the dominant culture or the migrant culture. This situation of being out of touch with either culture may be the result of actions by the dominant society—for example, when the U.S. government forced Native Americans to live apart from members of their nation. However, the term *marginalization* has come to describe, more generally, individuals who live on the margin of a culture, not fully able to participate in its political and social life, due to cultural differences.

Adapting on Reentry

When migrants return home to their original cultural contexts, the same process of adaptation occurs and may again involve culture shock, or reentry shock. Sometimes this adaptation is even more difficult because it is so unexpected. Coming home, we might think, should be easy. Students who return home from college, business people who return to corporate headquarters after working abroad, and Native Americans who return to their nations all notice the difficulty of readjusting (Martin & Harrell, 1996).

Scholars have referred to this process as the W-curve of adaptation, because sojourners seem to experience another U-curve: the anticipation of returning home, culture shock in finding that it's not exactly as expected, and the gradual adaptation that follows.

There are two fundamental differences between the first and second U-curves. These are of personal change and expectations (Martin, 1984). The first time, the sojourner is fundamentally unchanged and is experiencing new cultural contexts, perhaps for the first time. In the reentry phase, the sojourner has changed through the adaptation processes and has become a different individual. The person who returns home is not the same person who left home. Our own relationships with our native languages can change, for example. After returning to the United States from a lengthy stay in France, Tom (one of the authors) was visiting a friend. Having brought a bottle of wine to share, he tried to ask for a corkscrew, but the word that came to mind was *tire-bouchon*, the French word. These small word mishaps can be quite frustrating and can make the reentry process more difficult.

Secondly, the sojourner who returns home often does not expect to experience any culture shock. Family and friends usually do not expect the sojourner to have any difficulty. International students who study in the United States and return home talk about how their friends and families expect them to be a little different (more educated) but basically the same as before they went off to college (Martin, 1986; Uehara, 1986).

In addition, the cultural context of reentry is different. Depending on how long the person was away, political figures, popular culture, family, technology, and even language may have changed. When Tom's father went to Japan for the first time, a Japanese taxi driver said to him, "I don't know where you are from, but you have been away for a long, long time." Tom's father had never been to Japan before, so the taxi driver was responding to his use of Japanese. Many words in the Japanese language have changed from the 19th century, when Tom's family immigrated to the United States. Although the Japanese language has changed greatly since the 19th century, many old words and structures remain in use by Japanese speakers in the United States.

Living on the Border

When people travel back and forth between cultures, they develop a multicultural identity. As Denis, an international student from France, describes it:

> I have been living outside my home country for several years now, and it seems that the returns home are not as hard as they were in the past. I feel as if I am able to switch fairly easily between the two cultures without having a lot of anxiety. I have learned to just take things as they come and become nonjudgmental regarding people's actions and behaviors. This has been very hard to do in both countries: to be able to step back and also realize that in most interactions problems are rarely with the people who live in a country, but rather they are within your own framework of beliefs and behaviors that you have to mentally put aside in order to see the other culture or your own.

Technological developments have made the possibilities for travel much easier. With the availability of jets to take us to many places around the world, we can change cultural contexts as never before. Yet, the movement between cultures is never as simple as getting on a plane (Clifford, 1992). David Mura, a Japanese American from the Midwest, went to live in Japan and wrote about his experiences there. He concluded:

> Japan helped me balance a conversation which had been taking place before I was born, a conversation in my grandparents' heads, in my parents' heads, which, by my generation, had become very one-sided, so that the Japanese side was virtually silenced. My stay helped me realize that a balance, which probably never existed in the first place, could no longer be maintained. In the end, I did not speak the language well enough; I did not have enough attraction to the culture. In the end, the society felt to my American psyche too cramped, too well defined, too rule-oriented, too polite, too circumscribed. I could have lived there a few more years if I had had the money and the time, but eventually I would have left. I would not have become one of those Americans who finds in Japan a surrounding society which nourishes and confirms their own sense of identity. Either I was American or I was one of the homeless, one of the searchers for whom John Berger calls a world culture. But I was not Japanese. (1991, p. 370)

The entanglements with history, identity, language, nonverbal communication, and cultural spaces are all salient concerns for understanding these global movements.

SUMMARY

In this chapter, we have tried to highlight the main issues in moving from one culture to another. We stressed that migration can be understood at both an individual level and a sociopolitical level. Migrant groups vary in the length of the migration and the degree of voluntariness. Given these two criteria, there are four types of migrants: sojourners (short-term voluntary), immigrants (long-term voluntary), refugees (long-term involuntary and short-term involuntary).

We also discussed some of the individual adaptation issues associated with migration, particularly culture shock. Four models that attempt to explain adaptation issues are the anxiety and uncertainty management model, the U-curve model, the transition model, and the communication-system model. Communication plays a crucial role in migration. Individual characteristics such as age, gender, preparation, and expectations influence how well a person adapts to new cultures. They can affect the personal outcomes of adaptation, which include good psychological health, functional fitness, and an intercultural identity. Cultural adaptation and identity are interrelated in many ways. Migrants deal with issues of assimilation, separation, integration, and marginalization. Migrants who return to their original homes also face readjustment, or cultural reentry. Those who make frequent or multiple border crossings often develop multicultural identities.

REFERENCES

Adler, P. (1975). The transition experience: An alternative view of culture shock. *Journal of Humanistic Psychology, 15,* 13–23.

Bennet, J. M. (1977). Transition shock: Putting culture shock in perspective. in N. C. Jain (Ed.), *International and Intercultural Communication Annual, 4,* 45–52.

Berry, J. W. (1992). Psychology of acculturation: Understanding individuals moving between two cultures. In R. W. Brislin (Ed.), *Applied cross cultural psychology* (pp. 232–253). Newbury Park, CA: Sage.

Berry, J. W., Kim, U., Minde, T., & Mok, D. (1987). Comparative studies of acculturative stress. *International Migration Review, 21,* 491–511.

Brabant, S., Palmer, C. E., & Gramling, R. (1990). Returning home: An empirical investigation of cross-cultural reentry. *International Journal of Intercultural Relations, 14,* 387–404.

Chen, L. (1994). How we know what we know about Americans: How Chinese sojourners account for their experiences. In A. Gonzalez, M. Houston, & V. Chen (Eds.), *Our voices: Essays in culture, ethnicity and communication* (pp. 125–132). Los Angeles: Roxbury Publishing Co.

Clifford, J. (1992). Traveling cultures. In L. Grossberg, C. Nelson, & P. Treichler (Eds.), *Cultural studies* (pp. 96–116). New York: Routledge.

Festinger, L. (1957). *A theory of cognitive dissonance.* Stanford, CA: Stanford University Press.

Furnham, A., & Bochner, S. (1986). *Culture shock: Psychological reactions to unfamiliar environments* (pp. xv–xx). New York: Methuen.

Gudykunst, W. B. (1995). Anxiety uncertainty management (AUM) theory: Current status. In R. L. Wiseman (Ed.), *Intercultural communication theory* (pp. 8–58). Newbury Park: Sage.

Gullahorn, J. T., & Gullahorn, J. E. (1963). An extension of the U-curve hypothesis. *Journal of Social Issues, 14,* 33–47.

Hawes, F., & Kealey, D. J. (1981). An empirical study of Canadian technical assistance: Adaptation and effectiveness on overseas assignment. *International Journal of Intercultural Relations, 5,* 239–258.

Jun, J-K. (1980). Explaining acculturation in a communication framework. *Communication Monographs, 47,* 155–179.

Kealey, D. J. (1989). A study of cross-cultural effectiveness: Theoretical issues, practical applications. *International Journal of Intercultural Relations, 13,* 387–427.

Kim, Y. Y. (1977). Communication patterns of foreign immigrants in the process of acculturation. *Human Communication Research, 41,* 66–76.

———. (1988). *Communication and cross cultural adaptation.* Philadelphia: Multilingual Matters.

———. (1995). Cross cultural adaptation: An integrated theory. In R. L. Wiseman (Ed.), *Intercultural communication theory* (International and Intercultural Communication Annual 19). Newbury Park, CA: Sage.

Kim, Y. Y., & Gudykunst, W. B. (Eds.). (1988). *Cross cultural adaptation: Current approaches* (International and Intercultural Communication Annual 11). Newbury Park, CA: Sage.

Lysgaard, S. (1955). Adjustment in a foreign society: Norwegian Fulbright grantees visiting the United States. *International Social Science Bulletin, 7,* 45–51. Thousand Oaks, CA: Sage.

Martin, J. (1984). The intercultural reentry: Conceptualizations and suggestions for future research. *International Journal of Intercultural Relations, 8,* 115–134.

Martin, J. N. (1986). Communication in the intercultural reentry: Student sojourners' perceptions of change in reentry relationships. *International Journal of Intercultural Relations, 10,* 1–22.

Martin, J. N., & Harrell, T. (1996). Reentry training for intercultural sojourners. In D. Landis & R. S. Bhagat (Eds.), *Handbook of intercultural training* (2nd ed., pp. 307–326). Thousand Oaks, CA: Sage.

Martin, J. N., Bradford, L., & Rohrlich, B. (1995). Comparing predeparture expectations and post-sojourn reports: A longitudinal study of U.S. students abroad. *International Journal of Intercultural Relations, 19,* 87–110.

Morris, R. (1960). *The two way mirror: National status in foreign students' adjustment.* Minneapolis: University of Minnesota Press.

Mura, D. (1991). *Turning Japanese: Memoirs of a sansei.* New York: Anchor Books.

Nwanko, R. N., & Onwumechili, C. (1991). Communication and social values in cross-cultural adjustment. *Howard Journal of Communications, 3,* 99–111.

Oberg, K. (1960). Cultural shock: Adjustment to new cultural environments. *Practical Anthropology, 7,* 177–182.

Rohrlich, B., & Martin, J. N. (1991). Host country and reentry adjustment of student sojourners. *International Journal of Intercultural Relations, 15,* 163–182.

Ruben, B. D., & Kealey, D. J. (1979). Behavior assessment of communication competence and the prediction of cross-cultural adaptation. *International Journal of Intercultural Relations, 3,* 15–47.

Searle, W., & Ward, C. (1990). The prediction of psychological and sociocultural adjustment during cross cultural transitions. *International Journal of Intercultural Relations, 14,* 449–464.

Uehara, A. (1986). The nature of American student reentry adjustment and perceptions of the sojourn experience. *International Journal of Intercultural Relations, 10,* 415–438.

U.S. News & World Report. (1994). Refugees: The silent emergency. *Focus on change: World map companion guide* (pp. 22–23). Washington, DC: Author.

Ward, C. (1996). Acculturation. In D. Landis & R. S. Bhagat (Eds.), *Handbook of intercultural training* (2nd ed., pp. 125–147). Thousand Oaks, CA: Sage.

Ward, C., & Kennedy, A. (1992). Locus of control, mood disturbance, and social difficulty during cross-cultural transitions. *International Journal of Intercultural Relations, 16,* 175–194.

Ward, C., & Searle, W. (1991). The impact of value discrepancies and cultural identity on psychological and sociocultural adjustment of sojourners. *International Journal of Intercultural Relations, 15,* 209–225.

Weissman, D., & Furnham, A. (1987). The expectations and experiences of a sojourning temporary resident abroad: A preliminary study. *Human Relations, 40,* 313–326.

Witte, K. (1993). A theory of cognitive and negative affect: Extending Gudykunst and Hammer's theory of uncertainty and anxiety reduction. *International Journal of Intercultural Relations, 17,* 197–216.

CHAPTER NINE

POPULAR CULTURE AND INTERCULTURAL COMMUNICATION

We can experience new places through travel and by relocating and living elsewhere. But there will always be many places around the world that we have not visited and where we have not lived. Most of us do not even make it around the globe.

In the previous chapter, we discussed intercultural communication and traveling, visiting, and migrating to other places. What do we know of places we have never been? And how do these places affect intercultural communication?

Neither of us has ever been to Brazil, Nigeria, India, or China. Yet, both of us hold tremendous amounts of information about these places from the news, movies, television shows, advertisements, and more. The kind and quality of information we all have about other places is influenced by popular culture. We may have some knowledge of colonial Africa from John Huston's film *The African Queen,* or we may have some knowledge of rural China from Pearl S. Buck's novels. But the views that books and movies portray supplement the information we get from other sources. For example, audiences that view the movie *Havana* will also recall news reports of Fidel Castro, the Cuban Missile Crisis, the Mariel boat lift, and more.

The complexity of popular culture is often overlooked in our society. People express concern about the social effects of popular culture—for example, the influence of television violence on children, and the relationship between heterosexual pornography and violence against women. Yet, most people look down on the study of popular culture, as if it contains nothing of significance. This contradiction makes it difficult sometimes to investigate and discuss popular culture.

As U.S. Americans, we are in a unique position in relationship to popular culture. Products of U.S. popular culture are well known and circulate widely on the international market. The popularity of U.S. music stars, such as Michael Jackson and Madonna, and of Hollywood films and television shows creates an uneven flow of texts between the United States and other nations. Scholars Elihu Katz and Tamar Liebes (1987) noted the "apparent ease with which American television programs cross cultural and linguistic frontiers. Indeed, the phenomenon is so taken for granted that hardly any systematic research has been done to explain the reasons why these programs are so successful" (p. 419).

In contrast, U.S. Americans are rarely exposed to popular culture from outside the United States. Exceptions to this largely one-way movement of popular culture include rock stars who sing in English. Consider how difficult it is to find foreign films or television programs throughout most of the United States. Even when non-U.S. corporations market their products in the United States, they almost always use U.S. advertising agencies, collectively known as "Madison Avenue." The apparent imbalance of cultural texts globally not only renders U.S. Americans more dependent on U.S.-produced popular culture, but it also can lead to cultural imperialism, a topic we discuss later in this chapter.

The study of popular culture has become increasingly important in the communication field. Although intercultural communication scholars traditionally have overlooked popular culture, we believe that popular culture is a significant influence in intercultural interaction. In this chapter, we explore some of these influences.

WHAT IS "POPULAR CULTURE"?

In Chapter 3, we examined various approaches to the study of culture, including a distinction between "high culture" and "low culture," which has been reconceptualized as "popular culture." Barry Brummett, a contemporary rhetorician, offers the following definition: "Popular culture refers to those systems or artifacts that most people share and that most people know about" (1994, p. 21). According to this definition, television, music videos, and popular magazines would be systems of popular culture. In contrast, the symphony and the ballet would not qualify as popular culture because most people would not be able to identify much about them.

So, popular culture often is seen as populist, including forms of contemporary culture that are made popular by and for the people. As John Fiske, professor of communication arts, observes:

> *To be made into popular culture, a commodity must also bear the interests of the people. Popular culture is not consumption, it is culture—the active process of generating and circulating meanings and pleasures within a social system: culture, however industrialized, can never be adequately described in terms of the buying and selling of commodities. (1989, p. 23)*

There are four significant characteristics of popular culture.

- It is produced by culture industries.
- It is different from folk culture.
- It is everywhere.
- It fills a social function.

As Fiske points out, popular culture is nearly always produced within a capitalist system that sees the products of popular culture as commodities that can be economically profitable. They are produced by what are called culture industries. The Disney Corporation is a noteworthy example of a culture industry because it produces amusement parks, movies, cartoons, and a plethora of associated merchandise.

Folk culture arises in spite of the drive for financial profit. It emerges from needs that are not satisfied by the dominant culture. Consider folk dance, for example. As a "traditional" or folk form of culture, it is neither "high culture" nor "popular culture."

Popular culture is ubiquitous. We are bombarded with it, every day and everywhere. On average, U.S. Americans watch more than 40 hours of television per week. Movie theatres beckon us with the latest multimillion-dollar extravaganza, nearly all U.S.-made. Radio stations and music TV programs blast us with the hottest music groups performing their latest hits. And we are inundated with a staggering number of advertisements and commercials daily.

It is difficult to avoid popular culture. Not only is it ubiquitous, but it also serves an important social function. How many times have you been asked by friends and family to discuss your reactions to recent movies or television programs? Academicians Horace Newcomb and Paul Hirsch (1987) suggest that

Although the media has a powerful impact on our perceptions of people, I don't think it is the sole reason that problems in intercultural communication persist. I believe that we have been socialized to think and behave in a certain way, and that media reinforce some of the existing stereotypes that some people hold. I think it is wrong to blame the media for our problems in communicating with other people and for not treating people as individuals. I believe that if we're going to blame the media, then we should also blame ourselves for being held under their influence. The media have minds of their own, but so do we. We can prejudge just as well as media can. Again, because the media exist, and because of our socialization that has enabled us to categorize, there is an urgent need for effective communication among different cultures.

—Tara

television serves as a cultural forum for discussing and working out our ideas on a variety of topics, including those that emerge from television programs. Television, then, has a powerful social function—to serve as a forum for dealing with social issues.

The ways that people negotiate their relationships to popular culture are complex. It is this complexity that makes understanding the roles of popular culture in intercultural communication so difficult. Clearly, we are not passive receivers of this deluge of popular culture. We are, in fact, quite active in our consumption or resistance to popular culture, a notion that we turn to next.

CONSUMING AND RESISTING POPULAR CULTURE

Consuming Popular Culture

Faced with such an onslaught of cultural texts, people negotiate their ways through popular culture in quite different ways. Popular culture texts do not have to win over the majority of people to be "popular." People often seek out or avoid specific forms of popular culture. For example, romance novels are the best selling form of literature, but many people are not interested in reading these novels. Likewise, whereas you may enjoy watching soap operas or wrestling, many other people do not find pleasure in those forms of popular culture.

There is some unpredictability in the ways that people navigate through popular culture. However, some profiles emerge. Advertising offices of popular magazines even make their reader profiles available to potential advertisers. These reader profiles portray what the magazine believes its readership "looks" like. Although reader profiles do not follow a set format, they generally detail the average age, gender, individual and household incomes, and so on of their readership. The reader profile for *Vogue* would not look like the reader profile for *Esquire,* for example.

We are confronted, as is this woman, with a wide range of popular culture texts in everyday life. We often select and engage those texts that connect with different aspects of our cultural identities. People seek magazines and newspapers that give them information and provide insights into various aspects of their identities, including romance, hobbies, racial/ethnic issues, gay/lesbian politics, and foreign languages. Think about the various identity issues that would guide your selection of magazines from this newstand. (© David DeLossy/The Image Bank)

Each magazine targets a particular readership and then sells this readership to advertisers. The diversity of the U.S. American population generates very different readerships among a range of magazines. This happens in several different ways. Let's explore some of the ways that this diversity is played out in the magazine market.

How Magazines Respond to the Needs of Cultural Identities A wide range of magazines respond to the different social and political needs of cultural identities. You may already be familiar with magazines geared toward a male or a female readership. But there are many other kinds of magazines that serve important functions for other cultural identities. For example, *Ebony* is one of many magazines that cultivate an African American readership. Similar magazines exist for other cultural identities. For example, *A. Magazine*, published in New York City, boasts that it is the national magazine for Asian Americans; *The Advocate* claims to be the national newsmagazine for gays and lesbians. These magazines offer information and points of view that are unavailable in other magazines. They function as a forum for discussing concerns that mainstream magazines often overlook. They also tend to affirm, by their very existence, these other cultural identities that sometimes are invisible or are silenced in the mainstream culture.

In addition, many non-English language newspapers circulate among readers of specific ethnic groups. They serve the same function as the magazines just mentioned. However, because their production costs are low, they are able to survive more easily and reach their limited readerships. Newspapers printed in Cantonese, Spanish, Vietnamese, Japanese, French, Korean, Arabic, Polish, Navajo, and other languages reach non-English-speaking readers in the United States.

How Individuals Negotiate Consumption Readers actively negotiate their way through cultural texts such as magazines—consuming those that fulfill important cultural needs and resisting others that do not. Hence, it is possible to be a reader of many magazines that comprise a particular cultural configuration; that is, someone might read several women's magazines, Spanish language newspapers and magazines, as well as *Newsweek* and *Southern Living*.

Within the communications department at Arizona State University, many magazines and newspapers are passed around and shared among students and faculty members, including *France-Amérique* (the largest U.S. French language newspaper, produced by the publisher of Paris's *Le Figaro*), *The Rafu Shimpo* (the Los Angeles Japanese Daily News), *The Advocate*, *Shape*, *The Village Voice*, *The New Yorker*, *L'actualité* (a Montreal newsmagazine), and *Asian Week*. Whether or not we "fit" the reader profiles, these publications lend insight into the cultural realities of different groups in the United States and abroad.

Cultural Texts Versus Cultural Identities We must be careful not to conflate the magazines with the cultural identities they are targeting. After all, many publications offer different points of view on any given topic. In short, there is no single and unified "Asian American position" on immigration reform, or any "Latino/a position" on affirmative action. Rather, there can be a preponderance of opinions on some issues. These often are played out through popular culture forms.

It is important to remember that other cultural populations can participate in different cultural forums—with different discussions and information—than readers of mainstream texts. For example, an article in *The Rafu Shimpo*, the Los Angeles Japanese Daily News, highlighted yet another hate crime against an Asian American. In this case, a European American male repeatedly stabbed a Chinese American man at a grocery store in Novato, a city in the San Francisco Bay Area. The reality of living in a society that expresses racism, homophobia, xenophobia, and antisemitism through hate crimes is often lost on those who rely on mainstream media. These issues make a tremendous difference in the ways we perceive social reality on a day-to-day basis.

People come together through cultural magazines and newspapers, to affirm and negotiate their relationships with their cultural identities. In this way, the texts are like cultural spaces, which we discussed in Chapter 7. However, magazines are just one example of how popular culture can function. Not all popular culture texts are easily correlated to particular cultural groups. Think about the various television programs, movies, mass-market paperbacks, and tabloids that flood our everyday lives. The reasons that people enjoy some over others cannot easily be determined. People negotiate their relationships to popular culture in complex ways.

Resisting Popular Culture

At times, people actively seek out particular popular culture texts to consume. At other times, they resist cultural texts. Consider the mixed reaction to music star Madonna. Some people love Madonna and identify themselves as fans. Others reject her and her music.

Communication studies focusing on Madonna highlight some of the complexities of consumption and resistance. One communication study demonstrates the different meanings and interpretations that various racial and ethnic groups have of Madonna's music videos (Nakayama & Peñaloza, 1993). In this study, various groups offered interpretations that indicated different ways of resisting dominant social ideas. So, although Madonna may be a popular star, her texts are not simply popular. They are not clear reflections of mainstream U.S. culture. In fact, Madonna's popularity and what she supposedly represents are somewhat controversial. Many people actively and strongly dislike Madonna. So-called Madonna-haters are angered by the cultural values they see promoted by Madonna's texts (Schultze, White, & Brown, 1993). In the case of Madonna, the conflict of cultural values and cultural identities is apparent and leads us to think about resisting these popular culture texts. Resistance need not be seen as entirely unrelated and distinct from consumption.

Tom, one of the authors, spoke at a 1993 Madonna conference in West Hollywood, California. He was stunned by the magnitude of adoration some of her fans expressed. Some of them made explicit comparisons between Madonna and the Pope, noting that Madonna had much more to offer their lives than the Pope. These fans were more than ready to consume whatever they could about Madonna.

On the other hand, there are those who delight in hating Madonna. The appearance of *The I Hate Madonna Handbook* reflects the complexity of resistance and consumption. The handbook's author explains: "This is a book for people who love to hate Madonna and for those who hate to love her. It's also a book for everyone who wonders when this woman will have had enough, start a perfume line, and call it quits" (Rosenzweig, 1994, p. ix). The handbook attacks Madonna's character from a variety of angles, but most notably on sexual politics.

People often resist particular forms of popular culture by refusing to engage in them. For example, some people feel the need to avoid television completely; some even decide not to own televisions. Some people refuse to go to movies that contain violence because they do not find pleasure in such films. These kinds of conscious decisions are often based on concerns about the cultural politics at work.

Resistance to popular culture can also be related to social roles. Some teachers, for example, disliked the movie *Ferris Bueller's Day Off* for its anti-authoritarian stance vis-à-vis school teachers and principals. Likewise, some people have expressed concern about the homophobic or racist ideologies embedded in Disney films such as *Aladdin* (Boone, 1995). *Aladdin*, for example, plays into Western fears of homosexuality and the tradition of projecting those concerns on Arabic culture. Resistance stems mainly from concerns about the representation of various social groups. Popular culture plays a powerful role in how we think about and understand other groups.

REPRESENTING CULTURAL GROUPS

As we noted at the beginning of this chapter, people often are introduced to other cultures through the lens of popular culture. These introductions can be quite intimate, in ways that a tourist may not experience. For example, movies enter family homes and portray romance, familial conflict, or a death in the family. The audience sees and enters the private lives of people they do not know, in ways that they could never do simply as tourists.

Yet, we must also think about how these cultural groups are portrayed through that lens of popular culture. Not everyone sees the portrayal in the same way. For example, you may not think that the TV show *Melrose Place* represents quintessential U.S. American values and lifestyles. But some viewers may see it as their entree into the ways that U.S. Americans (or perhaps European Americans) live.

In his study of the martial arts movie *Showdown in Little Tokyo*, Tom Nakayama (1994) argued that popular culture representations help us understand identities in relationships to other identities. In this particular movie, the

Early in 1995, I sent out June calendars for my summer program for kids. The calendar page talked about June as "Multicultural Month." I had asked for art to be placed on each corner of the page, to represent children of different cultures. I was surprised to see that this calendar showed two African American children with ripped clothing, funky shoes, and enlarged facial features (especially the lips). Being African American myself, I immediately took offense at the representation. I called the District Office where the calendars were created and spoke with one of the staff. I pointed out that the calendar negatively represented African Americans and that I did not want my students or parents to see this. I also pointed out to her how the children of other cultures looked, by comparison. The others were portrayed as clean-cut. She said the computer generated the pictures with the only cultures they had. I said, "I want new calendars made." She dodged the subject. I said the calendars promoted a negative stereotype against African Americans. Her response shocked me. She said, "But isn't that how Blacks look?" I swallowed and held back from answering. Her stereotype of Blacks meant dirty, poor people with ragged clothes and large lips.

What is most interesting is I just received my calendar for November and the Blacks are represented quite nicely. Maybe they have a new computer program. Yeah, right. God will meet her on judgment day.

—Pamela

cultural identities of the Japanese (as the "bad guys") had to be understood in their narrative relationship to the "good guys" (two Los Angeles police officers). Images portraying other identities—based on race, gender, or sexual orientation—fueled the movie's narrative. In this way, the relationships among the various identities are negotiated and constructed by Hollywood.

Migrants' Perceptions of Mainstream Culture

Ethnographers and other scholars have been successful crossing international and cultural boundaries to examine the influence of popular culture. In an early study, Elihu Katz and Tamar Liebes (1987) set up focus groups to see how different cultural groups watch the TV show *Dallas:* "There were ten groups each of Israeli Arabs, new immigrants to Israel from Russia, first and second generation immigrants from Morocco, and kibbutz members. Taking these groups as a microcosm of the worldwide audience of *Dallas*, we are comparing their readings of the program with ten groups of matched Americans in Los Angeles" (p. 421).

In this study, Katz and Liebes found that the U.S. Americans in Los Angeles were much less likely to perceive *Dallas* as portraying life in the United States. In contrast, the Israelis, Arabs, and the array of immigrants were much more inclined to believe that this television show was indeed all about life in the United States. Katz and Liebes note: "What seems clear from the analysis, even at this

James Dean remains a popular cultural icon in the United States and abroad. This 1996 photo shows that one of his films, *East of Eden,* continues to play in Tokyo. How does Dean's popularity in Japan contrast with the absence of a similar popular Japanese male star in the United States? What might explain this disparity? Think about the issues of cultural imperialism raised in this chapter. *(T. K. Nakayama)*

stage, is that the non-Americans consider the story more real than the Americans. The non-Americans have little doubt that the story is about 'America'; the Americans are less sure" (p. 421). The results of this study are not surprising, but we should not overlook what we can learn about the intercultural communication process. We can see that these popular-culture images are often more influential in constructing particular ways of understanding cultural groups other than our own.

Another study (Lee & Cho, 1990) that focused on immigrants to the United States, found similar results. Researchers asked Korean women immigrants why they preferred watching Korean television shows (which they had to rent at the video store) to U.S. television programs. The women respondents felt that, because of the cultural differences, the Korean television shows were more appealing.

Yet, as one respondent noted:

"I like to watch American programs. Actors and actresses are glamorous and the pictures are sleek. But the ideas are still American. How many Korean women are that independent? And how many men commit incest? I think American programs

are about American people. They are not the same as watching the Korean pro-
grams. But I watch them for fun. And I learn the American way of living by
watching them" (p. 43)

Here, both consumption and resistance to U.S. television are evident. This
woman uses U.S. television to learn about U.S. American "way of living" but
prefers to watch Korean shows because they relate to her cultural identity.

The use of popular culture to learn about another culture should not be surprising. After all, many teachers encourage their students to use popular culture
in this manner, not only to improve their language skills, but also to help them
learn many of the nuances of another culture. When Tom (one of this book's authors) was first studying French, his French professor told the students that *Le
dernier métro* (*The Last Metro*), a film by director François Truffaut, was playing
downtown. The point, of course, was to learn to hear the French language at a
native rate. But Tom remembers being amazed at the subtle references to antisemitism, the treatment of lesbianism, and the film's style, which contrasted
sharply with that of Hollywood films.

Popular Culture and Stereotyping

In what ways does reliance on popular culture create and reinforce stereotypes
of different cultures? As we noted at the outset of this chapter, neither author
has had the opportunity to travel all over the world. Our knowledge about other
places, even places we have been, is largely influenced by popular culture. For
people who do not travel and interact in relatively homogeneous social circles,
the impact of popular culture may be even greater.

There are many familiar stereotypes of ethnic groups represented in the media. Scholar Jack Shaheen (1984), who is of Lebanese descent, went in search of
"real" Arabs after tiring of the way Lebanese and other Arabs were portrayed in
the media—as billionaires, bombers, and belly dancers. According to his research, "television tends to perpetuate four basic myths about Arabs: they are all
fabulously wealthy; they are barbaric and uncultured; they are sex maniacs with
a penchant for white slavery; and they revel in acts of terrorism" (p. 4). Shaheen
describes other untruths (for example, that Iranians are Arabs and that all Arabs
are Muslim).

Scholar Lisa Flores (1994) describes the portrayal in television documen-
taries of Mexicans responding to natural disasters. According to Flores, docu-
mentaries often show Mexicans as resilient, patient, and faithful—rather passive
and therefore acceptable. She connects this to the portrayal of Mexican Americans as not quite American, "although the difficulty in becoming American is
posited as not a lack of choice, but lack of ability" (p. 16).

African American women also have been portrayed stereotypically on TV,
especially in the 1950s and 1960s, when the roles they held were secondary (for
example, as domestics). Scholar Bishetta Merritt (1994) also reminds us of the
African American female characters who often appear as scenery in the background: the person buying drugs, the homeless person on the sidewalk, the hotel

lobby prostitute. Merritt points out that these women still project images, even if they aren't the focus.

> *If the majority of black women the television audience is exposed to are homeless, drug-addicted, or maids, and if viewers have no contact with African American women other than through television, what choice do they have but to believe that all women of this ethnic background reflect this television image? . . . It is, therefore, important, as the twenty-first century approaches and the population of this country includes more and more people of color, that the television industry broaden the images of African American women to include their nuances and diversity.*
> (*p. 52*)

What about those ethnic groups that simply don't appear except as infrequent stereotypes: Native Americans and Asian Americans? How do these stereotypes influence intercultural interaction? Do people behave any differently if they don't hold stereotypes about people with whom they are interacting? Two communication researchers, Valerie Manusov and Radha Hegde (1993), investigated these questions in a study in which they identified two groups of college students: those who had some preconceived ideas about India and those who didn't. It turns out that the preconceived ideas were pretty positive. Manusov and Hegde then asked all of the students to interact, one at a time, with an international student from India who was part of the study.

When the students with preconceptions talked with the Indian student, they interacted differently than those who had no expectations. Students from the former group relied less on small talk, covered more topics, and asked fewer questions within each topic. Overall, their conversations were more like those between people who know each other. The students with the preconceptions also were more positive about the conversation.

What can we learn from this study? It appears that having some information and positive expectations may lead to more in-depth conversations and positive outcomes than having no information. However, what happens when negative stereotypes are present? It is possible that expectations are fulfilled in this case, too.

For example, in several studies at Princeton University, Whites interviewed both White and Black "job applicants" who were actually part of the study and were trained to behave consistently, no matter how interviewers acted toward them. The interviews were videotaped. The interviewers clearly behaved differently toward Blacks; their speech deteriorated, they made more grammatical errors, they spent less time, and they showed fewer "immediacy" behaviors—that is, they were less friendly and less outgoing. In a second study, interviewers were trained to be either "immediate" or "nonimmediate" as they interviewed White job applicants. A panel of judges watched the videotapes and agreed that those applicants interviewed by the "nonimmediate" interviewer performed less well and were more nervous. This suggests that the African American applicants in the first study never had a chance: They were only reacting to the nonimmediate behavior of the interviewers. Mark Snyder summarizes: "Considered together,

Although I feel that race is an emotionally charged issue, I do feel that media have a lot to do with it. Whenever a crime is committed, if it is someone who is colored or from a different ethnic group than White America, the media always state what color the person is or what the person's ethnicity is. Unfortunately, this paints a bad picture of the rest of the group. This then leads to stereotyping. If the media would not focus so much on the color or ethnicity of the person committing the crime, and if people would not be so ignorant to the fact that this one person does not represent the whole group, then, in my opinion, prejudice would eventually decline.

I think stereotyping and prejudice also come about because of in-groups and reference groups. In-groups are the people who want to use the term we. Reference groups are the groups that we want to be part of, to belong to. If the media state that some Black man robbed a bank, then a White person may state that we (the in-group of Whites) should not put up with criminals from the Black community (the out-group). That person may say about his own racial or ethnic group "I don't know anyone who has ever committed a crime." Although this may be the case, it does not necessarily mean that no Whites have ever committed a crime. This leads back to the media. They seem to paint a negative picture of a whole race. Also, if a White person, for instance, committed a crime, this same man would try to use the scapegoat theory and/or make an excuse for the crime.

—Brad

the two investigations suggest that in interracial encounters, racial stereotypes may constrain behavior in ways to cause both blacks and whites to behave in accordance with those stereotypes" (1995, p. 373).

U.S. POPULAR CULTURE AND POWER

One of the dynamics of intercultural communication that we have highlighted throughout this text is power. In considering popular culture, we need to think about not only the ways that people interpret and consume popular culture, but also the ways that these popular culture texts represent particular groups in specific ways. If people largely view other cultural groups through the lens of popular culture, then we need to think about the power relations that are embedded in these popular culture dynamics.

Global Circulation of Images/Commodities

As we noted earlier, much of the international circulation of popular culture is U.S. popular culture. U.S.-made films, for example, are widely distributed by an industry that is backed by considerable financial resources. Some media scholars have noted that the U.S. film industry earns far more money outside the United

States than from U.S. box office sales (Guback, 1969; Guback & Varis, 1982). This situation ensures that Hollywood will continue to seek overseas revenue and that it will have the financial resources to do so.

Many other U.S. media are widely available outside of the United States, including television and newspapers. Cable News Network (CNN) was even available in Iraq during the Gulf War. MTV is also broadcast internationally. The *International Herald Tribune*, published jointly by the *New York Times* and the *Washington Post*, is also widely available in some parts of the world. The implications of the dominance by U.S. media and popular culture have yet to be determined, although you might imagine the consequences.

Not all popular culture comes from the United States. For example, the invention and rise of James Bond is a British phenomenon, but the famous character has been exported to the United States. In their study of the popularity of James Bond, scholars Tony Bennett and Janet Woollacott (1987) note that in the Bond film *A License to Kill*, "The threat to the dominance of white American male culture is removed not by a representative of that culture, and certainly not by a somewhat foppish English spy, but by the self-destruction of the forces ranged against it" (pp. 293–294). The appropriation of the British character into U.S. ideological and economic terrain complicates arguments about popular culture and intercultural communication.

Cultural Imperialism

It is difficult to measure the impact of the U.S. and Western media and popular culture on the rest of the world. But we do know that we cannot ignore this dynamic. The U.S. government in the 1920s believed that having U.S. movies on foreign screens would boost the sales of U.S. products because the production would be furnished with U.S. goods. The U.S. government worked closely with the Hays Office (officially, the Motion Picture Producers and Distributors of America) to break into foreign markets, most notably in the United Kingdom (Nakayama & Vachon, 1991).

The discussions about "media imperialism," "electronic colonialism," and "cultural imperialism," which began in the 1920s, continue today. The interrelationships between economics, nationalism, and culture make it difficult to determine with much certainty how significant cultural imperialism might be. The issue of cultural imperialism is complex because the definition of cultural imperialism is complex. In his survey of the cultural imperialism debates, scholar John Tomlinson (1991) identifies five different ways of thinking about cultural imperialism: (1) as cultural domination, (2) as media imperialism, (3) as nationalist discourse, (4) as a critique of global capitalism, and (5) as a critique of modernity (pp. 19–23). Tomlinson's analysis underscores the interrelatedness of issues of ethnicity, culture, and nationalism in the context of economics, technology, and capitalism—resources that are distributed unevenly throughout the world. To understand the concerns about cultural imperialism, therefore, it is necessary to consider the complexity of the impact of U.S. popular culture. There is no easy way to measure the impact of popular culture, but we should be

I grew up in northern central Canada. When I was a child, we had only two tele-vision channels: CBC (Canadian Broadcasting Corporation) in English, and CBC in French. I was 10 years old when we got our next channel—another small Cana-dian network. When I was 14, we got cable. The viewing choices seemed endless.

I remember spending less time watching my old favorite Canadian shows, and more time watching U.S. sit-coms, variety shows, and game shows. I went from Celebrity Cooks to M*A*S*H, from Radio on Television to Happy Days. The vari-ety shows had guests that we actually liked, not just had to put up with because they were the only ones willing to be interviewed on the CBC. In Canada, the top prizes on game shows were train trips for two, space heaters, and weekend getaways within your own city. The U.S. game shows had the big bucks. And thus, I became more and more interested in television. It seemed like a good thing, what with so many choices.

The nightly news stayed the same, though. Beginning with international news (which included, for the most part, news from Britain and the United States, and any major international "events"), followed by our Canadian and provincial news. We always had and still have great newspeople and anchors.

I no longer own a television. I am 26 and I haven't had one for four years. When I do watch television, I'm selective. I watch news, PBS, special shows, or a soap opera I haven't seen in years (just to keep up). I'm sure that I have been influenced by U.S. television in many ways, but the biggest influence, I think, is that I now know what is good and what is lame, pure "mind-candy" television.

—James

sensitive to its influences on intercultural communication. Let's look at some examples.

In the Gulf War of 1991 U.S. troops and allies fought the Iraqis for control of Kuwait. Demanding that Iraq relinquish Kuwait and reestablish its indepen-dence as a nation, the United States attacked Baghdad. Media coverage high-lighted the air strikes in these attacks. Many malls, homes, and businesses were saturated with yellow ribbons in support of U.S. and allied troops. At that time, French writer Jean Baudrillard published a series of articles (called "*La guerre du golfe n'aura pas eu lieu,*" or "The Gulf War did not take place") in a Paris-based newspaper, *Libération*. In these articles, he argued that the Gulf War was a media simulation, that we had no access to truth. Our reliance on media images, rather than on reality, made us very reliant on popular culture. Yet, as he argues, we need not play into that game:

The true belligerents are those who thrive on the ideology of the truth of this war, despite the fact that the war itself exerts its ravages on another level, through fak-ing, through hyper-reality, the simulacrum, through all those strategies of psycho-logical deterrence that make play with facts and images, with the precession of the virtual over the real, of virtual time over real time, and the inexorable confusion between the two. If we have no practical knowledge of this war—and such knowledge is out of the question—then let us at least have the skeptical intelligence to reject the probability of all information, of all images whatever their source. (quoted in Norris, 1992, pp. 193–194)

Baudrillard's rejection of the war coverage is one tactic for dealing with the media hype and barrage of images. Theorist Christopher Norris warns against such a position, because it encourages us to forget that many people, mostly Iraqis, were killed in the war; it was not simply a movie.

In early 1994, another international event drew media attention. U.S. American teenager Michael Fay was caned in Singapore as punishment for vandalism. From the time of his sentencing to the caning itself—a period of four months—the U.S. media and popular culture were riveted on this case. Unlike with the Gulf War, there appeared to be no consensus in the United States about Michael Fay's situation. Many were strongly in favor of Singapore's tough stance on crime and envied its low crime rate. Others felt that Fay's sentence was a clear example of cruel and unusual punishment. Whatever the issue, it seemed certain that it was not concern for Fay. Once he had been caned, there was little interest in him: "After his return to the U.S., there was hardly any attempt to get him to corroborate what had been said about Fay-beating Singapore. The columnists and commentators who had written about him had moved on to other issues" (Latif, 1994, p. 102).

The significance of the Michael Fay affair resides less in the personal event than in the popular culture construction of Singapore and this country's relations with the United States. Popular culture became an important forum for playing out the issues, whether it involved parodies on late night television or news stories that attempted to analyze the situation. As a small nation, Singapore did not have the resources to mount a strong defense of its position in the U.S. media, nor could it simply capitulate to the U.S. government's request to suspend the sentence if it was to retain its sovereignty. Thus, the media's discussion of the Fay event was dominated by U.S. social concerns, such as rising crime rates, particularly among youth. As journalist Asad Latif concludes:

The issue is a reminder to Singapore of the challenge a small state faces in trying to uphold its domestic system in an unequal world. If anything, the challenge will grow as the disappearance of the bipolar world reveals the ideological differences within the free world that Cold War solidarities had papered over. (1994, p. 100)

Sometimes the Western images are imported and welcomed by the ruling party of other countries. For example, the government of the Ivory Coast of West Africa has used the media and importation of foreign (mostly French) media to promote its image of a "new" Ivoirien cultural identity. The government purchased a satellite dish that permits 1400 hours of French programming annually, part of the 77% of foreign programming. It has been criticized by many for borrowing heavily from the Western media—for inviting cultural imperialism.

I arrived in Moscow, Russia, spent three days with my host family, and was then sent to what is called a Pioneer Camp. This camp was basically a scout camp designed to indoctrinate the youth in preparation for Communist Party membership. At that point I had no knowledge of the Russian language or culture and there wasn't a single person at the camp (of 300 students) who spoke English. Needless to say, I mastered the art of nonverbal communication very quickly.

In terms of the initial interaction, those around me and I lacked both linguistic and cultural competence. The frustration accumulated for a few days, until we had a little dance one evening. As it turned out, the Billy Joel song "We Didn't Start the Fire" was the favorite song of the older students and, although they didn't understand the lyrics, they could sing along. We played that song over and over again until we were all friends. We found similarity. That one similarity factor brought us to a level of closeness that was unbelievably intense.
—Katrina

While television, as mirror, sometimes reflects multiple Ivoirien cultures, the latter are expected to acquiesce to a singular national culture in the image of the Party, which is also synonymous with a Western cultural image. . . . The cultural priority is openness for the sake of modernization in the quest of the Ivoirien national identity. (Land, 1992, p. 25)

In all of these examples, popular culture plays an enormous role in understanding relations around the globe. It is through popular culture that we try to understand the dynamics of other cultures and nations. Although these representations are problematic, we also rely on popular culture to understand many kinds of issues: the invasion of Grenada, the vote to allow divorce in Ireland, the conflict in Bosnia-Herzegovina, the murders of homeless children in Brazil, the breakup of the former Soviet Union, the rise of nationalism in Quebec and Eritrea and Tahiti. For many of us, the world exists through popular culture.

SUMMARY

For many people, popular culture is one of the primary modes of intercultural experience. The images produced by culture industries such as film and television enable us to "travel" to many places. As a forum for the development of our ideas about other places, we rely heavily on popular culture. For example, many people who have never been to Japan or studied much about the Japanese economic system have incredibly strong ideas about these topics. Trade issues with Japan are foregrounded in many U.S. news reports and from the backdrop in U.S. films such as *Rising Sun* and *Black Rain*. The United States imports very little Japanese popular culture.

It is significant that much of our popular culture is dominated by U.S.-based culture industries, considering how we use popular culture as a form of intercultural communication. Not all popular culture emerges from the United States, though. But the preponderance is from the United States or Western Europe. And it contributes to a power dynamic—cultural imperialism—that affects intercultural communication everywhere.

There are four important characteristics of popular culture: Popular culture is produced by culture industries; it is distinct from folk culture; we find it everywhere; and it serves social functions. Individuals and groups can determine the extent to which they are influenced by popular culture. That is, we may consume or resist the messages of popular culture. Our cultural identities are significant in how we negotiate our interaction with popular culture.

Popular culture is an important force in the way we understand other cultural groups. We tend to rely more heavily on media images to think about cultural groups we have little or no personal experience with. Stereotypes are important to contend with in understanding intercultural communication interaction.

A great deal of popular culture is produced in the United States and circulates globally. The imbalance between the exchange of U.S. popular culture and other popular culture texts has raised concerns about cultural imperialism.

REFERENCES

Boone, J. A. (1995). Rubbing Aladdin's lamp. In M. Dorenkamp & R. Henke (Eds.), *Negotiating lesbian and gay subjects* (pp. 149–177). New York: Routledge.

Bennett, T., & Woollacott, J. (1987). *Bond and beyond: The political career of a popular culture hero.* New York: Methuen.

Brummett, B. (1994). *Rhetoric in popular culture.* New York: St. Martin's Press.

Fiske, J. (1989). *Understanding popular culture.* New York: Routledge.

Flores, L. (1994). *Shifting visions: Intersections of rhetorical and Chicana feminist theory in the analysis of mass media.* Unpublished dissertation. University of Georgia.

Guback, T. (1969). *The international film industry: Western Europe and America since 1945.* Bloomington: Indiana University Press.

Guback, T., & Varis, T. (1982). *Transnational communication and cultural industries.* Paris: Unesco.

Katz, E., & Liebes, T. (1987). Decoding *Dallas:* Notes from a cross-cultural study. In H. Newcomb (Ed.), *Television: The critical view* (4th ed., pp. 419–432). New York: Oxford University Press.

Land, M. (1992). Ivoirien television, willing vector of cultural imperialism. *The Howard Journal of Communications, 4,* 10–27.

Latif, A. (1994). *The flogging of Singapore: The Michael Fay affair.* Singapore: Times Books International.

Lee, M., & Cho, C. H. (1990, January). Women watching together: An ethnographic study of Korean soap opera fans in the U.S. *Cultural Studies, 4*(1), 30–44.

Leslie, M. (1992). Representation of blacks in Brazil on prime-time commercial television. *The Howard Journal of Communications, 4,* 1–9.

Manusov, V., & Hegde, R. (1993). Communicative outcomes of stereotype-based expectancies: An observational study of cross-cultural dyads. *Communication Quarterly, 41,* 338–354.

Merritt, B. D. (1994). Illusive reflections: African American women on prime-time television. In A. González, M. Houston, & V. Chen (Eds.), *Our voices* (pp. 48–53). Los Angeles: Roxbury.

Nakayama, T. K. (1994). Show/down time: "Race," gender, sexuality and popular culture. *Critical Studies in Mass Communication, 11,* 2, 162–179.

Nakayama, T. K., & Peñaloza, L. N. (1993). Madonna t/races: Music videos through the prism of color. In C. R. Schwichtenberg (Ed.), *The Madonna connection: Representational politics, subcultural identities, and cultural theory* (pp. 39–55). Boulder, CO: Westview.

Nakayama, T. K., & Vachon, L. A. (1991). Imperialist victory in peacetime: State functions and the British cinema industry. *Current Research in Film, 5,* 161–174.

Newcomb, H., & Hirsch, P. M. (1987). Television as a cultural forum. In H. Newcomb (Ed.), *Television: The critical view* (4th ed.). New York: Oxford University Press.

Norris, C. (1992). *Uncritical theory: Postmodernism, intellectuals, and the gulf war.* Amherst: University of Massachusetts Press.

Rosenzweig, I. (1994). *The I hate Madonna handbook.* New York: St. Martin's Press.

Schultze, L., White, A. B., & Brown, J. D. (1993). "A sacred monster in her prime": Audience construction of Madonna as low-other. In C. R. Schwichtenberg (Ed.), *The Madonna connection: Representational politics, subcultural identities, and cultural theory* (pp. 15–37). Boulder, CO: Westview.

Shaheen, J. G. (1984). *The TV Arab.* Bowling Green, OH: Bowling Green State University Press.

Snyder, M. (1995). Self-fulfilling stereotypes. In P. Rothenburg (Ed.), *Race, class and gender in the United States* (pp. 370–376). New York: St. Martin's Press.

Tomlinson, J. (1991). *Cultural imperialism.* Baltimore: Johns Hopkins University Press.

CHAPTER TEN

CULTURE, COMMUNICATION, AND INTERCULTURAL RELATIONSHIPS

Why and how do we develop relationships with other people? Think of how you got to know your friends—those you know as acquaintances as well as those with whom you have more intimate or even romantic relationships. What about your relationships with people who are different from you—in age, ethnicity, religion, sexual orientation? How did you get to know them? Are these relationships any different from those that are characterized by similarity?

There may be almost as many reasons for relationships as there are relationships. Perhaps some of your relationships developed because of circumstances—for example, when you had to work on a course project together with another student. Some relationships develop because of proximity or repeated contact (for example, with neighbors in dorms or apartments). Others develop because of a strong physical attraction, or because of a strong similarity (same interests, attitudes, or personality traits). Sometimes relationships develop between dissimilar people, simply because they are different. There seems to be some truth to both adages, "birds of a feather flock together" and "opposites attract."

How do we develop relationships with others who are culturally different? What is the role of communication in these relationships? And how do contexts (social, historical, political) influence our relationships?

These are some of the questions to explore in this chapter. First, we will discuss four principles of attraction that may explain how relationships develop and three stages of relational development. Then we examine some cross-cultural differences in relational development and maintenance. Finally, we examine intercultural relationships—both friendships and romantic relationships. For each of these topics, we'll examine contextual issues.

PRINCIPLES OF RELATIONAL ATTRACTION

Why do we enter into relationships with some people and not others? There seem to be four primary principles of relational attraction: proximity, physical attraction, similarity, and complementarity. Although cultural communities may apply these principles in different priorities, they seem to be applicable to most cultural contexts, across race, class, and ethnicity.

Proximity

One of the most powerful principles of relational attraction is proximity. People form relationships with those who are in close proximity: people with whom they work, play, worship, or share other activities. The Hollywood portrayal of relationships between people who randomly find each other in chance meetings is romantic but is not often substantiated in real life. Films like *Pretty Woman* show relationships developing across class and cultural backgrounds, in which upper middle class men fall in love with working class women. This makes good fantasy; however, in real life people tend to meet and develop relationships with other people whom they encounter in their daily lives. This usually, but not always, means that we tend to be attracted to individuals from similar social, economic, and cultural backgrounds.

However, this principle alone does not explain relational attraction. It is particularly limited in explaining attraction in some cultural contexts. As communication scholars Akbar Javidi and Manoochehr Javidi (1991) point out, in many Eastern countries a person's background (family, ethnicity, religion, and so on) is much more important than who he or she is as an individual. In the United States, although background is also important, we assume that we can become friends and develop relationships with anyone we meet. The proximity principle may explain the initial stages of relational development in the United States better than it explains relational development in Eastern countries. The same may be true in other cultural contexts. Communication scholar Kristine Fitch (1990/1991) describes similar patterns in Colombia, where individual compatibility is not key to romantic relationships. Rather, the major factor that determines whether the relationship will work is whether friends and family like each other.

We must remember to recognize the context in which relationships happen. In the way that many societies are structured, individuals do not often come in contact with people who are quite different from them. When they do, it is usually in highly imbalanced power situations—for example, when someone hires a maid or a gardener. The structures of society often determine the people with whom we come in contact. There is considerable evidence that, in the United States, people live in neighborhoods and work in places that are segregated by race and class.

The principle of proximity has implications for intercultural relationships. How many people do you meet in the course of a day who are different from you in age, gender, ethnicity, socioeconomic status, and sexual orientation? According to this principle, the more diverse your daily contacts, the more opportunities you have to develop intercultural relationships.

Physical Attraction

Another reason we're attracted to specific people is that we like the way they look. In fact, physical attraction may be the most important aspect in the very beginning of a relationship, at least in the United States. However, if this were the most important aspect, then only those considered very attractive would ever form relationships. Evidence suggests, however, that we are attracted to people whom we think have approximately the same level of attractiveness as we have. This phenomenon is described as the *matching hypothesis*.

The principle of physical attraction has implications for intercultural relationships, as does the principle of proximity. Every cultural community has standards for physical attractiveness, but these standards are culturally based. Notions of attractiveness are defined for us and reinforced by what we see on TV and in other media. The specific use of models in advertising, popular TV shows, and other media reinforces cultural standards of beauty. These standards can be so strong as to encourage anorexia and bulimia in young people, particularly young women.

When we look at the cultural constructions of sexuality and racial groups, we find how truly complex are the problems of culturally influenced standards of beauty. Popular culture often depicts ethnic and racial characteristics in un-truthful ways. For example, African American men are often depicted as highly sexually driven. Kobena Mercer's (1994) critique of Robert Mapplethorpe's pho-tographs of nude black men exposes this stereotype. Mercer argues that these photographs play into racist stereotypes about black male sexuality as a fetish.

Melissa Chan (1990) explains that the "Caucasian male's irrefutable prefer-ence for Asian women" (p. 1) is reflected in the many popular culture texts and discourses that portray Asian women as erotic, exotic, and submissive. This kind of attraction has spawned an entire business of mail-order Asian brides. In her work, Rona Halualani (1995) analyzed how these businesses perpetuate and market stereotypes. Asian men are often stereotyped in ways that downplay their masculinity. In response to these social discourses, some Asian American groups have hosted Asian male beauty pageants and produced calendars with at-tractive Asian men.

Of course, we all want to believe that we choose our relational partners out-side of the influences of these social discourses. We all want to believe that we fell in love with this man or this woman because he or she is "special." Yet, if we are serious about understanding the problems and dynamics of intercultural communication, we must be attentive to these larger social discourses about racial and sexual identities. Our relationships are strongly influenced by social and cultural ideas about interracial, intercultural, heterosexual, gay, lesbian, and intergenerational romance. In whatever ways people view their own relation-ships, other people can be quite influential in the development of those relation-ships through their support, silence, denial, or hostility.

And what about the larger social discourses on racial sexualities? As colum-nist Hoyt Sze notes:

> Naturally, people outmarry [marry outside their racial group] for love. But we must ask ourselves how much of this love is racist, unequal love. Unfortunately, in-terracial love is still inextricably linked to colonialism. How else does one explain the disproportional rates at which Asian American women and African American men marry out? Is it just a coincidence that the mainstream media objectify the same groups as "exotic-erotic" playthings? I know that Asian American men and African American women aren't fundamentally lacking in attractiveness or desir-ability. (1992, p. 10)

If we only try to understand romantic love on an interpersonal level, how might we explain the high rates of outmarriage by some groups and not others?

There seems to be great agreement on which physical characteristics are considered attractive, especially for females. One British researcher asked over 4,000 people of different ages, gender, occupation, and geographical location to rank pictures of 12 women. Male and female respondents of all ages and occu-pations showed similar rankings with the pictures (Iliffe, 1960). There is much less agreement on the stereotypes of male attractiveness (Lavrakas, 1975).

The higher levels of agreement on female beauty probably reflect the greater social emphasis on standards of female attractiveness. However, although the social discourses that construct attractiveness are increasingly turning toward male attractiveness, those discussions lag far behind the focus on female beauty. Think, for example, about the Miss America beauty pageant; its national exposure far outstrips the focus on the Mr. Male America beauty pageant.

Similarity

A third principle of relational attraction is similarity. According to this principle, we tend to be attracted to people whom we *perceive* to be similar to ourselves. Social psychologist Donn Byrne and his associates conducted a series of studies on this principle of attraction. They discovered that many individuals didn't really *know* if the people they were attracted to were similar to themselves. Most of the studies concentrated on similarity of attitudes (belief in God, political opinions, and so on).

There are several reasons why it makes sense to choose partners who hold similar views. Finding people who agree with our beliefs confirms our own beliefs and provides us with cognitive consistency. (If we like ourselves, we should like others who share our views.) In addition, an individual may explicitly seek a partner who holds the same beliefs and values due to deep spiritual, moral, or religious convictions. Also, if we're friends with people who are like us, we can better predict their behavior than if they are different from us. We also may be attracted to people whom we perceive to be similar in personality, although the research is less conclusive on this point. In addition, we may perceive greater similarity with people we like. For example, romantic partners often perceive each other to be more similar in attitude than they actually are (Byrne & Blaylock, 1963).

Similarity is based not on whether people actually *are* similar, but on the recognition or *discovery* of a similar trait. This process of discovering is crucial in developing relationships (Duck & Barnes, 1992). In fact, when people think they're similar, they have higher expectations about future interactions (La-Gaipa, 1987).

Attraction breeds attraction. If we like people we perceive to be similar, and they discover we like them, they may also be attracted to us. They then may express this liking, which makes them seem even more attractive. This phenomenon is described as the reciprocal liking hypothesis. It works only in some situations, though. If we have low self-esteem or feel that the other person is not genuinely interested in us, we may be suspicious of someone who seems attracted to us.

Complementarity

Sometimes we are attracted to persons who are somewhat different from ourselves. This principle of attraction, complementarity, seems contradictory to the similarity principle. The differences that form the basis of attraction may involve personality traits and may contribute to complementarity, or balance, in a relationship. For example, an introverted individual may seek a more outgoing

I had a friend who was lesbian, and with whom I used to work at a car dealership. In class, we talked about the theory that we are attracted by dissimilarities, but only after we interact with the dissimilar person. I can relate to this theory. When I first met Yvette, I was nervous and wasn't sure whether I wanted to become friends with her. Before I even met her, I made fun of her behind her back, along with my other co-workers. It was only after I got to know her that I realized a person's sexuality is insignificant in developing a relationship. I was threatened by what I didn't understand or know.

After I got to know Yvette, I came to appreciate our differences. She has become a real friend and confidante. I found her sexuality to be not only interesting but refreshingly different. I met her girlfriend and went out to dinner with them. Because I have allowed myself to let down my barriers with her, it has become easier to let down my barriers with other people whose culture is different from mine. However, sometimes I still make the mistake of patronizing on the basis of dissimilarities without fully getting to know the person. This is something I have a feeling we all need to work on!

—Shannon

partner, or a spendthrift may be attracted to an individual who is more careful with money.

This principle seems particularly relevant to intercultural relationships—relationships that assume cultural differences. Some individuals are attracted to people simply because they have a different cultural background. Intercultural relationships present intriguing opportunities to experience new things, new ways of looking at the world.

Most of us probably seek a balance between novelty and predictability in our relationships. The degree to which we seek more or less novelty is due to individual differences and social influences. When Judith, one of the authors, was in college, she wanted to socialize with international students. Their backgrounds and experiences seemed so different from hers and so intriguing. Growing up, Judith had had little opportunity to be with people who were different from her. In contrast, Tom, the other author, sought out other Asian Americans when he was in college. This difference may be due more to the paucity of Asian Americans in the Deep South during the 1970s than any substantial traits of ours.

Most people are attracted to some differences but not others. In fact, society seems to accept some relationships of complimentarity better than others. For example, dating international students tends to be more acceptable than dating across class lines.

These two principles (similarity and complementarity) may operate differently in Eastern countries, where people tend to shape their interpersonal relations in accordance with various levels of hierarchy, which is determined by gender, age, and background. Some fairly explicit guidelines govern these vertical relationships. For example, in most Eastern cultures, respect and loyalty toward older people is absolute. Difference in sex, status, and rank are maximized (Dodd, 1983; Javidi & Javidi, 1991). In family and work relationships, then, the complementarity principle works in that the differences are a given. In other relationships, like friendships, the similarity principle may be stronger.

The complementarity/similarity dialectic is at the heart of understanding intercultural relationships. It seems likely that *both* similarity and complementarity principles operate at the same time in intercultural relationships. Although we may be attracted initially by differences, some common ground or similarity must be established in order for the relationship to develop, flourish, and be mutually satisfying over time (Hatfield & Rapson, 1992).

STAGES OF RELATIONAL DEVELOPMENT

Relationships seem to develop in phases. You probably have friends that you don't know very well, with whom you are in the early stages of a friendship, just getting to know each other. On the other hand, you probably have some friends you know very well, and with whom you have passed through several friendship phases. These phases are continuous, fluid, overlapping. They have been given many different labels by researchers. We identify three phases, or stages, that seem to characterize both friend and romantic relationships in many cultural contexts: the orientation phase, the exploratory phase, and the stability phase. We are especially interested in the communication that may characterize each phase and in how these phases may vary in cross-cultural communities.

In the *orientation phase*, individuals are just getting to know each other. During this developmental stage, people use categorical or noninterpersonal information about each other to guide their interaction. For example, when teachers walk into the classroom for the first time of the semester, they don't know each individual student, but they rely on information about the student role and expect students to behave accordingly. In the same vein, if you were to meet a friend of your uncle, you probably would draw some conclusions about how people of his age behave; you even may infer that he or she may be similar to your uncle because they are friends. This categorical information is all we have to go on before we actually get to know a particular person.

In the *exploratory phase*, people try to discover more about each other by talking about nonintimate topics. They make "small talk," and try to find commonality. It's almost an audition for future interaction. Most relationships don't go beyond this stage.

In the *stability phase*, as we get to know people better, we rely on more idiosyncratic information to guide our actions and our expectations. For example, Judith (one of the authors of this book) knows that if she asks her friend Monica's opinion on how to deal with a very personal problem, Monica will readily give advice. On the other hand, Judith's friend Marge will be more guarded and less open. Judith has to probe much further to get an "honest" opinion from Marge. The interaction in this phase of development is more intense; there is more active participation and greater awareness of each other. Conversations are more indepth and cover more topics. The communication becomes more personal.

CULTURAL DIFFERENCES IN RELATIONAL DEVELOPMENT

What role does culture play in relational development? How do contexts influence relationships? To address these questions, let's identify some cultural differences in relational development.

Differences in Orientation Interactions

Cultural differences often come into play in the very beginning stages of relational development, in initial interactions. Different cultural rules address how to regard strangers. In some communities, all strangers are regarded as potential relationships. In other cultural communities, relationships can develop only after introductions—after long and careful scrutiny. For example, in German Mennonite society, strangers, especially those outside the religious group, are often regarded with suspicion and not as potential friends. In contrast, some communities regard any stranger as a potential friend. Many U.S. Americans are known to disclose personal information in very public contexts. As a student from Colombia observed, "I couldn't believe what this guy was telling me. I had just met him and he was telling me that he had been divorced, and that he had three kids. In my country we would never tell a stranger this kind of information" (quoted in Ogami, 1987).

A renowned communication scholar, Dean Barnlund (1989), along with his colleagues found many differences in relational development in their students in Japanese and U.S. American colleges. Students in both countries were asked about their interactions with strangers and friends, about their ideas on friendship and more intimate relationships. There were both similarities and differences between Japanese and U.S. American students in their ideas about relationships. U.S. students were more open and receptive to strangers; they said they talked to strangers in many different contexts—perhaps waiting at a bus stop, the line at the grocery store, or in classes. In contrast, the Japanese students talked to significantly fewer strangers than did U.S. Americans over the same period of time.

Barnlund suggests that these differences may be due to different cultural patterns, like preferences for high- or low-context communication. Many cultures in the United States emphasize low-context communicating, in which information is contained more in the words than the background of the situation. In other communities, like those of Japan, characterized as more high context, background (contextual) information about someone is important in determining whether (or how) to pursue a relationship with him or her.

Members of high context cultures such as most non-Western cultures, are interested in gathering background (demographic) information, such as what high school or university a person attended, his or her hometown, the company for which he or she works, the father's occupation, and religious background. . . . People are able to reduce uncertainty and obtain a high level of accuracy in predicting others' future behaviors by making a rich array of dependable inference from these types of information. (Javidi & Javidi, 1991, p. 135)

In a high-context culture, relationships will not develop as easily without background or contextual information. For example, Yuichi, a Japanese student, had just begun his graduate work at a university in the midwestern United States. The department held its annual "get-acquainted potluck," at which graduate students and faculty chatted informally. Yuichi was panic stricken in this situation because he couldn't tell who was a member of the faculty and who was a student. Because he had no prior information about the individuals present (and couldn't determine their status from the way they dressed), he was uncertain about how to act and communicate. He was worried that he would make a mistake, address someone too informally or formally. The difficulty he experienced was not shared by others at the potluck, to whom status and position were less important in communication. Similar cultural differences affect communication at other stages of relational development.

Forming Friendships

What are the characteristics of a friend? How does a relationship develop to more intimate stages? To some people, a friend is someone to see or talk with occasionally, someone to do social things with—go to a movie, discuss interests, maybe share some problems. The person might be one of many friends. If the friend moves away they might eventually lose contact, and both might make new friends. To other people, a friendship is taken much more seriously. A friendship takes a long time to develop, includes many obligations (perhaps lending money or doing many small favors), and is a life-long relationship.

Dean Barnlund's study (1989) of Japanese and U.S. students revealed many similarities in how the two groups defined and developed friendships. In general, the principles of similarity and proximity played some role. Both groups tended to be attracted to those similar in age and nationality, and to those around them. Both groups used the same words to describe characteristics of a friend: *trust*, *respect*, *understanding*, and *sincerity*.

However, the study revealed differences in the important characteristics of friends. Whereas both U.S. and Japanese students described similar characteristics of "friend," they ordered these characteristics differently. The Japanese students listed togetherness, trust, and warmth as the top characteristics. The U.S. students named understanding, respect, and sincerity as the most important characteristics. Barnlund links these different priorities to cultural values: The Japanese list emphasizes relational harmony and collectivism, whereas the U.S. list reflects the importance of honesty and individuality. For many U.S.

Intercultural friendships provide great opportunities. Through these relationships we can learn about other areas of the world and even about our own experience and background. The number of intercultural friendships people have depends on how multicultural their social networks are. How many times a day do you come in contact with people who are different from you? How often do you pursue intercultural friendships? (© Bill Bachmann/Tony Stone Images, Inc.)

Americans, relationships are based on and strengthened by honesty and understanding, even if it hurts sometimes.

Barnlund's study focused on European American students. Researcher M. J. Collier (1991) conducted a similar study that investigated Mexican, Anglo, and African American students' notions about friendships. She found that these three groups had many notions in common regarding the characteristics of close friendship. Their definitions of friendship focused on two characteristics, trust and acceptance.

It would seem that most cultural groups characterized friendship in similar ways. However, Collier found some differences. She found that, "Anglo Americans emphasized freedom in expressions of ideas. African Americans emphasized problem solving, and Mexican Americans emphasized support and expression of feeling" (p. 149). Collier correlates this distinction with earlier research that describes Anglo Americans' emphasis on honesty and confidentiality, African Americans' stress on the importance of sincerity and respect for the individual, and Latinos' focus on respect and support for the relationship. Clearly, these distinctions would affect how people of different cultural groups would develop friendships.

Developing Verbal and Nonverbal Intimacy

Friendships As relationships develop in intimacy in the stability phase, the friends share more personal and private information. Researchers Tamar Katriel and Gerry Philipsen (1990) describe a "communication ritual" in U.S. American speech between good friends, in which the individuals "sit down and talk" or "talk it out." This is a particular kind of communication that is different from "mere talk," and we recognize it as such. The ritual involves particular phases: One person presents a problem, the other person affirms the problem, and a discussion ensues. Although there is some attempt at resolution, the primary function of this ritual is to affirm participants' identities and engender intimacy. Katriel and Philipsen describe how this ritual functions also to reinforce the unspoken but understood cultural rules that define many intimate relationships in the United States.

Kurt Lewin (1981), a renowned psychologist, conducted a cross-cultural study in self-disclosure. (The conclusion of this dated but classic study still holds true.) Lewin proposed that the personal/private self can be modeled as three concentric circles representing three areas of information we share with others. The first circle is an outer boundary that includes superficial information about ourselves and our lives: our general interests, our daily life, and so on. The middle circle includes more personal information—perhaps our life history, our family background, and so on. Then there is the inner core, which includes very personal and private information, some of which we share with no one.

These spheres of information may correspond with the three phases in relational development. At the orientation phase, individuals share superficial information. At the exploratory stage, they exchange more personal information. And in the stability phase, they may disclose more intimate information.

Lewin's cross-cultural study revealed the most variation in the degree to which the outer area is more or less permeable. For example, for many European Americans, the outer boundary is very permeable; they may disclose a wide range of relatively superficial information with many people, even those they don't know well, in many contexts. The middle, or second, area is less permeable; this information is shared with fewer people and in fewer contexts. Information in the inner area is shared with very few.

In contrast, for many other cultural and ethnic groups, the outer boundary is much more closed. International students in the United States often remark that U.S. American students seem superficial. That is, U.S. students welcome interaction with strangers and share information of a superficial nature—for example, at a party. When some international students experience this, they assume that they are in the middle area, or moving into the exploratory "friend" phase, only to discover that the U.S. student considers the international student just an acquaintance, not really a friend at all.

A student from Singapore describes her relationships with American students:

I learned in the first couple months that people are warm yet cold. For example, I would find people saying "Hi" to me when I'm walking on campus or asking me how I am doing. It used to make me feel slighted that even as I made my greeting back to them, they are already a mile away. Then when real interaction occurs, for example, in class, somehow I sense that people tend to be very superficial and false. Yet they disclose a lot of information, for example, talking about personal relationships, which I wasn't comfortable with. I used to think that because of such self-disclosure, you would share a special relationship with the other person, but it's not so because the same person who was telling you about her personal relationship yesterday has no idea who you are today. Now I have learned to not be offended or feel slighted by such incidences.

There also are cultural differences in how much nonverbal expression is encouraged. Again, Barnlund's studies revealed that U.S. Americans expressed much more intimacy nonverbally than did the Japanese respondents.

Romantic Relationships   Some intimate relationships develop into romantic relationships. Few studies compare the development of these types of intimate relationships across cultures. One such study, though, was conducted by communication researcher Gao Ge (1991), who compared romantic heterosexual relationships among Chinese and U.S. American young people. Through interviews with students about their romantic relationships, she found common themes of openness, involvement, shared nonverbal meanings, and relationship assessment. However, there were some variations between the two groups. The U.S. American students emphasized the importance of physical attraction, passion, and love. Gao interprets this as a reflection of a more individualistic orientation. In contrast, the Chinese students stressed the importance of their partners' connectedness to their family and other relational connections, reflecting a more collectivistic orientation.

One day during the first few months of our relationship, my American girlfriend and I went to a beach that was famous for sunsets. We walked up to the top of a sand dune and stood there to enjoy the sunset. I did not find it as romantic as she did because I saw such sunsets every day. "It is not different from the other sunsets I have seen in my life," I thought. Slowly she got closer to me while we were talking about anything we could talk about. Then her hand held my hand. I froze and looked around to see if people were watching us. It seemed people did not really care, or maybe they pretended not to notice our presence. After a while, she started hugging me. I pretended it was OK, though my eyes tried to find out if people were looking at us. When it came to the point that she wanted to kiss me, I held her arms and slowly pushed her away from me.

She was at least discouraged, if not disappointed, hurt, and confused. We did not talk to each other. It seemed as if we did not know each other. When we had dinner at a nearby restaurant, I saw tears in her eyes. "Just tell me the truth if you do not love me," she said. I did not really understand what she meant, because the fact that I did not kiss her at the top of the dunes did not mean I didn't love her. I felt uncomfortable with the people who seemed to watch us. Maybe one of them knew us, our friends, our colleagues, relatives, and so on. It would be embarrassing if those people knew what we were doing at the beach. Public displays of affection are not accepted by my community.

—Api

Research in the United States that investigates the development of romantic relationships has focused on the importance of the individual's autonomy. Togetherness is important as long as it doesn't interfere too much with one's own freedom. Communication scholar Virginia Kidd (1975) identifies the vision of most intimate relationships: Change is the norm for relational behavior; relational meanings are flexible; and deviation from norms can be seen as creative, a way to negotiate new types of relationships. Openness, talking things out, and retaining a strong sense of self are seen as specific strategies for maintaining a healthy intimate relationship.

However, there are many cultural differences in how people relate to one another. Therefore, this prescription for relational intimacy probably doesn't hold for most cultural groups. Researchers like Gao Ge will continue to identify and describe similarities across cultures.

Gay Relationships

Most of the information discussed so far has been derived from research on heterosexual friendships and romantic relationships. Much less information is available about gay relationships. What we know is that gay relationships are a fact of society. Homosexuality has existed in every society and in every era. As

After we had been going out for a few months, I took her to the village to see my family and relatives. I introduced her as my friend, instead of my girlfriend. She was able to communicate with people because she speaks the national language—although not the local language, which is very different. My mother commented that she was so big compared with Indonesian women. My father did not say anything. At the end of the day we decided to return to the city because it would be a scandal if we spent the night in my parents' house even if we slept in different rooms, which was what we would probably do. It was a nice introduction. The next time I went home I was by myself. My parents did not say anything about us. My young sisters teased me a little bit about us. "Is she your friend or your 'friend'?" they teased.

Time went by and we came home to my parents more frequently. I assumed that my parents already knew that we went out together. They had ears, eyes, and other senses. Even if I did not verbally tell them about our relationship, they knew it through what they heard and observed about us. Yet, to show my respect to them indirectly, I had to let them know. When we were socializing in our living room, talking about my sister's wedding, I half-jokingly said to my parents, "So, what are you gonna give us for our wedding present?" My father humorously replied, "Anything you want." We knew that my parents would not be able to give us an expensive present and we did not expect them to. From his answer I knew that my father already knew or at least thought about us. He was not surprised when we eventually got married.

—Api

communication scholar James Chesebro explains: "In cultures other than that of the United States—the majority, as a matter of fact—homosexuality is not considered a problematic behavior" (1981, p. x).

What we know about gay relationships is often in contrast to the "model" of heterosexual relationships. Gay relationships may be intracultural or intercultural. Although there are many similarities between gay and straight relationships, there are several areas where they may differ: in the role of same-sex friendships, the role of cross-sex friendships, and in the relative importance of friendships.

Same-sex friendship relationships may have different roles for gay and straight males in the United States. Typically, U.S. males are socialized toward less self-expression and emotional intimacy. Most heterosexual men turn to women for emotional support; often, a wife or female romantic partner, rather than a same-sex friend, is the major source of emotional support.

This was not always true in the United States, and it is not true today in many countries where male friendship often closely parallels romantic love. Both types of relationship may involve expectations of undying loyalty, devotion, and intense emotional gratification (Hammond & Jablow, 1987). This seems to be true also for men in gay relationships; they tend to seek emotional support from same-sex friendships (Sherrod & Nardi, 1988).

This differentiation doesn't seem to be true for straight women and lesbians, though. Individuals in these groups seem to seek intimacy more often through same-sex friendships. That is, they seek an intimate level of friendship more often with women than with men.

The role of sexuality also may be different in heterosexual relationships compared to gay friendships. In heterosexual relationships, friendship and sexual involvement sometimes seem mutually exclusive. As the character Harry said to Sally in the film *When Harry Met Sally . . .* "Men can never be friends with women. The sex thing always gets in the way." Cross-sex friendships always seem ambiguous because of the "sex thing."

This ambiguity does not seem to hold true in gay relationships. Friendships often start with sexual attraction and involvement but often last after sexual involvement is terminated. There is often a clear distinction between "lover" and "friend" for both gay men and women, almost like an "incest taboo" among the family of friends (Nardi, 1992, p. 114). Close friendships may play a more important role for gay people than for straight people. Gay people often suffer discrimination and hostility from the straight world. In addition, they often have strained relationships with their families. For these reasons, the social support from friends in the gay community often plays a special role. Sometimes friends fill in as family, as described by a young man interviewed for a study. He explained:

> *Friends become part of my extended family. A lot of us are estranged from our families because we're gay and our parents don't understand or don't want to understand. That's a separation there. I can't talk to them about my relationships. I don't go to them; I've finally learned my lesson: family is out. Now I've got a close circle of good friends that I can sit and talk to about anything. I learned to do without the family. (quoted in Nardi, 1992, p. 110)*

Many of the issues in romantic relationships apply to both heterosexual and gay couples. However, some relational issues, including permanent relationships and relational dissolution, are unique to gay partners.

The fact is that in the United States, there is no legal recognition of permanent gay relationships. At the time of this writing, a legislative commission has recommended to the legislature of the state of Hawaii that same-sex marriages be legalized. If this occurs, there will be many implications for the development and maintenance, as well as termination, of gay and lesbian relationships. Yet, no U.S. state currently allows two people of the same sex the benefits—legal, cultural, economic—of marriage. Regardless of one's position on the desirability of gay and lesbian marriage, it is important to understand the implications for same-sex relationships.

The dissolution of heterosexual relationships often is delayed due to family and society pressures, religious beliefs, custody battles, and so on. However, some gay relationships probably terminate at a much earlier time because they are not subject to these pressures. This also may mean that, even though they are shorter lived, gay relationships are happier and mutually productive (Bell & Weinberg, 1978).

There is certainly no reason to believe that the development of same-sex relationships has been the same around the world. Same-sex relationships, like heterosexual relationships, are profoundly influenced by the cultural contexts in which they occur. In Denmark, for example, gay and lesbian couples are allowed to marry (Bech, 1992). Also, same-sex relationships are recognized in Australia for purposes of immigration (Hart, 1992). That is, a gay or lesbian citizen may sponsor his or her long-term partner for residency in Australia.

RELATIONSHIPS ACROSS DIFFERENCES

Now that we have discussed a variety of ways in which relationships may vary in different cultural contexts, what can we learn about *intercultural* relationships? Intercultural relationships may be very similar to intracultural relationships. The same factors probably influence whether we are initially attracted to someone who is culturally different from us: physical attraction, similarity, complementarity. As we noted, the principles of complementarity and similarity probably operate in tandem in intercultural relationships. But what are the unique characteristics of intercultural relationships?

Characteristics of Intercultural Relationships

Intercultural relationships are unique in several ways. First, intercultural relationships, by definition, are often characterized by cultural differences in communication style, values, and perceptions. The dissimilarities probably are most outstanding in the early stages of the relational development—when people tend to use more noninterpersonal categorical information. However, if some commonality is established and the relationship develops beyond the initial stages, these cultural differences may have less impact because all relationships become more idiosyncratic as they move to more intimate stages.

Secondly, expectations and stereotyping often come into play in intercultural relationships. We may not be encouraged by our parents and social group to form relationships with those who are different. One student described her parents' stereotypes:

> *My parents always explained to me that the Native Americans were the ones who committed the crimes in the city and for me to stay away from them. When I entered junior high school, I started meeting these so-called "bad Native Americans." At first, I had a preconceived notion that they were all bad people. But as time went by, I started realizing that they were not bad people. You just had to get to know them first before you could actually judge them. I explained this to my parents and they understood this concept but said that every Native American that they had ever met before had done something wrong to make my parents not like them. Eventually, I started bringing home some of my Native American friends and proved to my parents that all Native Americans are not bad people and that they do not commit crimes.*

POINT OF VIEW

Young people often find strong disapproval for interethnic relationships, often from both sides. Brian Jarvis was a young, White high school student when he wrote this article, in which he talks about the good times he and his best friend (an African American) had when they were kids. Things are different, though, when they get to high school. He explains that many parents think it's okay for children from different ethnic groups to be friends. But parents do not encourage interracial friendships among adolescents, who might start dating.

AGAINST THE GREAT DIVIDE

The commons is a gathering spot where students relax on benches and talk with friends. They also buy candy and soda, watch TV and make phone calls. It's a place where all sorts of things happen. But you'll never find a white student and a black student talking to each other.

After three years, I still feel uncomfortable when I have to walk through the "black" side to get to class. It's not that any black students threaten or harass me. They just quietly ignore me and look in the other direction, and I do the same. But there's one who sometimes catches my eye, and I can't help feeling awkward when I see him. He was a close friend from childhood.

Ten years ago, we played catch in our backyards, went bike riding and slept over at one another's houses. By the fifth grade, we went to movies and amusement parks, and bunked together at the same summer camps. We met while playing on the same Little League team, though we attended different grade schools. We're both juniors now at the same high school. We usually don't say anything when we see each other, except maybe a polite "Hi" or "Hey." I can't remember the last time we talked on the phone, much less got together outside of school.

Since entering high school, we haven't shared a single class or sport. He plays football, a black-dominated sport, while I play tennis, which is, with rare exception, an all-white team. It's as if fate has kept us apart; though more likely it's peer pressure.

In the lunchroom, I sit with my white friends and my childhood friend sits with his black ones. It's the same when we walk through the hallways or sit in the library. If Michael Jackson thinks, "It don't matter if you're black or white," he should visit my high school.

Source: Brian Jarvis, "Against the Great Divide," *Newsweek* (1993, May 3), p. 14.

Thirdly, there may be more anxiety in the early stages of intercultural relationships compared to intracultural relationships. (Some anxiety always exists in the early stages of a relationship.) The level of anxiety may be higher if one or both parties has negative expectations based on a previous interaction or on stereotypes (Stephan & Stephan, 1992).

In interviews with U.S. and Japanese students who were friends, researcher Sandra Sudweeks and colleagues (1990) found that several themes emerged.

One intercultural relationship that I have been involved in is with a man named Jim. Maybe you would still consider him a boy; he's 19 years old. I've known him for one year. I met him through work and we have been good friends ever since. He is from Taiwan and came to the United States about eight years ago.

At first he was very shy, which strengthened the stereotype I had of him. I never really tried to get any information out of him, because I figured that if he even knew I existed that he would have confronted me. But now I know that he thought the same of me. Because of certain stereotypes and expectations, I didn't think I'd be able to communicate with him. Even if he knew my language or I knew his, I thought we were so different that he would just not be able to even understand my thoughts. (How naive I was!) I thought that he would be too intelligent to even understand some of my beliefs. (There's another stereotype!) I guess I thought of him as a bookish nerd with no social skills. Well, as I began to have more questions and more uncertainty about him, I became more interested in him. I approached him every once in a while and began asking him questions about himself and his life. (You can use uncertainty reduction theory to explain this situation. I decided to finally communicate with him to reduce my uncertainty of him.)

He was awesome—not only intelligent, but extremely well equipped in social contexts. He was the type of person that appeared to have no social skills and also appeared to be shy. But once stimulated, the words flowed right out of his mouth. I felt that I had known him forever. It was so strange for me at first to accept how much we had in common. More than anything, I couldn't understand our bond.

This situation has really opened my eyes. I'm not afraid to admit that I stereotyped him. We all have our flaws, and my flaw in this situation has been remedied. He taught me that everyone is a person and that one of the only things that really differentiates us is our language. It is definitely a barrier that we can overcome. Through this relationship I have learned to treat everyone as an equal and to give everyone a chance. Don't be close-minded and automatically assume that a person with a different ethnic, religious, or social background cannot relate to you. You may be surprised.

—Jennifer

Themes of competence, similarity, involvement, and turning points characterized some aspect of the intercultural relationships. For example, the students talked about the importance of linguistic and cultural competence. At first, language was often an issue. Even when people speak the same language, they sometimes have language difficulties that can prevent relationships from flourishing. The same holds true for cultural information.

Dissimilarity may account for the initial attraction, but these students talked about the importance of finding some *similarity* in their relationship that transcended the cultural differences. For example, they looked for a shared interest in sports or other activities. Or they were attracted by similar physical appearance, lifestyle, or attitude.

While I was hanging out at my best friend's apartment, his roommate came home with a friend. His friend's name is Reita and he is from Algeria, I believe. In the course of the evening, I had the opportunity to talk with Reita. He is a hard worker and a great person. At first, though, I did not think he was very intelligent. Because he has such a heavy accent, I had difficulty understanding him. It was obvious that he could see my dilemma and that it was not the first time it had occurred. He tried to help me by using shorter words during our discussion, which led me to do the same. After our conversation, I came away thinking and feeling that I had to talk down to him because of the vocabulary he was using with me. I have spoken with Reita many times since then and now know that my first impression about his education was way off. Once I became familiar with his accent and could understand him better, he began to speak to me as normal. He no longer feels the need to use short words for me to comprehend. He just speaks a little slower using his regular vocabulary.
—Heather

Relationships take time to develop; students mentioned how important it was that the other person make time for the relationship. This is one aspect of involvement. Intimacy of interaction is another element of involvement. So are shared friendship networks. Sharing the same friends was more important for Japanese students than for American students, because the Japanese students had left their friendships behind.

Finally, students mentioned significant points that were related to perceived changes in the relationship—turning points that moved the relationship forward or backward. For example, asking the friend to do a favor, or to share an activity, might be a turning point. They remarked that if the other refused, the relationship often didn't develop beyond that point. On the other hand, a point of understanding (self-disclosure) may move the relationship to a new level.

Benefits of Intercultural Relationships

Although intercultural relationships may present unique challenges, the potential rewards and opportunities are tremendous. Once common ground is established, it is possible to build a relationship based on differences and similarities. An example of this is the relationship between Judith, one of the authors, and a Chicana colleague. When they first met, they thought they had little in common. They came from very different ethnic and cultural backgrounds. But soon they found commonality in their academic work. They became friends and discovered they had a great deal in common in their backgrounds. Both came from large religious families, both have parents who contributed a great deal to their communities, and both are close to their older sisters and their nieces. Through the relationship, they also have learned a lot about each other's different world.

This kind of relationship provides "relational learning," learning that comes from a particular relationship but generalizes to other contexts. We can identify some of the benefits of such relationships. Benefits include:

- Acquiring knowledge about the world
- Breaking stereotypes
- Acquiring new skills

You can probably think of a lot more.

In intercultural relationships, we often learn specific information about unfamiliar cultural patterns and language. Anneliese, a graduate student who lived in Guatemala, explained that she learned a new way of looking at time, that "meeting at 9 o'clock" might mean 9:30 or 10:00, not because someone forgot or wasn't "on time," but because there was a completely different definition for "9:00." She also learned a different language than the Spanish she learned in the university setting.

Intercultural relationships also can help break stereotypes. Andy, a student at Arizona State University, told us he used to think that Mexicans were lazy. This opinion was formed from media images, discussions with friends, and political speeches about immigration in the Southwest. However, when he met and made friends with immigrants from rural Mexico, his opinion changed. He saw that the everyday life of his friends was anything but indolent. They had family responsibilities and sometimes worked two jobs to make ends meet.

We often learn how to do new things in intercultural relationships. Through her friendships with students in the United States and abroad, Judith (one of the authors) has learned to make paella (a Spanish dish) and *nopalitos con puerca* (a cactus-and-pork stew), to play bridge in French, and to downhill ski. Through intercultural relationships, newcomers to the society can acquire important skills. Andy's immigrant friends often ask him for help with new things, like buying car insurance or shopping for food. When Tom, one of the authors, first moved to France, his new French friends helped him navigate the university cafeteria. All of these potential benefits can lead to a sense of interconnectedness with others and can establish a life-long pattern of communication across differences. We also hope that it helps us become better intercultural communicators.

Writer Letty Cottin Pogrebin (1987) discusses the challenges of communicating across differences of color, culture, sexual orientation, physical ability, and age. She emphasizes that intercultural relationships take more "care and feeding" than do those relationships between people who are very similar. Intercultural relationships are often more work than in-group relationships. A lot of the work has to do with explaining—explaining to themselves, to each other, and to their respective communities.

First, in some way, conscious or unconscious, we ask ourselves: What is the meaning of being friends with someone who is not like me? Am I making this friend out of necessity, for my job or because everyone I'm around is different from me in some way? Am I making this friend because I want to gain entree into this group for personal benefit? Because I feel guilty?

The best example of an intercultural relationship that I have had is with a French girl named Sandrine. She came to my house as an exchange student while I was in high school. She lived with me for a month and then invited me to her house the next summer. When she came to my house, she spoke English very well and had taken many English classes. When I went to her house, I had taken only two years of French. I understood it but did not speak very well. It has been five years since I have seen Sandrine, but we write letters often. I consider her a good friend. I will apply this relationship to the stages of an interpersonal relationship and talk about how it has been harder to progress in this relationship because of our different cultures.

Most of the summer that Sandrine visited me was spent in the orientation and exploratory stages. We talked a lot (in English) about our families and school and about where she lived. I think it was really hard to get out of this stage because of language differences. I had taken one year of French, so I knew simple sentences but not conversational ones. So Sandrine could not talk to me at all in French. (We used dictionaries a lot!)

When I went to her house the next summer, it was a real culture shock to me not to have anyone around who spoke English. I listened a lot and wondered if this was how Sandrine felt when she came to my house. I think this experience brought us to the stability stage. We were able to talk about how strange and scary it is to go into another culture with another language. Once I learned more French, I could tell Sandrine much more and we could talk in either French or English. We helped each other with language, and I learned so much about Sandrine personally.

I don't think we are deeply into the stability stage, though, especially because of the great distance between us and because we have not seen each other in so long. We still write each other letters and she is one of my best friends. I think the language barrier was the hardest thing to overcome. Once we did that, and once I came to her country and felt all the feelings she felt coming to my country, we shared something unique.
—Stephanie

Secondly, we explain to each other. This is the process of "ongoing mutual clarification," one of the healthiest characteristics of intercultural relationships. It is the process of learning to see from the other's perspective. One example is when Judith's African American friend explained how her community viewed the O. J. Simpson trial. Judith grew to understand the event from a different perspective, to find that others can interpret events in a completely different way.

People who cross boundaries often have to explain this to their respective communities. Your friends may question your close relationship with someone who is much older or is of a different ethnicity. For example, in the film *Mississippi Masala*, Mina, a young Indian woman from Uganda who settled with her family in the southeastern United States, fell in love with a young African

American man. They each tried to explain their relationship to their respective families and friends. Mina's family questioned why she had to go outside her group to find a boyfriend, why Indian boys weren't good enough for her. Her boyfriend's family accused him of making trouble for himself and his family. Both families said that their relationship caused nothing but trouble.

Pogrebin points out that historically the biggest obstacles to boundary-crossing friendships have come not from minority communities but from majority communities. Those in the majority (for example, Whites) have the most to gain by maintaining social inequality and are less likely to initiate boundary-crossing friendships. On the other hand, minority groups have more to gain. Developing intercultural relationships can help them survive, particularly economically and professionally.

Finally, in intercultural relationships individuals recognize and respect the differences. In these relationships, we often have to remind ourselves that we can never know exactly what it is to walk in another person's shoes. Furthermore, those in the majority group tend to know less about those in minority groups than vice versa. As Pogrebin stated, "Mutual respect, acceptance, tolerance for the faux pas and the occasional closed door, open discussion and patient mutual education, all this gives crossing friendships—when they work at all—a special kind of depth" (quoted in Gudykunst & Kim, 1992, p. 318).

Intercultural Dating and Marriage

Researcher Phillip E. Lampe (1982) investigated the reasons for and against interethnic dating among students attending a college in Texas. He discovered that the reasons people gave for dating within and outside their own ethnic group were very similar: they were attracted to the other person, physically and/or sexually.

In contrast, the reasons people gave for not dating someone in or out of their own ethnic group were very different. The main reason given for not dating within the ethnic group was lack of attraction. However, the reasons given for not dating outside the ethnic group were lack of opportunity and not having thought about it. Lampe interprets this distinction in responses as reflecting the social and political structure of U.S. American society—that most individuals, by the time they reach adolescence, have been taught that it is better to date within one's ethnic and racial group and probably have very little opportunity to date interethnically. Other studies confirm that families often instill negative attitudes regarding interracial friendships or romantic relationships (Kauri & Lasswell, 1993; Mills et al., 1994).

The authors of this book have replicated Lampe's study every semester at Arizona State University for the past five years and have found the same results. Like Lampe's respondents, about 60% of our students surveyed say they have dated interculturally. Many of the remaining 40% give the same reasons as those in Lampe's study for not dating interculturally: no desire and/or no opportunity. So, even though Lampe's study was conducted more than 10 years ago, the same conditions seem to hold, at least in some areas of the United States.

Whenever we were together in Indonesia, I saw people staring at us. It bothered me at the beginning. I just felt uncomfortable with the way people looked at us. Sometimes in a subtle way I pretended that I was not with her, especially when there were other people with us. Other times, when people asked me about us, I even denied that I went out with her because I did not want to be perceived as conceited. I never said to other people "This is my girlfriend." I thought people would think I was showing off because I was dating a foreigner. My behaviors often bothered my girlfriend. She thought I intentionally hid our relationship from other people, as if I was embarrassed of it. She saw me as a man who did not have the courage to admit that we were in a serious relationship. We argued very often about it and only after I explained the reasoning behind it could she understand and accept it.

In Indonesia, people's reactions toward our relationship were sometimes very negative. They thought that our relationship was only temporary. It would end when she had to return home to her country. These reactions were based on the negative perception that people in Indonesia have of Western women. "Easy come, easy go," they would say. Western women are projected negatively through movies and magazines. One evening I was riding a motorcycle with her. Two men on a motorcycle came close to us and the passenger said to me, "Can we share her?" I did not say anything to him. This offensive question really hurt my feelings. Yet, I had to understand those who did not understand us. I had to control my emotion. My girlfriend did not understand his question, because it was in the local language. Only later when I felt more comfortable did I tell her the experience.

—Api

Permanent Relationships

According to studies conducted in Canada and the United States, women are more likely than men to marry outside their ethnic group. Likewise, individuals who are older or who have a higher level of education are more likely to marry outside their ethnic group (Jensen, 1982; Kouri & Lasswell, 1993; Sung, 1990).

What are the major concerns of couples who marry interculturally? Their concerns, like those of dating couples, often involve dealing with pressures from the family and society in general. In addition, some issues involve the raising of children. Sometimes these concerns are intertwined. Although many couples are concerned with raising children and dealing with family pressures, those in intercultural marriages deal with these issues to a greater extent. They are more likely to disagree about how to raise the children and are more likely to encounter opposition and resistance from their families about the marriage.

Writer Dugan Romano interviewed many couples in which one spouse came from another country. She outlines 17 challenges of these international marriages. Some are common problems faced by most couples, including friends, politics, finances, sex, in-laws, illness and suffering, and raising children. The following issues are exacerbated in these intercultural marriages: values, eating

There are increasing numbers of intercultural couples in the United States. Intercultural couples blend their cultural backgrounds in various ways. What are some of the unique challenges and opportunities that these relationships face? *(© Joel Gordon)*

and drinking habits, gender roles, attitudes regarding time, religion, place of residence, dealing with stress, and ethnocentrism.

Of course, every husband and wife develop their own idiosyncratic way of relating to each other, but intercultural marriage poses consistent challenges. Romano also points out that most couples have their own systems for working out the power balance in their relationships, for deciding who gives and who takes. She identifies four styles of interaction: submission, compromise, obliteration, and consensus. Couples may adopt different styles depending on the context.

Submission is the most common style. One partner submits to the culture of the other partner, abandoning or denying his or her own. The submission may occur in public, whereas in private life the relationship may be more balanced. Romano points out that this model rarely works in the long run. People cannot erase their core cultural background, even though they may try.

Compromise occurs when each partner gives up some parts of his or her culturally bound habits and beliefs to accommodate the other. Although this may seem fair, it really means that both people sacrifice important aspects of their life. The Christian who gives up having a Christmas tree and all of the celebration of Christmas for the sake of a Jewish spouse may eventually come to resent the sacrifice.

In the third model, obliteration, both partners deal with differences by attempting to erase their individual cultures. They may form a new culture, with new beliefs and habits, especially if they live in a country that is home to neither of them. It may seem like the only way for people whose backgrounds are completely unreconcilable. However, because it's difficult to be completely cut off from one's own cultural background, obliteration is not a particularly good long-term solution.

The model that is the most desirable, not surprisingly, is the consensus model, one based on agreement and negotiation. It is related to compromise in that both partners give and take, but it is not a tradeoff. It is a win-win proposition. Consensus may incorporate elements of the other models. On occasion, one spouse might temporarily "submit" to the other's culture: For example, while visiting her husband's Muslim family, a Swiss wife might substantially change her demeanor, dressing more modestly and acting less assertive. On occasion, each spouse might temporarily give up something to accommodate the other. Consensus requires flexibility and negotiation.

Romano stresses that couples who are considering permanent international relationships should prepare carefully for the commitment: live together, spend extended time with the other's family in the home, learn the partner's language, study the religion, and learn the cuisine. The couple should also consider legal issues like citizenship, children's citizenship, finances and taxation, ownership of property, women's rights, divorce, and issues regarding death.

CONTEXTUALIZING INTERCULTURAL RELATIONSHIPS

It is often easy to see the differences, but not the similarities, in intercultural relationships. As you may have noticed from the studies discussed in this chapter, much of the research on intercultural friendships and romantic relationships has focused on comparing Japanese with U.S. Americans. Much of the interest in Japan has arisen due to its economic and political importance in U.S. life. Nevertheless, these studies help us understand some of the basic differences in how people of each cultural group think about romance and friendship.

Unfortunately, it is easy to begin stereotyping the Japanese, or any group, when we compare their families, marriages, friendships, and work relationships, with our own. Developing a dialectical way of thinking about relationships, and intercultural communication in general, will help avoid stereotyping. A dialectical approach recognizes the tension between two sides of any issue, where truth rests somehow with both.

Researcher Leslie A. Baxter (1988) suggests that a dialectical model explains the dynamics of relationships. She identifies three basic dialectical tensions in relationships: novelty–predictability, autonomy–connection, and openness–closedness.

The *novelty–predictability dialectic* is perhaps the most relevant to intercultural relationships. This dialectic suggests that some predictability in a relationship is necessary but that too much can lead to boredom. In contrast, too much

I am involved in an intercultural experience at this very moment and have been for several years. I have been dating my boyfriend for five years and we have recently become engaged. Both families were thrilled until one fateful word sent the thrill and happiness of an engagement to confusion and animosity . . . religion! My family is Jewish and, although we are not very religious, I am very proud of my religion and would never contemplate converting to another religion. Herein lies the rub: My boyfriend is Catholic and, although he does not practice, he would not convert to Judaism because he does not believe in any organized religion. Over the years, we have discussed our different views on religion but never have come to any agreement. I suppose I thought it would all "magically work itself out." It is a difficult situation, but when you add to the mix both our families' viewpoints, it becomes almost impossible. My parents want to see me married in a temple, at the very least by a rabbi. Patrick's parents want him to be married with a full Catholic mass. Both sets of parents find the other party's wishes completely unacceptable, as do Patrick and I. So here I sit with a big, shiny ring and a family in turmoil. I believe the main factor in this problem was our lack of communication. If Patrick and I had communicated our positions effectively, instead of merely glossing over the issue onto more pleasant topics, we would not be in this situation. I also believe that fear is playing a major role in this intercultural conflict. Both sets of parents and Patrick and I are probably fearful of losing our identities, our cultural and religious identities. I remain hopeful because, if there can be peace in the Middle East, anything is possible.
—Lisa

novelty, or unpredictability, can lead to frustration and misunderstandings. Dialectic tensions like these run throughout our relationships.

Furthermore, in our relationships we look toward connections with others, but at the same time we sacrifice some of our own autonomy. Baxter calls this the *autonomy–connection dialectic*. One partner may want to go to the *Dia de los muertos* (Day of the Dead) celebration, while the other may wish to go to the *O-Bon* celebration (which also honors ancestors). One might want to go to the gay and lesbian pride festival, while the other wishes to see a baseball game. Both may express their autonomy and do what they wish as individuals, but they also need to find connection by sharing experiences. Sometimes in our relationships we may feel the need to be more autonomous, and at other times we may want to feel more connected.

In both private and public communication, it is necessary to balance the kinds of information we reveal to other people. Sometimes too much openness can hurt a relationship, especially if one partner discloses what the other partner considers to be private information. Yet, relationships need public recognition, so complete privacy is often not a positive choice. This balance is called the *openness–closedness dialectic*.

As authors, we feel compelled to extend the notion of dialectical tensions to encompass the entire relational sphere. Rather than trying to understand relationships by examining the relational partners alone, we believe it is helpful to consider as well the larger contexts in which such relationships occur. Let's examine some of those contexts.

As we noted in Chapter 5, history is always an important context for understanding intercultural interactions. The same is true with intercultural relations. Many U.S. men in military service during various wars have returned to the United States with women they met and married while stationed abroad. Many others left without their partners and/or children. Many of the servicemen who experienced such intercultural relationships argued successfully against miscegenation laws, or laws that prohibited interracial marriages.

Colonialist histories constructed somewhat different relationships. The British, for example, constructed myriad intercultural relationships, recognized or not, within the places they colonized. Writer Anton Gill (1995) discusses in his book *Ruling Passions* various ways in which the colonialists tried to engage in or to avoid intercultural relations: he also discusses the legacy of interracial children left in the wake.

The dialectical tension rests, on the one hand, between the social, political, and economic contexts that make some kinds of intercultural relationships possible and, on the other hand, the desires and motives of the partners involved. There are no easy answers to explain whom we meet, when we meet them, and under what conditions we might have a relationship. Different cultural groups have different demographics, histories, and social concerns. Scholar Harry Kitano and his colleagues (1984) discuss some of these issues for Asian Americans. Scholars Anderson and Saenz (1994) apply the demographics of Mexican American communities to argue for the importance of larger structural factors—such as proximity—in understanding interracial marriage.

It is important to consider intercultural relationships in the contexts in which they emerge. What kinds of persecution might intercultural relationships encounter? What social institutions might discourage such relationships? Think, for example, how much more difficult it would be to have an interracial relationship if such marriages were illegal, if you attended racially segregated educational institutions, if your church leaders preached against it, or if your family discouraged it. Some of these contexts no longer apply, of course. For example, public schools no longer can segregate based on race. But what kinds of social restrictions continue to exist to discourage the development of intercultural relationships? And who benefits today, on a social level, from such relationships? These difficult questions are all worth reconsidering. There are no easy answers.

SUMMARY

In this chapter, we have examined some aspects of being attracted to and forming relationships with people who are both similar to and different from ourselves. The four principles of attraction—proximity, physical attraction, similarity, and complementarity—seem to operate for most people in most cultures. Similarity and complementarity are especially important for intercultural relationships, in that individuals are simultaneously drawn to the similarity and differences of other people.

Gay relationships are probably similar in many ways to heterosexual relationships, but they may differ in other aspects. In gay relationships, friendship and sexual involvement are not mutually exclusive, as seems often to be the case for heterosexuals. Gay men seem to seek more emotional support from same-sex friends than heterosexual men do. Friendships may play a special role in gay relationships, because the individuals often experience strained relationships with their families.

Developing relationships with people who are different from ourselves offers special challenges: the tendency to stereotype and the anxiety that sometimes accompanies these relationships. Although intercultural relationships may take more "care and feeding," there are tremendous benefits. Through intercultural relationships, we can acquire knowledge beyond our local communities, break stereotypes, and acquire new skills.

Intercultural dating relationships, particularly in the United States, are still not very common and are often disapproved of by family and society. Due to societal structures, there is little opportunity or desire to date across differences.

Finally, all of these relationships can be viewed dialectically through competing tensions of novelty–predictability, autonomy–connecting, and openness–closedness. The social environment in which relationships develop must be taken into account. The contexts in which we move and live may or may not provide us with opportunity and support for developing intercultural relationships.

REFERENCES

Anderson, R. N., & Saenz, R. (1994). Structural determinants of Mexican American intermarriage, 1975–1980. *Social Science Quarterly, 75*(2), 414–430.

Barnlund, D. C., & Yoshioka, M. (1990). Apologies: Japanese and American styles. *International Journal of Intercultural Relations, 14,* 193–206.

Barnlund, D. S. (1989). *Communication styles of Japanese and Americans: Images and reality.* Belmont, CA: Wadsworth.

Baxter, L. A. (1988). A dialectical perspective on communication strategies in relationship development. In S. Duck (Ed.), *A handbook of personal relationships* (pp. 257–273). New York: John Wiley & Sons.

Bech, H. (1992). Report from a rotten state: "Marriage" and "homosexuality" in "Denmark." In K. Plummer (Ed.), *Modern homosexualities: Fragments of lesbian and gay experience* (pp. 134–150). New York: Routledge.

Bell, A. P., & Weinberg, M. S. (1978). *Homosexualities: A study of diversity between men and women.* New York: Simon & Schuster.

Berscheid, E., & Walster, E. H. (1978). *Interpersonal attraction* (2nd ed.). Reading, MA: Addison-Wesley.

Byrne, D. (1971). *The attraction paradigm.* New York: Academic Press.

Byrne, D., & Blaylock, B. (1963). Similarity and assumed similarity of attitudes between husbands and wives. *Journal of Abnormal and Social Psychology, 67,* 636–640.

Chan, M. (1990, December 19). Gentlemen prefer Asians: Why some Anglos are only attracted to Asian women. *The Rafu Shimpo*, pp. 1, 4.

Chesebro, J. W. (Ed.). (1981). *Gayspeak: Gay male and lesbian communication.* New York: Pilgrim Press.

Collier, M. J. (1991). Conflict competence within African, Mexican and Anglo American friendships. In S. Ting-Toomey & F. Korzenny (Ed.), *Cross cultural interpersonal communication* (pp. 132–154). Newbury Park, CA: Sage.

Collier, M. J., Ribeau, S., & Hecht, M. L. (1986). Intracultural communication rules and outcomes with three domestic cultures. *International Journal of Intercultural Relations, 10,* 439–457.

DeVito, J. A. (1981). Educational responsibilities to gay male and lesbian students. In J. W. Chesebro (Ed.), *Gayspeak: Gay male and lesbian communication* (pp. 197–208). New York: Pilgrim Press.

Dodd, H. C. (1983). *Dynamics of intercultural communication.* Dubuque, IA: Wm. C. Brown.

Duck, S., & Barnes, M. K. (1992). Disagreeing about agreement: Reconciling differences about similarity. *Communication Monographs, 59,* 199–208.

Duffy, S. M., & Rusbult, C. E. (1986). Satisfaction and commitment in homosexual and heterosexual relationships. *Journal of Homosexuality, 12,* 1–23.

Fitch, K. (1990/1991). A ritual for attempting leave-taking in Colombia. *Research on Language and Social Interaction, 24,* 204–224.

Gao, G. (1991). Stability of romantic relationships in China and the United States. In S. Ting-Toomey & F. Korzenny (Eds.), *Cross-cultural interpersonal communication* (pp. 99–115). Newbury Park, CA: Sage.

Gill, A. (1995). *Ruling passions: Sex, race and empire.* London: BBC Books.

Graham, M. A., Moeai, J., & Shizuru, L. S. (1985). Intercultural marriages: An intrareligious perspective. *International Journal of Intercultural Relations, 9,* 427–434.

Gudykunst, W. B., & Kim, Y. Y. (Eds.). (1992). *Readings on communicating with strangers* (pp. 318–336). New York: McGraw-Hill.

Halualani, R. T. (1995). The intersecting hegemonic discourses of an Asian mail-order bride catalog: Pilipina 'oriental butterfly' dolls for sale. *Women's Studies in Communication, 18*(1), 45–64.

Hammond, D., & Jablow, A. (1987). Gilgamesh and the Sundance Kid: The myth of male friendship. In H. Brod (Ed.), *The making of masculinities: The new men's studies* (pp. 241–258). Boston, MA: Allen & Unwin.

Hart, J. (1992). A cocktail of alarm: Same-sex couples and migration to Australia, 1985–1990. In K. Plummer (Ed.), *Modern homosexualities: Fragments of lesbian and gay experience* (pp. 121–133). New York: Routledge.

Hatfield, E., & Rapson, R. L. (1992). Similarity and attraction in close relationships. *Communication Monographs, 59,* 209–212.

Hecht, M. L., Ribeau, S., & Alberts, J. K. (1989). An Afro-American perspective on interethnic communication. *Communication Monographs, 56,* 385–410.

Hecht, M. L., Ribeau, S., & Sedano, M. V. (1990). A Mexican American perspective on interethnic communication. *International Journal of Intercultural Relations, 14,* 31–55.

Hecht, M. L., Larkey, L., Johnson, J., & Reinard, J. C. (1992). African American and European American perceptions of problematic issues in interethnic communication effectiveness. *Human Communication Research, 19*, 209–236.

Iliffe, A. M. (1960). A study of preferences in feminine beauty. *British Journal of Psychology, 51*, 267–273.

Javidi, A., & Javidi, M. (1991). Cross-cultural analysis of interpersonal bonding: A look at East and West. *Howard Journal of Communications, 3*, 129–138.

Jensen, C. (1982). Interethnic marriages. *International Journal of Comparative Sociology, 23*, 225–235.

Katriel, T., & Philipsen, G. (1990). What we need is communication: Communication as a cultural category in some American speech. In D. Carbaugh (Ed.), *Cultural communication and intercultural contact* (pp. 77–94). Hillsdale, NJ: Lawrence Erlbaum.

Kidd, V. (1975). Happily ever after and other relationship styles: Advice on interpersonal relations in popular magazines, 1951–1973. *Quarterly Journal of Speech, 61*, 31–39.

Kitano, H. H. L., Yeung, W.-T., Chai, L., & Hatanaka, H. (1984). Asian-American interracial marriage. *Journal of Marriage and the Family*, 179–190.

Knapp, M. (1984). *Interpersonal communication and human relationships*. Boston: Allyn & Bacon.

Kouri, K. M., & Lasswell, M. (1993). *Black-white marriages*. Hayworth Press.

LaGaipa, J. J. (1987). Friendship expectations. In R. Burnett, P. McGee, & D. Clarke (Eds.). Accounting for relationships (pp. 134–157). London: The Methuen.

Lampe, P. (1982). Interethnic dating: Reasons for and against. *International Journal of Intercultural Relations, 6*, 115–126.

Lavrakas, P. J. (1975). Female preferences for male physiques. *Journal of Research in Personality, 9*, 324–334.

Lewin, K. (1948). Some social psychological differences between the United States and Germany. In G. Lewin (Ed.), *Resolving social conflicts*. New York: Harper.

Mercer, K. (1994). *Welcome to the jungle*. New York: Routledge.

Mills, J. K., Daly, J., Longmore, A., & Kilbride, G. (1995). A note on family acceptance involving interracial friendships and romantic relationships. *The Journal of Psychology, 129*(3), pp. 349–351.

Nardi, P. M. (1992). That's what friends are for: Friends as family in the gay and lesbian community. In K. Plummer (Ed.), *Modern homosexualities: Fragments of lesbian and gay experience* (pp. 108–120). New York: Routledge.

Ogami, N. (Producer). (1987). *Cold water* [Videotape]. (Available from Intercultural Press, P.O. Box 700, Yarmouth, ME 04096)

Peplau, L. A. (1988). Research on homosexual couples: An overview. In J. P. DeCecco (Ed.), *Gay relationships*. New York: Haworth Press.

Plummer, K. (Ed.). (1992). *Modern homosexualities: Fragments of lesbian and gay experience*. New York: Routledge.

Pogrebin, L. C. (1987). *Among friends*. New York: McGraw-Hill.

Romano, D. (1988). *Intercultural marriage: Promises and pitfalls*. Yarmouth, ME: Intercultural Press.

Rose, T. L. (1981). Cognitive and dyadic process in intergroup contact. In D. L. Hamilton (Ed.), *Cognitive processes in stereotyping and intergroup behavior* (pp. 280–302). Hillsdale, NJ: Lawrence Erlbaum.

Sanders, J. A., Wiseman, R. L., & Matz, S. I. (1991). Uncertainty reduction in acquaintance relationships in Ghana and the United States. In S. Ting-Toomey & F. Korzenny (Eds.), *Cross-cultural interpersonal communication* (pp. 79–98). Newbury Park, CA: Sage.

Sherrod, D., & Nardi, P. M. (1988). *The nature and function of friendship in the lives of gay men and lesbians.* Paper presented at the annual meeting of the American Sociological Association, Atlanta, GA.

Stephan, W., & Stephan, C. (1985). Intergroup anxiety. *Journal of Social Issues, 41,* 157–166.

Stephan, W., & Stephan, C. (1992). Reducing intercultural anxiety through intercultural contact. *International Journal of Intercultural Relations, 16,* 89–106.

Sudweeks, S., Gudykunst, W. B., Ting-Toomey, S., & Nishida, T. (1990). Developmental themes in Japanese–North American relationships. *International Journal of Intercultural Relations, 14,* 207–233.

Sung, B. L. (1990). Chinese American intermarriage. *Journal of Comparative Family Studies, 21,* 337–352.

Sze, H. (1992, July 24). Racist love. *Asian Week,* pp. 10, 24.

Ting-Toomey, S. (1991). Intimacy expression in three cultures: France, Japan and the United States. *International Journal of Intercultural Relations, 15,* 29–46.

Walster, W., Aronson, V., Abrahams, D., & Rottman, L. (1966). Importance of physical attractiveness in dating behavior. *Journal of Personality and Social Psychology, 4,* 508–516.

White, E. (1983, June). Paradise found: Gay men have discovered that there is friendship after sex. *Mother Jones,* 10–16.

Wu, S. (1990, April 15). In search of Bruce Lee's grave. *New York Times Magazine,* pp. 20, 22.

CULTURE, COMMUNICATION, AND CONFLICT

Many people are raised to think that "Peace on Earth" is a Christian ideal to express at Christmastime. The significance of peace crosses many cultures and religions, though. It is hardly unique to Christianity. Yet, one thing we can be sure of is that conflict is unavoidable. Conflicts are happening around the world, as they always have, and they occur at many different levels: interpersonal, social, national, and international.

There are three complementary approaches to understanding conflict. One is the interpersonal approach, which focuses on how cultural differences cause conflict and influence the management of the conflict. The other two approaches, interpretive and the critical, focus more on intergroup relationships and on cultural, historical, and structural elements as the primary sources of conflict.

Cultural differences can lead to conflict at different levels. For example, at the interpersonal level friends or romantic partners from different cultural backgrounds may disagree about their relationships with respective friends and family. At a societal level, cultural differences regarding the importance of preserving the environment versus the importance of economic development may fuel conflict between environmentalists and business interests.

Social (and sometimes national) conflicts often arise from differences in the definition of land use. In Hawaii, for example, Caucasian Americans want to use land that is deemed sacred by native Hawaiians. This modern-day conflict is familiar to many Native American peoples, too.

Cultural differences also can result in conflict on an international level—for example, when the U.S. and Singapore governments disagreed on what constituted appropriate punishment for a specific crime. Singapore authorities imposed incarceration and caning as punishment for a given crime, whereas U.S. authorities would have imposed a fine and perhaps incarceration for the same crime.

Understanding intercultural conflict seems especially important because of the relationship between culture and conflict. That is, cultural differences can cause conflict and, once conflict occurs, cultural backgrounds and experiences influence how individuals deal with conflict. We should say up front that there is little known about how to deal effectively with intercultural conflict. Most research to date in the United States applies almost exclusively to majority culture members. Our challenge is to review this knowledge, take what can be applied in intercultural contexts, and perhaps come up with some new ways to think about conflict.

In this chapter, then, we'll first identify two general orientations to interpersonal conflict and identify types of conflict, responses, and styles of managing conflict. We will then examine how cultural background can influence conflict management. Then we'll look at conflict in contexts, incorporating more interpretive and critical theories into our understanding of conflict. Finally, we will describe unique characteristics of intercultural conflict and guidelines for viewing and engaging in conflict across cultural borders.

There are many different kinds of conflicts; this particular conflict reflects elements of both interpersonal and social conflict. Usually, conflicts arise because of incompatibilities of values, interests, or goals. How would the two orientations (conflict as opportunity versus conflict as destructive) view this type of conflict? *(© Robert Brenner/ PhotoEdit)*

TWO ORIENTATIONS TO INTERPERSONAL CONFLICT

What is interpersonal conflict? Is conflict good or bad? Should conflict be welcomed because it provides opportunities to strengthen relationships? Or should it be avoided because it can only lead to problems for relationships? What is the best way to handle conflict when it arises? Should we talk about it directly, deal with it indirectly, or avoid it?

Everyone experiences interpersonal conflict from time to time. For example, you may want to spend your day off going hiking in the mountains when your partner wants to go to a movie. Or you may feel pressured by your fiancé to have sex, whereas you want to wait until you are married. Or your parents may want you to enroll in the state college in your hometown, whereas you want to attend college out of state and live in a dorm.

Although you probably have experienced interpersonal conflicts like these at some time or another, it's not always easy to figure out the best way to deal with conflict. And what does culture have to do with it? To what extent does your cultural background (gender, age, ethnicity, and so on) influence how you manage

My conflict with my son is that he feels that he is old enough to come and go as he pleases, without ever having to report in to us. My culture of the older generation has caused some intercultural conflicts in setting up house rules; one rule is that if you are going to be home later than 1:30 in the morning, you have to call and let us know what you are doing and where you are. I have discussed this "checking in" conflict with my son's friends. None of the girls his age has the freedom he insists "all of his friends" have. Many of the boys do have this freedom.

   —Marcia

conflict? To answer some of these questions, we'll first describe two very different ways of thinking about interpersonal conflict and outline some of the ways in which culture and conflict are related.

Conflict as Opportunity

This orientation to conflict is the one most commonly represented in U.S. interpersonal communication texts. In this view, conflict is sometimes difficult but ultimately offers an opportunity for strengthening relationships. Interpersonal conflict is usually defined as involving a perceived or real incompatibility of goals, values, expectations, processes, or outcomes between two or more individuals (Donohue & Kolt, 1992; Hocker & Wilmot, 1991; Trenholm & Jensen, 1992).

As relational communication scholars Sandra Petronio and Jess Alberts (In press) suggest, most definitions imply three elements of interpersonal conflict: interdependence, incompatibility, and interference. First, interpersonal conflict can occur only in relationships in which the individuals are interdependent. For example, if you want to go to a movie and someone unconnected to you wants to go hiking, there is no conflict. Secondly, conflict implies some kind of incompatibility—perhaps in goals, values, or expectations. Thirdly, the conflict implies that one person has the power to interfere with the other's wishes, values, and so on—for example, if you and your partner want to do two different activities and you have only one car.

This approach suggests a fairly neutral to positive orientation to conflict. Conflict is seen as "natural" and pervasive. Although it recognizes that many people don't enjoy conflict, this orientation emphasizes the potentially positive aspects. The main idea is that working through conflicts constructively results in a stronger, healthier, and more satisfying relationship (DeVito, 1992). From this perspective, there are additional benefits for groups working through conflict: They can gain new information about people or other groups, they are able to diffuse more serious conflict, and they can increase cohesiveness when engaging in conflict with other groups (Filley, 1975).

The most desirable response, then, is to recognize the conflict and work through it in a productive way. Doing so can also help clarify ideas and commitment in the relationship. In fact, many people consider conflict-free relationships as not very healthy and potentially problematic. Relationships without conflict may mean that partners are not dealing with issues that need to be dealt with. However, not all cultural groups share this neutral to fairly positive orientation to conflict.

Conflict as Destructive

Many cultural groups view conflict as ultimately unproductive for relationships. This perspective may stem from spiritual or cultural values. For example, most Amish think of conflict not as an opportunity for personal growth but as almost certain to destroy the fabric of interpersonal and community harmony. When conflict does arise, the strong spiritual value of pacifism dictates a nonresistant response—often avoidance.

> *The nonresistant stance of Gelassenheit [yieldedness] forbids the use of force in human relations. . . . [L]egal and personal confrontation is avoided wherever possible. Silence and avoidance are often used to manage conflict. (Kraybill, 1989, p. 26)*

Avoidance of conflict extends even to a refusal to participate in military confrontation, which led to negotiations with the U.S. government for conscientious-objector status. Amish children are instructed to turn the other cheek in any conflict situation, even if it means getting beat up by the neighborhood bully. This emphasis extends to personal and business relationships; Amish would prefer to lose face or money rather than escalate conflict. This value for nonviolence and pacifism may contrast with mainstream values, but it can contribute to what we think about conflict. A nonviolent approach to human and group relations has been practiced by many cultural groups through the ages, including contemporary groups such as the Quakers and Amish.

What are the basic principles of nonviolence applied to interpersonal relations? As Hocker and Wilmot (1991) point out, our language makes it difficult even to talk about this approach. Words and phrases like *passive resistance*, and *pacifism* sound lofty and self-righteous. Actually, nonviolence is *not* the absence of conflict, and it is *not* a simple refusal to fight. Rather, it is a difficult (and sometimes very risky) orientation to interpersonal relationships. The "peacemaking" approach:

- Values strongly the other person and encourages his or her growth
- Attempts to de-escalate conflicts or keep them from escalating once they start
- Attempts to find creative negotiation to resolve conflicts when they arise

We'll discuss more of the specific elements of this approach later.

This general orientation to conflict also may be rooted in cultural values. For example, most Japanese (like the Amish) would say that from their vantage point interpersonal conflicts are not opportunities for personal growth. Rather, interpersonal conflicts are more damaging than useful to their relationships. This view is shared by many Asian cultures.

From this perspective, low-level conflict is often avoided. However, another appropriate response is to seek intervention from a third party. There are both formal and informal interventions. On an informal level, a friend or colleague may be asked to intervene. For example, a Taiwanese international student at a U.S. university was offended by the People's Republic of China flag that her roommate unwittingly displayed in their room. The Taiwanese student went to the international student advisor and asked him to please talk to the U.S. American student and ask her to remove the flag.

Intermediaries are also used by those who think that interpersonal conflict provides opportunities. However, in those cases they are most often used in formal settings. People hire lawyers to mediate disputes or negotiate commercial transactions (for which they can also hire real estate agents). Or they engage counselors or therapists to help families or individuals resolve or manage relational conflicts. Whereas confronting conflict is ultimately desirable, intervention is a less desirable option.

Researcher Stella Ting-Toomey and her colleagues (1991) describe how these two orientations are based on different underlying cultural values involving identity and face saving. In the more individualistic approach, espoused by most interpersonal communication textbooks, the concern is with the individual saving his or her own dignity. The more communal approach espoused by both Amish and Japanese cultures and by other collectivist groups is more concerned with maintaining the harmony of interpersonal relationships and saving the dignity of others.

INTERPERSONAL CONFLICT

Perhaps if everyone agreed on the best way to view conflict, there would be less of it. The reality is that different orientations to conflict may result in more conflict. In this section, we identify five different types of conflict and some strategies for responding to conflict.

Types of Conflict

There are many different types of conflict, and we may manage these types in different ways (Rahim, 1986). Communication scholar Mark Cole (1996) conducted interviews with Japanese students about their views on conflict and found most of the same general categories as those identified in the United States. These categories of conflict include:

- Affective conflict
- Conflict of interest

My boyfriend and I have been seeing each other for over five years now. When we first started going out, we had a real problem to deal with. His family is very family oriented, and most things are focused around the family. My family, on the other hand, is not family oriented. In fact, I'm not really close to my family at all. This caused a real problem for my boyfriend, because he had a hard time understanding why we never spent time with my family and why I didn't base any decisions on family. I really didn't think it caused a conflict for me, because I loved having the family togetherness of my boyfriend's family; it was a feeling and experience I'd never had before. But now I realize that it did cause a conflict for me in a couple of ways. First, I came to realize that my own life didn't really have a family orientation. Secondly, I questioned why my boyfriend would do so much for people based solely on their being part of his family.

I believe that our different ethnic backgrounds are responsible for our different views on family. The reason I focus on our ethnicity is that, from what I have seen, the characteristics of different cultural groups are different. My boyfriend is Mexican American. His family came to the United States many generations ago. My family came from England many generations ago.

One way in which my boyfriend and I have dealt with this conflict is through experience and understanding. We have learned through understanding that our cultures are different. It isn't that one is better than the other. They are different.

—Corinne

- Value conflict
- Cognitive conflict
- Goal conflict

Affective conflict occurs when individuals become aware that their feelings and emotions are incompatible. For example, suppose an individual finds that his or her romantic love for a close friend is not reciprocated. The disagreement over their different levels of affection causes conflict.

A conflict of interest describes a situation in which people have incompatible preferences for a course of action or plan to pursue. For example, suppose someone makes plans for a friend to go out and sing karaoke when the friend has already made plans to stay home and study for an exam. Another example of conflict of interest is when parents disagree on the appropriate curfew time for their children.

Value conflict, a more serious type, occurs when people differ in ideologies on specific issues. Mario and Melinda have been dating for several months and are starting to argue frequently about their religious views, particularly on abortion. Melinda is pro-choice and has volunteered to do counseling in an abortion clinic. Mario, a devout Catholic, is opposed to abortion under any circumstances and is very unhappy about Melinda's choice to volunteer. This situation illustrates value conflict.

245

Girls are brought up to look forward to their own weddings, to enjoy planning weddings. If I look at a bridal magazine and just fantasize, my boyfriend thinks I am pressuring him to get married. Recently, my three-year-old cousin showed him a dress and said that this was the dress she was going to get married in. That helped him understand how girls are socialized regarding weddings. This helped illustrate my point to him. But he is still uncomfortable when I look at wedding stuff.
   —Wendy

Cognitive conflict describes a situation in which two or more people become aware that their thought processes or perceptions are incongruent. For example, Marissa and Derek argue frequently about whether Marissa's friend Bob is paying too much attention to her; Derek suspects that Bob really wants a sexual encounter with Marissa. Their different perceptions of the situation constitute cognitive conflict.

Goal conflict occurs when people disagree about a preferred outcome or end state. Bob and Ray, who have been in a relationship for 10 years, have just bought a house. Bob wants to furnish the house slowly, making sure that money goes into the savings account for retirement. Ray wants to furnish the house immediately, using money from their savings. Bob and Ray's individual goals are in conflict with each other.

Strategies and Tactics

The ways in which people respond to conflict may be influenced by their cultural backgrounds. Most people deal with conflict in the way they learned while growing up and watching those around them deal with contentious situations. Conflict strategies usually consider how people manage self-image in relational settings. For example, they may prefer to preserve their own self-esteem rather than help the other person save face (Ting-Toomey, 1994).

Although individuals may have a general predisposition to deal with conflict in particular ways, they may choose different tactics in different situations. People are not necessarily locked into a particular style of conflict strategy (Folger, Poole, & Stutman, 1993). There are at least five specific styles of managing conflicts (Thomas & Kilmann, 1974; Rahim, 1986). These styles include:

- Dominating
- Integrating
- Compromising
- Obliging
- Avoiding

The *dominating* style reflects a high concern for the self and a low concern for others. It has been identified with a win-lose orientation or with forcing behavior to win one's position. The behaviors associated with this style include loud and forceful expressiveness, which may be counterproductive to conflict resolution. However, this view may reflect a Eurocentric bias, because members of some cultural groups (including African Americans) see these behaviors as appropriate in many contexts (Speicher, 1995).

The *integrating* style reflects high concern for both the self and the other person and involves an open and direct exchange of information in an attempt to reach a solution that is acceptable to both parties in the conflict. This style is seen as most effective in most conflicts because it attempts to be fair and equitable. It assumes collaboration, empathy, objectivity, recognition of feelings, and creative solutions. However, it requires a lot of time and energy (Folger, Poole, & Stutman, 1993).

The *compromising* style reflects a moderate degree of concern for the self and others. This style involves sharing and exchanging information in such a way that both individuals give up something to find a mutually acceptable solution. Sometimes this style is less effective than the integrating approach because people feel forced to give up something they value and so have less commitment to the solution.

The *obliging* style describes a situation in which one person in the conflict plays down the differences and incompatibilities and emphasizes commonalities that satisfy the concerns of the other person. Obliging may be most appropriate when one person is more concerned with the future of the relationship than with the issues. This is often true of hierarchical relationships in which one person has more status or power than the other.

The final style, *avoiding*, supposedly reflects a low concern for the self and others. In the dominant U.S. cultural contexts, a person who uses this style attempts to withdraw, sidestep, deny, and bypass the conflict. However, in some cultural contexts, this is an appropriate strategy style that, if used by both parties, may result in more harmonious relationships.

There are many reasons that we tend to prefer a particular conflict style in our interactions. A primary influence is our family background; some families prefer a particular conflict style, and children come to accept this style as normal. The family may have settled conflict in a dominating way, with the person having the strongest argument (or muscle) getting his or her way.

Sometimes people try very hard to reject the conflict styles they saw their parents using. Consider the following two examples. Bill remembers hearing his parents argue long and loud, and his father often used a controlling style of conflict management. He vowed he would never deal with conflict that way in his own family, and he has tried very hard to use other ways of dealing with conflicts when they arise in his family. Stephanie describes how she has changed her style of dealing with conflict as she has gotten older:

> *I think as a child I was taught to ignore conflict and especially to not cause conflict. When I was growing up, I saw my mom act this way toward my father and probably learned that women were supposed to act this way toward men. As a teenager I figured out that this just wasn't how I wanted to be. Now I like conflict, not too much of it, but I definitely cannot ignore conflict. I have to deal with it or else I will worry about it. So I deal with it and get it over with.*

When I was back home in Singapore, my parents never really taught me about how to deal with conflict. I was never encouraged to voice my opinions, and, I guess because I'm a girl, sometimes my opinions are not highly valued. I think society also taught me to maintain harmony and peace, and that meant avoiding conflict. I practiced silence and had to learn quietly to accept the way things are at school and especially at work.

When I first came to the United States I tried to be more vocal and to say what was on my mind. But even then I would restrain myself to a point where I couldn't help it any longer and then I would try to come across as tactfully as possible. I used to think about when I was back in Singapore, when I dealt with conflict in such a way: If I could not remove the situation, then I would remove myself from the situation. But now after learning to be more independent, more vocal, and more sure of myself, I know that I can remain in the situation and perhaps try to resolve some if not all of it.

—Jacqueline

It is important to recognize that people use a variety of ways to deal with conflict. People do not have the same reasons for using the conflict management styles that they choose. These five styles offer some options.

CULTURE AND INTERPERSONAL CONFLICT

Gender, Ethnicity, and Conflict

This section explores the ways in which gender and ethnicity influence how we handle conflict. Many studies have shown that men and women in the United States have different communication styles. Researcher Deborah Tannen explains, "Communication between men and women can be like cross cultural communication, prey to a clash of conversational styles," with different purposes, rules, and ways of interpreting rules (1990, p. 42). These different ways of speaking sometimes lead to conflict and can influence how men and women handle conflict.

Differences in conversational style that lead to misinterpretation and conflict include different ways of showing support. For example, sometimes women make sympathetic noises in response to what a friend says, whereas men say nothing, to show respect for independence. Women may interpret men's silence as not caring. Another area of misinterpretation is the reaction to "troubles talk." Typically, women commiserate by talking about a similar situation they experienced. However, men who follow rules for conversational dominance interpret this as stealing the stage. Another difference occurs in telling stories. Men tend to be more linear in their storytelling; women tend to give more details and offer tangential information, which men interpret as an inability to get to the point.

My conflict style is very much like my father's, which is very different from my mother's and sisters' styles. It is a style that relies heavily on verbal offense and defense to justify one's opinion and position, to build up credibility, to articulate one's emotions, and to raise objections. I am very verbal. I am not a silent person, and I do not use restraint toward a conflict situation.
—Nikki

Men and women also often misinterpret relationship talk. Women may express more interest in the relationship process and may feel better just discussing it. Men who are problem-solving oriented may see little point in discussing something if nothing is identified as needing fixing (Wood, 1994, pp. 145–148).

The relationship between ethnicity, gender, and conflict communication is even more complex. Do males and females of different ethnic backgrounds prefer different ways of dealing with conflict? Somewhat contradictory evidence exists. Some studies contrasting African American and White American male and female conflict styles show that Black females tend to engage in somewhat more controlling conflict strategies than White females and that White females tend to engage in more active, solution-oriented conflict strategies than Black females (Ting-Toomey, 1986).

Mary Jane Collier (1991) investigated this topic in a study in which she asked African American, White Americans, and Mexican American students to describe conflicts they had had with a close friend and how they dealt with the conflict. She also asked them what they should (and should not) have said, and whether they thought that males and females handle conflict differently.

She found that male and female ethnic friends differ in their ideas about the best ways to deal with conflict. African American males and females offered generally similar descriptions of problem-solving approach (integration style) as appropriate behavior in conflict management. (One friend said, "I told him to stay in school and that I would help him study." Another explained, "We decided together how to solve the problem and deal with our friend.") African American males tended to emphasize that appropriate arguments should be given, information should be offered, and opinions should be credible, whereas African American females generally emphasized appropriate assertiveness without criticism. (One man complained, "She pushed her own way and opinion and totally disregarded mine" [p. 147].) Some of these findings seem to contradict earlier studies comparing African American and White communication styles. Contradictions might be due to differences among groups studied (for example, comparing working class African Americans and middle-class Whites). Further, because these studies are based on very small samples, we should interpret their findings tentatively.

White males and females generally seemed to focus on the importance of taking responsibility for behavior. Males mentioned the importance of being direct.

The way that I was raised to handle conflict was influenced by my mother's perception of the role of females. She always told us not to yell or express anger but to hold in what is bothering us. She used to say, "When you do express how you feel, do it calmly and softly, not causing a fight." This is not the behavior we learned, though, because we observed how my Dad always voiced his opinions and spoke boldly about what upset him. Somehow, I found a happy medium between the two views and learned to tell exactly how I feel about things without totally yelling but without speaking softly either.
　　—Victoria

(They used expressions like "getting things in the open" and "say right up front [p. 145].) Females talked about the importance of concern for the other person and the relationship and for situational flexibility. (One woman explained, "She showed respect for my position and I showed respect for hers" [p. 146].)

Mexican American males and females tended to differ in that males described the importance of talking to reach a mutual understanding. (One man wanted to "make a better effort to explain." Another said that he and his partner "stuck to the problem until we solved it together" [p. 147].) Females described several kinds of reinforcement of the relationship that were appropriate. In general, males and females in all groups described females as more compassionate and concerned for feelings, and males as more concerned with winning the conflict and being "right."

It is important to remember that, whereas ethnicity and gender may be related to ways of dealing with conflict, it is inappropriate (and inaccurate) to assume that any one person will behave in a particular way because of his or her ethnicity or gender.

Value Differences and Conflict Styles

Another way of understanding cultural variations in intercultural conflict resolution is to look at how cultural values influence conflict management. Cultural values in individualistic societies differ from those in collectivistic societies. Individualism places greater importance on the individual rather than on groups like the family or professional work groups. Individualism is often cited as the most important of European American values and is seen in the autonomy and independence encouraged in children. For example, children in the United States are often encouraged to leave home after age 18, and older parents often prefer to live on their own rather than with their children. In contrast to individualism, people from collectivistic societies often emphasize extended families and loyalty to groups. Although these values have been related to national differences, they also may be true for other groups. For example, European Americans may value individualism more than Latinos, and women may value collectivism more than males.

These contrasting value differences may influence communication patterns. Several studies have established that people from individualistic societies tend to be more concerned with saving their own self-esteem during conflict; tend to be more direct in their communication; and tend to use more controlling, confrontational, and solution-oriented conflict styles. In contrast, people from collectivistic societies tend to be more concerned with preserving group harmony and with saving the other person's dignity during conflict. They may use a less direct conversational style and may use avoiding and obliging conflict styles instead (Ting-Toomey et al., 1991). However, the particular way that one chooses to deal with conflict in any situation depends on the type of conflict and the relationship one has with the other person.

A recent study found that Japanese college students used avoiding style more with acquaintances more than with best friends in certain types of conflicts (conflicts of values and opinions). In contrast, they used integrating conflict styles more with best friends than with acquaintances. In interest conflicts, they used a dominating style more with acquaintances than with best friends.

This suggests that with outgroup members, like acquaintances, where harmony is not as important, Japanese use dominating or avoiding styles (depending on the conflict type). However, with ingroup members like best friends, the way to maintain harmony is to work through the conflict with an integrating style (Cole, 1996).

INTERPRETIVE AND CRITICAL APPROACHES TO SOCIAL CONFLICT

Both the interpretive and critical approaches tend to emphasize the social and cultural aspects of conflict. Conflict from these perspectives is far more complex than the ways that interpersonal conflict is enacted. It is deeply rooted in cultural differences in the context of social and historical conflict. Consider, for example, the conflict in northern Wisconsin between many Whites and Native Americans over fishing rights. Communication theorist Brad Hall concluded, in part, that "actual intercultural interactions which display the conflict (and generally receive the bulk of attention) are but the tip of the iceberg in understanding the complexities of such conflicts" (1994, p. 82). Let's look more closely at the social, economic and historical contexts of this contemporary conflict. This area of Wisconsin is heavily dependent on tourism and fishing. The fishing of Anishinabe (Chippewa) is being blamed for economic downturns in these areas, leading to uneasy social relationships. A treaty was signed in 1837 giving the Anishinabe year-round fishing rights in exchange for the northern third of Wisconsin. Understanding these forces is necessary to understanding the complexities of the current conflict.

These complexities are embedded in cultural differences. In addition, the conflict may be motivated by a desire to bring about social change. In social movements, individuals work together to bring about social change. They often use confrontation as a strategy to highlight the injustices of the present system. So, for example, when African American students in Greensboro, North Carolina sat down at White-only lunch counters in the 1960s, they were pointing out the injustices of segregation. Although the students were nonviolent, their actions drew a violent reaction that, for many people, legitimized the claims of the injustice.

Historical and political contexts also are sources of conflict. Many international conflicts have arisen over border disputes. For example, Argentina and the United Kingdom both claimed the Malvinas (or Falkland) Islands in the South Atlantic, which led to a short war in 1982. Disputes between France and Germany over Alsace-Lorraine lasted much longer—from about 1871 to 1945. Similar disputes have arisen between Japan and Russia over islands north of Japan. The historical reasons for such conflicts help us understand the claims of both sides. Contextualizing intercultural conflict can help us understand why the conflict occurs and to identify opportunities for resolving those conflicts.

Social Context

The choice of how we manage conflict may depend on the particular context or situation. For example, we may choose to use an avoiding style if we are arguing with a close friend about serious relational issues in a quiet movie theater. In contrast, we may feel freer to use a more confrontational style in a social movement rally.

Nikki, a student with a part-time job at a restaurant, described an incident in serving a large group of German tourists. The tourists thought she had added a 15% tip to the bill because they were tourists; they hadn't realized it was the policy when serving large groups. Nikki explained privately that she was much more conciliatory when dealing with this group in the restaurant than if it had been a more social context. She thought the people were rude, but she practiced good listening skills and took a more problem solving approach than she would have otherwise.

Jacqueline, from Singapore, is often very annoyed with U.S. Americans who comment on how well she speaks English, because English is her first language even though she is ethnically Chinese. She used to say nothing in response; now sometimes she retorts, "So is yours." Jacqueline may believe that she is engaging part of a longer antiracism struggle against the stereotype that Asians cannot speak English. Viewed in this context, the social movement of antiracism gives meaning to the conflict that arises for Jacqueline.

Many conflicts arise and must be understood against the backdrop of existing social movements. Social movements are large-scale efforts designed to change something in contemporary society. For example, the women's suffrage movement was not an individual effort, but a mass effort to give women the right to vote in the United States. Many similar contemporary social movements give meaning to conflicts. They include movements against racism, sexism, and homophobia; movements to protect animal rights, the environment, free speech, civil rights; and so on. College campuses are likely locations for much activism. Journalist Tony Vellela commented on activism: "It may have subsided, and it certainly changed, reflecting changing times and circumstances, but progressive student political activism never really stopped after the much-heralded anti-Vietnam War era" (1988, p. 5).

There is, of course, no comprehensive list of existing social movements. They arise and dissipate, depending on the opposition, the attention, and the strategies they use. As part of social change, social movements need confrontation to highlight whatever injustice is being done.

Confrontation, then, can be seen as an opportunity for social change. In arguing for a nonviolent approach to change, Dr. Martin Luther King, Jr., emphasized that this strategy used nonviolent confrontation.

> *Nonviolent resistance is not a method for cowards; it does resist. . . . [It] does not seek to defeat or humiliate the opponent, but to win his friendship and understanding. The nonviolent resister must often express his protest through noncooperation or boycotts, but he realizes that these are not ends themselves; they are merely means to awaken a sense of moral shame in the opponent. (1984, pp. 108–109)*

This type of confrontation exposes the injustices of a society and opens the way for social change, to avert the continuation of this injustice. Although nonviolence is not the only form of confrontation employed by social movements, its use has a long history—from Mahatma Gandhi's struggle for India's independence from Britain to the civil rights struggle in the United States to the struggle against apartheid in South Africa. Images of the violent confrontations that arose from nonviolent marches tended to legitimize the social movements and delegitimize the existing social system. For example, the televised images of police dogs attacking schoolchildren, and riot squads turning fire hoses on protesters in Birmingham, Alabama, in the civil rights movement swung public sentiment in favor of the social movement.

Some social movements have also used violent forms of confrontation. Groups such as *Action Directe* in France, the Irish Republican Army, the environmental group Earth First, and independence movements in Corsica, Algeria, and Chechnya have all been accused of using violence, which tends to label them as terrorists rather than social movement protesters. Even the suggestion of violence can be threatening to the public. For example, in 1964 Malcolm X spoke in favor of civil rights: "The question tonight, as I understand it, is 'The Negro Revolt and Where Do We Go From Here?' or 'What Next?' In my little humble way of understanding it, it points toward either the ballot or the bullet" (X, 1984, p. 126). Malcolm X's rhetoric terrified many U.S. Americans who then refused to give legitimacy to Malcolm X's movement. To understand communication practices such as these, it is important to study the social context in which the movement operated. Social movements highlight many issues relevant to intercultural interaction.

Historical and Political Contexts

Stephanie, a young college student, was outraged at a male classmate who, during the heat of an argument, hurled a racial slur at her. Because the event occurred during class and the instructor asked them to be quiet, Stephanie couldn't

The historical and social forces that produce conflicts are not always apparent. For example, the aftermath of the Los Angeles rebellion masks the complexity of intercultural social conflict. Can you identify different ways to view the Los Angeles rebellion?
(© Ted Soqui/Impact Visuals)

take a confronting approach to settle the conflict. She complied with the teacher's request but later told some of her male friends what the classmate had said. They confronted him and asked him never to use that kind of language again.

The pejorative term used against Stephanie gains its meaning and power from the historical relations between Blacks and Whites in the United States. Many derogatory words have power and force from their historical usage and the history of oppression that they reference. As we noted in Chapter 5, much of our identity comes from history. It is only through understanding the past that we can understand what it means to be a member of a particular cultural group. For example, understanding the history of Ireland helps give meaning to Irish identity.

Sometimes identities are constructed in opposition or in conflict with other identities. When people identify as members of particular cultural groups, they are marking their difference from others. These differences, when infused with historical antagonism, can lead to future conflicts. Consider, for example, the modern-day conflicts in Bosnia-Herzegovina; they did not emerge from interpersonal conflicts among the current inhabitants. In large part, they are re-enacting centuries-old conflicts between cultural groups. The contemporary participants are caught in a historical web that has pitted cultural identities against one another.

These dynamics are at work all around the world. Historical antagonisms become part of cultural identities and cultural practices that place people in positions of conflict. Whether in the Middle East, Northern Ireland, Rwanda, Uganda, Nigeria, Sri Lanka, or Chechnya, we can see these historical antagonisms lead to various forms of conflict.

When people witness conflict, they often assume that it is caused by personal issues between individuals. By reducing conflict to the level of interpersonal interaction, we lose sight of the larger social and political forces that contextualize these conflicts. People are in conflict for reasons that extend far beyond personal communication styles.

INTERCULTURAL CONFLICTS IN INTERPERSONAL CONTEXTS

Given all of these variations in how people deal with conflicts, what happens when there is conflict in intercultural relationships? One way of understanding conflict management in intercultural interaction is to identify unique characteristics of dealing with conflict in relationships that are characterized by differences.

Characteristics of Intercultural Conflict

Intercultural conflict is often characterized by ambiguity, language issues, and by various communication styles. Let's explore these three aspects of conflict.

Ambiguity   Intercultural conflict may be characterized by ambiguity, which causes us to resort quickly to our default style—the style that we learned in our family. If your preferred way of handling conflict is to deal with it immediately and you are in a conflict situation with someone who prefers to avoid it, the conflict may become exacerbated as you both retreat to your preferred style. The confronting person becomes increasingly confrontive, the avoider retreats further.

Language Issues   The issues surrounding language may be important ones. For example, one student, Stephanie, described a situation that occurred when she was studying in Spain. She went to an indoor swimming pool with her host family sisters. Being from Arizona, she was unaccustomed to swimming in such cold water, so she went outside to sun. Her "sisters" asked her why she didn't swim with them. Stephanie explained:

> *At that point I realized they thought I should really be with them. . . . I didn't know how to express myself well enough to explain to them. . . . I tried, but I don't think it worked very well. So I just apologized. . . . I did basically ignore the conflict. I would have dealt with it, but I felt I did not have the language skills to explain myself effectively, so I did not even try. . . . That is why I had such a problem, because I could not even express what I would have liked to.*

So when you don't know the language well, it is very difficult to handle conflict effectively. On the other hand, some silence is not bad. Sometimes it provides a "cooling off" period for things to settle down. Depending on the cultural context, silence can be very appropriate.

Combination of Conflict Styles   Intercultural conflict also may be characterized by a combination of orientations to conflict and conflict management styles. Sociologist Thomas Kochman (1981) has written extensively about the differences in the ways in which Blacks and Whites communicate in the United States. He is especially insightful about how these styles are at cross-purposes in conflict situations. In interracial conflicts, African Americans are said to engage in loud interaction and intense language interaction to display their emotion, whereas Whites tend to engage in overly solicitous and friendly communication strategies in negotiating differences.

Kochman explains that loudness holds a positive value for African Americans in that it reflects sincerity and conviction of action, whereas an avoidance style or compromise style in a confrontation means defeat. Interpreted from an Afrocentric perspective, this orientation reflects an emphasis on Nommo—the importance of the well-articulated spoken word, which reflects oral traditions of Africa. Whereas Whites tend to view loudness as indicating aggression and hostility, African Americans interpret Whites' overly solicitous or friendly style of communication in conflict as masking hypocrisy and weakness (Ting-Toomey, 1986).

My very first roommate last year as a transfer student was a cultural experience. She was quiet and kept to herself, which is very unlike me. She was neat and kept things clean, which is something we had in common.

A major difference was that she was very disciplined. She worked according to a schedule and studied consistently. This was strange for me, because I am very spontaneous and always on the go. We got along, but we were just different people. Our strong bond was based on our both being new to Arizona and having to adjust to the culture.

The one major thing that was difficult to get used to was her cooking. I don't what it was, but the smell would linger around the house for hours. She knew it bothered me, so she cooked when I wasn't around and left all of the windows open. We got along because we respected each other's backgrounds and feelings. Most of all, we were experiencing a new course of life together.

—Jennifer

Managing Intercultural Conflict

There are no easy answers for dealing with intercultural conflict. At times, we can apply the principles of dialectic. At times, we may need to step back and show self-restraint. Occasionally it may be more appropriate to assert ourselves and not be afraid of strong emotion. Here, we offer several suggestions: First, recognize the existence of various styles and identify your preferred style; then expand your conflict style repertoire, understand the importance of conflict context, and be able to forgive.

Recognizing the Existence of Different Styles   Conflict is often exacerbated because of the unwillingness of partners to recognize style differences. Barbara L. Speicher (1994) analyzes a conflict that occurred between two student leaders: the committee chair, Peter, an African American male; and Kathy, a European American female, who was president of the organization. The two had a history of interpersonal antagonism. They disagreed on how the meeting should be run and specifically on how data should be collected in a particular project they were working on. They interviewed the meeting participants afterwards and learned that most thought the conflict was related mainly to the interpersonal history of the two and somewhat to the issue at hand, but not to either race or gender.

Speicher goes on to describe how her analysis of videotapes of the conflict showed that both Kathy and Peter adhered to the cultural norms described by Kochman.

Peter was assertive, took the floor when he had an important point to make and became loud and emphatic as the conflict accelerated. . . . The Eurocentric discomfort with and disapproval of his adamancy led to either silence (avoidance) or attempts to calm him down and diminish rather than resolve the conflict. Throughout, the Eurocentric responses coincided with Kochman's description of their low tolerance for strong emotions. (Speicher, 1994, p. 204)

Speicher goes on to say that part of the problem was due to the differences in perceptions of rationalism, "the sacred cow of Western thought" and emotionalism. In Western thought these two often are seen as mutually exclusive. But this is not so in Afrocentric thinking. For Peter, he was being rational, giving solid evidence for each of his claims, and he was also emotional.

For his Eurocentric colleagues, high affect seemed to communicate that he was taking something personally, that vehemence precluded rationality or resolution. Speicher suggests that perhaps we need to rethink the way we define conflict competence. From an Afrocentric point of view, one can be emotional and rational and still be deemed competent.

Speicher also points out the danger of attributing individual behavior to group differences: "While such work can help us understand one another, it can also encourage viewing an interlocutor as a representative of a group (stereotyping) rather than as an individual" (p. 206). However, she goes on to say that in this particular case

failure to recognize cultural differences led to a negative evaluation of an individual. The problems that emerged in this exchange were attributed almost exclusively to Peter's behavior. The evaluation was compounded by the certainty on the part of the European Americans, as expressed in the interviews, that their interpretation was the correct one, a notion reinforced by the Eurocentric literature on conflict. (p. 206)

This particular combination of complementary styles often results in damaged relationships and frozen agendas—the avoiding "rational"/confronting "dance." Other combinations may be difficult but less overtly damaging. Two people with assertive emotional styles may understand each other and know how to work through the conflict. Likewise, it can also work if two people both avoid open conflict, particularly in long-term committed relationships (Pike & Sillars, 1985). However, jointly avoiding conflict does not necessarily mean that it goes away. But it may give people time to think about how to deal with the conflict and talk about it.

Identifying Your Preferred Style   Although we may change our way of dealing with conflict, based on the situation and the type of conflict, most of us tend to use the same style in most situations. For example, the authors of this book, Tom and Judith, both prefer an avoiding style. If we are pushed into conflict or feel strongly that we need to resolve a particular issue, we can speak up for ourselves. However, we both prefer more indirect means of dealing with current and potential conflicts. We often choose to work things out on a more personal, indirect level.

It is also important to recognize which conflict styles "push your conflict button." Some styles are more or less compatible; it's important to know which styles are congruent with your own. If you prefer a more confronting style and you have a disagreement with someone like Tom or Judith, it may drive you crazy.

Expanding Your Repertoire If a particular way of dealing with conflict is not working, be willing to try a different style. This is easier said than done. As conflict specialists Joyce Hocker and William Wilmot (1991) explain, people often seem to get "frozen" into a conflict style. For example, some people consistently deny any problems in any relationship; conversely, some people consistently escalate small conflicts into large ones.

There are many reasons for getting stuck in a conflict management style, according to Hocker and Wilmot; the style may have developed during a period of time when the person felt good about him- or herself—when the particular conflict management style worked well. Consider, for example, the high school athlete who develops an aggressive style on and off the playing field—a style that people seem to respect. A limited repertoire may be related to gender differences; some women get stuck in an avoiding style, whereas some men get stuck in a confronting style. A limited repertoire also may come from cultural background—a culture that encourages confronting conflict or a culture (like Judith and Tom's) that rewards avoiding conflict. A combination of these reasons is the likely cause of being stuck using one style of dealing with conflict.

In most aspects of intercultural communication, adaptability and flexibility serve us well. Conflict communication is no exception. This means that there is no so-called objective way to deal with conflict. Occasionally, you may find that a style contrasting yours feels just as right to someone else. Recognizing this condition may promote conflict resolution.

This is where the dialectic comes in. It is helpful to be prepared, as in other aspects of relationships, to listen sometimes and not say anything. One strategy that mediators use is to allow one person to talk for an extended period of time while the other person listens. Some guidelines based on the principles of nonviolence can assist in de-escalating or resolving intercultural conflict. Hocker and Wilmot outline three such guidelines.

1. Practice self-restraint. It's OK to get angry, but it's important to move past the anger—to refrain from acting out feelings.
2. Join your opponent "in forming a team of persons struggling together to find a solution to a common problem. . . . [M]oving toward enemies as if they were friends exerts a paradoxical force on them and can bring transcendence" (1991, p. 191).
3. Engage in dialogue.

Dialogue differs from normal conversation. As Hocker and Wilmot point out:

> *In dialogue, both people speak and listen to help the other clarify what is being said. . . . [Q]uality dialogue is slow, careful, full of feeling, respectful, and attentive. . . . This movement towards an opposing viewpoint must be learned; few*

When anyone offends against you, let your first thought be, under what conception of good and ill was this committed? Once you know that, astonishment and anger will give place to pity. For either your own ideas of what is good are no more advanced than his, or at least bear some likeness to them, in which case it is clearly your duty to pardon him; or else, on the other hand, you have grown beyond supposing such actions to be either good or bad, and therefore it will be so much the easier to be tolerant of another's blindness.

Source: Marcus Aurelius, *Meditations* (translated by Maxwell Staniforth), 1964, pp. 109–110, New York: Penguin. (Original work written about 180 C.E.)

develop this approach to others without a deep sense of the importance of each human being, and a belief in the possibility of coming together to search for new solutions that honor each person. (p. 191)

Dialogue offers an important opportunity for coming to a richer understanding of your own intercultural conflicts and experiences.

Recognizing the Importance of Context   As we noted earlier in this chapter, it is important to understand the larger social, political, and historical contexts that give meaning to many types of conflict. Conflict arises for many reasons, and it would be misleading to think that all conflict could be understood within the interpersonal context alone.

People often act in ways that cause conflict. However, it is important to let the context explain their behavior as much as possible. Otherwise, their behaviors may not make sense to you. Once you understand the contexts that frame the conflict, whether cultural, social, historical, or political, you will be in a better position to understand and conceive of the possibilities for resolution.

Being Willing to Forgive   A final suggestion for facilitating conflict is to examine options when conflict results in very bad feelings, particularly with long-term relationships. One such option is forgiveness. This means letting go of—not forgetting—feelings of revenge (Lulofs, 1994). This may be particularly useful in intercultural conflict (Augsburger, 1992).

Teaching forgiveness between estranged individuals is as old as recorded history. It is present in every culture and is part of the human condition (Arendt, 1954). Forgiveness can be a healthy reaction. Psychologists point out that blaming others and feeling bitter resentment lead to a victim mentality. Lack of forgiveness may actually lead to stress, burnout, and physical problems (Lulofs, 1994).

There are several models of forgiveness. Most include an acknowledgment of hurt, anger, and healing. In a forgiveness loop, forgiveness is seen as socially constructed and based in communication. If someone is in a stressed relationship, he or she can create actions and behaviors that make forgiveness seem real; then he or she can communicate this to the other person, enabling the relationship to proceed and move forward.

Forgiveness may take a long time. It is important to distinguish between what is forgiveness and what is not, because false forgiveness can be self-righteous and obtrusive; it almost nurtures past transgression. As Lulofs describes, forgiveness is not

> *simply forgetting that something happened. It does not deny anger. It does not put us in a position of superiority. It is not a declaration of the end of all conflict, of ever risking again with the other person (or anybody else). It is not one way. . . . We do not forgive in order to be martyrs to the relationship. We forgive because it is better for us and better for the other person. We forgive because we want to act freely again, not react out of past pain. . . . [It] is the final stage of conflict and is the one thing that is most likely to prevent repetitive, destructive cycles of conflict. (Lulofs, 1994, pp. 283–284, 289)*

SUMMARY

There are three approaches to understanding conflict. The interpersonal approach focuses on cultural differences. The interpretive and critical approaches focus on intergroup relationships. Conflict can be seen as opportunity or it can be seen as destructive. There are many different types of conflict, including conflicts of interests, values, and goals, as well as cognitive and affective conflicts. There are at least five different ways of dealing with conflict, and individuals tend to have a preference for one of these five styles: a dominating style, which shows high concern for self; integrating and compromising styles, which demonstrate concern for self and others; and obliging and avoiding styles, which demonstrate low concern for self and others.

The choice of conflict style depends on cultural background as well as gender and ethnicity. For example, people from individualistic cultures may tend to use dominating styles, whereas people from collectivist cultures may prefer more integrating, obliging, and avoiding styles. However, the type of conflict and the relationship the disputants have will mediate these tendencies.

It is important to examine conflict in its context. Conflicts arise against the backdrop of existing social movements—for example, in reaction to racism, sexism, and homophobia. Some social movements use nonviolent means of dealing with these conflicts; others confront conflict with violence.

Intercultural conflict is often characterized by ambiguity, language issues, and variations in communication style. Suggestions for dealing with intercultural conflicts include recognizing the existence of different styles, identifying a preferred style, expanding one's repertoire for dealing with conflicts, recognizing the importance of context, and being willing to forgive.

REFERENCES

Arendt, H. (1954). *The human condition.* Chicago: University of Chicago Press.

Arnett, R. (1980). *Dwell in peace: Applying nonviolence to interpersonal relationships.* Elgin, IL: The Brethren Press.

Augsburger, D. (1981a). *Caring enough to forgive.* Ventura, CA: Regal Books.

Augsburger, D. (1981b). *Caring enough to not forgive.* Ventura, CA: Regal Books.

Augsburger, D. (1992). *Conflict mediation across cultures.* Louisville, KY: Westminster/John Knox Press.

Aurelius, M. (1964). *Meditations* (M. Staniforth, Trans.). New York: Penguin. (Original work written about 180 c.e.)

Canary, D. J., & Spitzberg, B. H. (1989). A model of the perceived competence of conflict strategies. *Human Communication Research, 15,* 630–649.

Cathcart, R. S. (1983, Spring). A confrontation perspective on the study of social movements. *Central States Speech Journal, 34,* 69–74.

Cole, M. (1996). *Interpersonal conflict communication in Japanese cultural contexts.* Unpublished dissertation, Arizona State University, Tempe.

Collier, M. J. (1991). Conflict competence within African, Mexican, and Anglo American friendships. In S. Ting-Toomey & F. Korzenny (Eds.), *Cross-cultural interpersonal communication* (pp. 132–154). Newbury Park, CA: Sage.

DeVito, J. (1992). *The interpersonal communication book* (6th ed.). New York: HarperCollins.

Donohue, W. A., & Kolt, R. (1992). *Managing interpersonal conflict.* Newbury Park, CA: Sage.

Filley, A. C. (1975). *Interpersonal conflict resolution.* Glenview, IL: Scott, Foresman.

Folger, J. P., Poole, M. S., & Stutman, R. K. (1993). *Working through conflict: Strategies for relationships, groups, and organizations* (2nd ed.). New York: HarperCollins.

Hall, B. "J." (1994). Understanding intercultural conflict through kernel images and rhetorical visions. *The International Journal of Conflict Management, 5*(1), 62–86.

Hocker, J. L., & Wilmot, W. W. (1991). *Interpersonal conflict* (3rd ed.). Dubuque, IA: William Brown.

King, M. L., Jr. (1984). Pilgrimage in nonviolence. In J. C. Albert & S. E. Albert (Eds.), *The sixties papers: Documents of a rebellious decade* (pp. 108–112). New York: Praeger. (Original work published 1958)

Kochman, T. (1981). *Black and White styles in conflict.* Chicago: University of Chicago Press.

Kozan, M. K. (1989). Cultural influences on styles of handling interpersonal conflicts: Comparisons among Jordanian, Turkish, and U.S. managers. *Human Relations, 42,* 787–799.

Kraybill, D. (1989). *The riddle of Amish culture.* Baltimore, MD: Johns Hopkins University Press.

Leung, K. (1987). Some determinants of reactions to procedural models for conflict resolution: A cross-national study. *Journal of Personality and Social Psychology, 53*, 898–908.

Leung, K. (1988). Some determinants of conflict avoidance. *Journal of Cross Cultural Psychology, 19*, 125–136.

Lulofs, R. S. (1994). *Conflict: From theory to action.* Scottsdale, AZ: Gorsuch Scarisbrick Publishers.

Nadler, L. B., Nadler, M. K., & Broome, B. J. (1985). Culture and the management of conflict situations. In W. B. Gudykunst, L. Stewart, & S. Ting-Toomey (Eds.), *Communication culture, and organizational processes* (pp. 77–96). Beverly Hills, CA: Sage.

Petronio, S., & Alberts, J. K. (In press). *Exploring interpersonal communication: An introduction.* Boston: Houghton Mifflin.

Pike, G. R., & Sillars, A. L. (1985). Reciprocity of marital communication. *Journal of Social and Personal Relationships, 2*, 303–324.

Rahim, A. (1986). *Managing conflict in organizations.* New York: Praeger.

Shuter, R. (1982). Initial interaction of American blacks and whites in interracial and intraracial dyads. *Journal of Social Psychology, 117*, 45–52.

Speicher, B. L. (1994). Interethnic conflict: Attribution and cultural ignorance. *Howard Journal of Communications, 5*, 195–213.

Tannen, D. (1986). *That's not what I meant! How conversational style makes or breaks relationships.* New York: Ballentine.

Tannen, D. (1990). *You just don't understand: Women and men in conversation.* New York: William Morrow.

Thomas, K. W. (1975). Conflict and conflict management. In M. Dunnette (Ed.), *Handbook of Industrial Psychology* (pp. 889–935). Chicago: Rand McNally.

Thomas, K., & Kilmann, R. H. (1974). *Thomas-Kilmann conflict MODE instrument.* Tuxedo, NY: Xicom.

Ting-Toomey, S. (1986). Conflict communication styles in Black and white subjective cultures. In Y. Y. Kim, (Ed.), *Interethnic communication: Current research* (pp. 75–88). *International and Intercultural Communication Annual 10.* Newbury Park, CA: Sage.

Ting-Toomey, S. (Ed.). (1994). *The challenge of facework: Cross-cultural and interpersonal issues.* Albany: State University of New York Press.

Ting-Toomey, S., Gao, G., Trubisky, P., Yang, Z., Kim, H. S., Lin, S. L., & Nishida, T. (1991). Culture, face, maintenance and styles of handling interpersonal conflicts: A study in five cultures. *International Journal of Conflict Management, 2*, 275–296.

Trenholm, S., & Jensen, A. (1992). *Interpersonal communication* (2nd ed.). Belmont, CA: Wadsworth.

Trubisky, P., Ting-Toomey, S., & Lin, S. L. (1991). The influence of individualism-collectivism and self monitoring on conflict styles. *International Journal of Intercultural Relations, 15*, 65–84.

Vellela, T. (1988). *New voices: Student political activism in the '80s and '90s.* Boston: South End Press.

Wood, J. T. (1994). *Gendered lives: Communication, gender, and culture.* Belmont, CA: Wadsworth.

X, Malcolm. (1984). The ballot or the bullet. In J. C. Albert & S. E. Albert (Eds.), *The sixties papers: Documents of a rebellious decade* (pp. 126–132). New York: Praeger. (Original work published in 1965)

THE OUTLOOK FOR INTERCULTURAL COMMUNICATION

265

Now that we have come to the end of our journey through this textbook, how do we really know whether we are good at intercultural communication? We've covered a lot of topics and discussed some ideas that might help you be a better communicator. You can't learn how to be a good communicator just by reading books, though. Just like learning to be a good public speaker, or a good relational partner, it takes experience.

This chapter begins with a discussion of individual components of competence: motivation, knowledge, attitudes, behaviors, and skills. We then turn to the contextual issues in competence. Then we discuss ethical issues in applying knowledge about cultures. Finally, we offer a dialectical way to think about culture and communication.

THE COMPONENTS OF COMPETENCE

What are the things we have to know, the attitudes that are most useful, and the behaviors that will make us be the most competent as communicators? Do we have to be motivated to be good at intercultural communication? Communication scholars Brian Spitzberg and William Cupach (1989) studied interpersonal communication competence in U.S. contexts, and other scholars have tried to apply their findings in intercultural contexts (Hammer, 1987; Imahori & Lanigan, 1989; Spitzberg, 1989; Dinges, 1996; Martin & Hammer, 1989). Their studies resulted in a list of basic components, or building blocks, of intercultural communication competence (for example, having respect for others). We will present these components because we think they can be useful as a starting point. However, we would like to offer two cautionary notes. First, this is only a starting point. Secondly, the basic components are interrelated; it is difficult to completely separate motivation, knowledge, attitudes, behaviors, and skills.

Individual Components

Motivation   Motivation is perhaps the most important dimension of communication competence. If we aren't motivated to communicate with others, it probably doesn't matter what other kinds of skills we possess. We can't assume that people always want to communicate. This is particularly important in contexts in which historic events or political circumstances have resulted in communication breakdowns. For example, it is understandable, given the history of animosity in the Middle East, why Israeli and Arab students would not be motivated to communicate. It is also understandable why a Taiwanese student would not want to room with a student from the People's Republic of China.

Knowledge   The knowledge component comprises various cognitive aspects of communication competence: it is what we know about ourselves, others, and various aspects of communication. Perhaps most important is self-knowledge, knowing how you may be perceived as a communicator, and knowing your

Intercultural communication competence requires motivation, knowledge about other cultures, and attitudes such as tolerance and empathy. In addition, one should exhibit communication behaviors that are meaningful to the other person. *(© Joel Gordon)*

strengths and weaknesses. How can you know what these are? Sometimes you can learn by listening to what others say and by observing how they perceive you. One student described her attempts to become a better intercultural communicator. She explained:

> *But honestly, I feel it begins within yourself. I feel that if each person in our class opens his or her eyes just a little more than what they were before coming into class it will make a difference. This class has really opened my eyes to other people's opinions and feelings.*

Acquiring self-knowledge is a long and sometimes complicated process. It involves being open to information coming in many different ways. As Rita, a young college student, reveals, "It's only after a solid friendship was formed that my Chicana friends told me about perceptions of their community regarding Anglos. Their perceptions are not always favorable and they said it reluctantly. But it has opened my eyes." We often don't know how we're perceived because we don't search for this information, or there is not sufficient trust in a relationship to reveal such things.

Of course, knowledge about how other people think and behave will help you be more effective. In this book we have tried to describe different cultural variations in language, both verbal and nonverbal communication. Unfortunately, this can lead to rigid categorization and stereotyping. Perhaps it is better just to be aware of the range in thought and behavior, and not to assume that just because someone belongs to a particular group that he or she will behave in a particular way. One way to approach this is to expand one's mental "category width," or the range of things we can include in one category. For example, can *snake* be included in the category of "foods" as well as the "unattractive, thing-to-be-avoided" category? Psychologist Richard Detweiler (1980) measured category width among Peace Corp volunteers and discovered that those with more flexible categories tended to be more successful in their work as volunteers.

Linguistic knowledge is another important aspect of intercultural competence. Knowing something about the difficulty of learning a second language also helps us appreciate the extent of the challenges that sojourners and immigrants face in their new cultural contexts. Also, knowing a second or third language expands one's communication repertoire and empathy for culturally different individuals. As Judith struggles through her conversational Spanish class, she is reminded again of how difficult it is to do ordinary things in a second language. And when she sits in class and worries that the instructor might call on her, she is reminded of the anxiety of many international students and immigrants trying to navigate a new country and language.

Attitudes Many attitudes contribute to intercultural communication competence, including tolerance for ambiguity. Two other significant qualities are empathy and nonjudgmentalness.

Tolerance for ambiguity refers to the ease in dealing with situations in which much is unknown. Whether we are abroad or at home, interacting with people who look different from us and behave in ways that are strange to us calls for a tolerance for ambiguity. This is one of the most difficult things to attain. As we've mentioned earlier, people have a natural preference for predictability; uncertainty can be disquieting.

Empathy is the ability to know what it's like to "walk in another person's shoes." Empathic skills are culture bound. We cannot really view the world through another person's eyes without knowing something about his or her experiences and life. As scholar William Howell states:

> *Empathy does not transcend the limits imposed by culture and knowledge and has no magic power to overcome differences in personality and background. What has not been experienced cannot be perceived. . . . Let us say that an American and a*

Japanese have been introduced and are conversing. The Japanese responds to the American's first remark with a giggle. An interested American observer feels plea-surable empathic sensations. The impulsive laughter indicates a congenial, accept-ing reaction. A Japanese observer feels intensely uncomfortable. (1982, p. 108)

What the American doesn't realize is that the giggle may not mean that the Japanese is feeling pleasure, and the empathy is missing the mark. So empathy is the capacity to imagine oneself in another role, within the context of one's cul-tural identity.

Magoroh Maruyama, an anthropologist-philosopher, describes empathy across cultures as transpection, a postmodern phenomenon. Achieving transpec-tion, trying to see the world exactly as the other person sees it, is a difficult process. It often involves trying to learn foreign beliefs, foreign assumptions, foreign perspectives, and foreign feelings in a foreign context (Maruyama, 1970). Transpection, then, can only be achieved by practice and requires struc-tured experience, self-reflection, and practice.

Being nonjudgmental is much easier said than done. We would like to think that we do not judge according to our own cultural frames of reference. But it is very difficult.

One of our colleagues recalls being at a university meeting at which a group of Icelandic administrators and a group of U.S. American faculty discussed im-plementing a study abroad exchange program. The Icelandic faculty were par-ticularly taciturn, and our colleague wanted to lighten up the meeting a little. Eventually she realized that the taciturnity probably reflected different norms of behavior. She had unknowingly judged the tenor of the meeting based on her own style of communication.

The D.I.E. exercise is helpful in developing a nonjudgmental attitude (Wendt, 1984). It involves making a distinction between description, interpreta-tion, and evaluation in the processing of information. Descriptive statements comprise factual information that can be verified through the senses. Examples are, "There are 25 chairs in the room," and "I am five feet tall." Interpretive statements attach meaning to the description. An example might be, "You must be tired." Evaluative statements clarify how we feel about something. An ex-ample might be, "When you're always tired, we can't have any fun together." Only descriptive statements are nonjudgmental.

It is sometimes helpful to use this device in intercultural communication—to be able to recognize whether we are processing information on a descrip-tive, interpretive, or evaluative level. Confusing the different levels can lead to misunderstanding and ineffective communication. For example, if I think a student is standing too close to me, I may interpret the behavior as, "This stu-dent is pushy," or I may evaluate it as, "This student is pushy and I don't like pushy students." However, if I force myself to describe the student's behavior, I may say to myself, "This student is standing 8 inches away from me, whereas most students stand farther away." This observation enables me to search for other (perhaps cultural) reasons for the behavior. The student may be worried about a grade and may feel anxious to get some questions answered. Perhaps the

I participated in a week-long cross-cultural seminar last summer in which the participants were from a mix of domestic and international cultural groups. On the first day, as an ice-breaker, we took turns introducing the person to the left. There were several international students including an older Japanese woman who had a little trouble with English. She introduced her partner in halting English but made only one mistake; she said that her partner (a White American woman) was "Native American." She meant to say that her partner was born in America, but her English wasn't quite fluent.

Immediately, one of the other members of the group raised her hand and said "I have an ouch" and proceeded to tell the group how important it was that we be honest and tell others when things were bothering us. She said, further, that it bothered her that this woman had been called a Native American when she was not. She emphasized how important it was that people be labeled accurately. She meant well. But the Japanese woman was mortified. She was embarrassed about her English to begin with, and she was really embarrassed at being singled out as being incorrect in her language. She did not say anything at the time. None of the rest of us in the group knew how distressed she was. As soon as the session was over, she went to the workshop leaders and asked to be transferred out of the group.

—Mary

student is used to standing closer to people than I am. Or perhaps the student *is* pushy.

It is impossible to always stay at the descriptive level. But it is important to know when we are describing and when we are interpreting. Most communication is at the interpretive level. For example, have you ever gone on a blind date and asked for a description of the person? The descriptions you might get (tall, dark, handsome, nice, kind, generous) are not really descriptions; rather, they are interpretations that reflect individual and cultural viewpoints (Wendt, 1984).

Behaviors and Skills Behaviors and skills are another component of intercultural competence. What are the most competent behaviors? Are there any universal behaviors that work well in all cultural contexts? At one level, there probably are. Communication scholar Brent D. Ruben (1976, 1977) devised a list of universal "behaviors" that actually includes some attitudes. These behaviors are: a display of respect, interaction management, ambiguity tolerance, empathy, relational rather than task behavior, and interaction posture (Ruben & Kealey, 1979).

Some general behaviors seem applicable to many cultural groups and contexts (Koester & Olebe, 1988; Olebe & Koester, 1989). However, these skills become problematic when we try to apply them in very specific ways. For example, being respectful works well in all intercultural interactions. Many scholars identify this particular skill as important (Collier, 1988; Martin & Hammer,

1989). However, how one expresses respect behaviorally may vary from culture to culture and from context to context. European Americans show respect by direct eye contact. Some Native Americans show respect by avoiding eye contact. In one research project, we asked Anglo and Chicano students to identify nonverbal behaviors that they thought would be seen as competent. They identified some of the same behaviors (smiling, direct eye contact, nice appearance, and so on), but they gave different importance to various behaviors depending on the context (Martin, Hammer, & Bradford, 1994).

There seem to be two levels of behavioral competence then. The macro level includes many culture-general behaviors: be respectful, show interest, be friendly, be polite. Then there is the micro level, at which these general behaviors are implemented in culture-specific ways.

It is important to know these different levels of behaviors and be able to adapt. Let's see how this works. In one study, Mitch Hammer and his colleagues evaluated the effectiveness of a cross-cultural training program for Japanese and U.S. American managers in a joint venture (a steel company) in Ohio. One goal was to determine if the managers' intercultural communication skills had improved significantly. The research team used a general behavioral framework of communication competence that included the following dimensions: immediacy, involvement, other orientation, interaction management, and social relaxation (Hammer, 1987; Hammer, Martin, Otani, & Koyama, 1990).

The two groups (Japanese managers and U.S. American managers) rated these dimensions differently. The U.S. Americans said that the most important dimension was involvement (how expressive one is in conversation), whereas Japanese managers said that other orientation (being tuned in to the other person) was most important.

Researchers also judged how well the managers adapted to the other group's communication style. They videotaped the interaction and asked Japanese raters to judge the American managers on how well they adapted to the Japanese style and vice versa. For example, good interaction management for Japanese meant initiating and terminating interaction, and making sure everyone had a chance to talk; for Americans it meant asking opinions of Japanese, being patient with silence, and avoiding strong disagreement and assertive statements. As this example shows, intercultural communication competence means being able to exhibit or adapt different kinds of behaviors, depending on the other person's cultural background.

William Howell (1982), a renowned intercultural scholar, investigated how top CEOs made high-quality decisions. He found, to his surprise, that they did not follow the analytic process prescribed in business school courses—conscious analysis of cost benefits, and so on. He discovered that they made decisions in a very holistic way. They reflected on the problem, talked about the decision with their friends and counterparts in other companies, and often mulled over the problem for a while. They would then come back to it when their minds were fresh and they would have the answer. He emphasized that intercultural communication was similar, that only so much could be gained by conscious analysis, and that the highest level of communication competence required a combination of holistic and analytic thinking. He identified four levels of intercultural communication competence:

1. unconscious incompetence
2. conscious incompetence
3. conscious competence
4. unconscious competence

Unconscious incompetence is the "be yourself" approach, in which the person is not conscious of differences and does not need to act in any particular way. Sometimes this works. However, being ourselves works best in interactions with people who are very similar to us. In intercultural contexts, being ourselves often means that we're not very effective and we don't realize our ineptness.

At the level of conscious incompetence, we realize that things may not be going very well in the interaction, but we're not sure why. Most of us have experienced intercultural interactions in which we felt that something wasn't quite right but we couldn't quite figure out what it was. This describes the feeling of conscious incompetence.

As instructors of intercultural communication, Judith and Tom (the authors) teach at a conscious, intentional level. Our instruction focuses on analytic thinking and learning. This describes the level of conscious competence. Reaching this level is a necessary part of the process of becoming a competent communicator. Howell would say that reaching this level is necessary but not sufficient.

Unconscious competence is the level at which communication goes smoothly but is not a conscious process. You've probably heard of marathon runners "hitting the wall," or reaching the limit of their endurance. Usually, inexplicably, they continue running past this point. Communication at the unconscious competent level is like this. This level of competence is not something we can acquire by consciously trying. It occurs when the analytic and holistic parts are functioning together. When we concentrate too hard or get too analytic, things don't always go easier.

Have you ever prepared for an interview by trying to anticipate every question and worrying about what answers to give, and then not doing very well? This silent rehearsing—worrying and thinking too hard—is called the "internal monologue." According to Howell, people should avoid it. This extraneous and obstructive activity prevents people from being successful communicators (Howell, 1979).

You've also probably had the experience of trying unsuccessfully to recall something, letting go of it, and then remembering it as soon as you're thinking about something else. This is what unconscious competence is—being well prepared cognitively and attitudinally, but knowing when to "let go" and rely on your holistic cognitive processing.

Contextual Components

As we have stressed throughout this book, an important aspect of being competent is understanding the context in which communication occurs. Intercultural communication happens in many contexts. A good communicator is sensitive to these contexts.

We also have emphasized that many contexts can influence intercultural communication. By focusing only on the historical context, you may overlook the relational context; by emphasizing the cultural context, you may be ignoring the gender or racial contexts of the intercultural interaction. And so on. It may seem difficult to keep all of these shifting contexts in mind. However, by analyzing your own intercultural successes and failures, you will come to a better understanding of intercultural communication.

Another aspect of context is the communicator's position within a speech community. Reflect on your own social position in relation to various speech communities and contexts. For example, if you are the only woman in a largely male environment, or the only person of color in an otherwise White community, you may face particular expectations or have people project motivations on your messages. Recognizing your own relation to the speech community and the context will help you better understand intercultural communication.

ETHICS AND INTERCULTURAL COMMUNICATION

In the first chapter we mentioned that one reason for studying intercultural communication was to learn guidelines for dealing with clashes of ethical systems, which involves the following issues:

1. How to assess cultural behavior

2. How to study culture in an ethical way

3. How to apply knowledge ethically about intercultural communication

Let's take a closer look at each of these issues.

Assessing Cultural Behavior

Ethics tell us what is right and wrong, and our cultures tell us what is right and wrong. They both provide absolutist frameworks. Not every cultural pattern is a statement of ethics, but many are. In this book, we have stressed the relativity of cultural behavior, that no cultural pattern is inherently right or wrong. So, is there any universality in ethics? Are any cultural behaviors always right or always wrong?

The answers depend on one's perspective. A universalist might try, for example, to identify acts and conditions that most societies think of as wrong: killing and stealing within the group, treason, and so on. Someone who takes an extreme universalist position would insist that cultural differences are only superficial, that fundamental notions of right and wrong are universal. Some religions take universal positions—for example, that the Ten Commandments are a universal code of behavior. Christian groups often disagree about the universality of the Bible. For example, are the teachings of the New Testament mainly guidelines for the Christians of Jesus' time, or can they be applied to Christians

An important guideline for the ethical intercultural communicator is to strive for empathy. Although it is difficult to really understand what it is like to walk in another person's shoes, an important first step is to really listen and then initiate and engage in a dialogue. *(© Mark Richards/PhotoEdit)*

in the 20th century? These are difficult issues for many people searching for ethical guidelines (Johanesen, 1990). The philosopher Immanuel Kant believed in the universality of moral laws. His well-known "categorical imperative" states that people should act only on maxims that apply universally to all (1949). The extreme relativist position holds that any cultural behavior can be judged only within the cultural context in which it occurs. This means that only those members of a community can truly judge the ethics of their own.

Intercultural scholar William S. Howell represents the relativist position. He explains:

> *Ethical principles in action operate contingently. Circumstances and people exert powerful influences. To say it differently, applied ethics constitute a necessarily open system. The environment, the situation, the timing of an interaction, human relationships all affect the way ethical standards are applied. Operationally, ethics are a function of context. . . .*
>
> *The concept of universal ethics, standards of goodness that apply to everyone, everywhere, and at all times, is the sort of myth people struggle to hold onto. . . . All moral choices flow from the perceptions of the decision maker, and those perceptions are produced by unique experiences in one person's life, in the context in which the choices are made. (pp. 182, 187)*

In his book *Last Watch of the Night*, author Paul Monette points out that it is important to recognize the many forms of intolerance with which most of us grow up. Think about how the intolerance around you may affect you and how difficult it is sometimes to be tolerant of the many diversities.

> *Most of our families do the very best they can to bring us up whole and make us worthy citizens. But it's a very rare person who manages to arrive at adulthood without being saddled by some form of racism or sexism or homophobia. It is our task as grownups to face those prejudices in ourselves and rethink them. The absolute minimum we can get out of such a self-examination is tolerance, one for another. We gay and lesbian people believe we should be allowed to celebrate ourselves and give back to the larger culture, make our unique contributions—but if all we get is tolerance, we'll take it and build on it.*
>
> *We don't know what history is going to say even about this week, or where the gay and lesbian revolution is going to go. But we are a revolution that has come to be based very, very strongly on diversity. We have to fight like everyone else to be open in that diversity; but I love Urvashi Vaid's idea that it's not a matter of there being one of each on every board and every faculty and every organization. It's a matter of being each in one. You'll pardon my French, but it's not so hard to be politically correct. All you have to do is not be an ——.*

Source: Paul Monette, *Last Watch of the Night* (1994), pp. 122–123, New York: Harcourt Brace.

These are not easy issues, and philosophers and anthropologists have struggled to develop ethical guidelines that seem universally applicable but also recognize the tremendous cultural variability in the world. For example, the humanistic principle advocated by anthropologist Elvin Hatch (1983) assumes that people can evaluate culture without succumbing to ethnocentrism, that all individuals and cultural groups share a fundamental humanistic belief, and that people should respect the well-being of others.

A related example is scholar David W. Kale's (1994) proposal of a universal code of ethics for intercultural communicators. This code is based on a universal belief in the sanctity of the human spirit and the goodness of peace. Perhaps the dialectical stance we advocated earlier can apply here too. Although we recognize some universal will toward ethical principles, we may have to live with the tension of not having easy answers for imposing our "universal" ethic on others.

How to Be an Ethical Student of Culture

Related to the issue of judging cultural patterns as ethical or unethical are the issues surrounding the study of culture. Part of learning about intercultural communication is learning about cultural patterns and cultural identity: our own and others. There are two issues to address here—self-reflexivity and learning about others.

In his book *The Rage of a Privileged Class*, author Ellis Cose describes the many practical ways in which race affects the everyday lives of people. This excerpt illustrates how difficult it is to know what it's like to be somebody else, because our very knowledge is shaped by our experiences.

> *In the workplace, the continuing relevance of race takes on a special force, partly because so much of life, at least for middle-class Americans, is defined by work, and partly because even people who accept that they will not be treated fairly in the world often hold out hope that their work will be treated fairly—that even a society that keeps neighborhoods racially separate and often makes after-hours social relations awkward will properly reward hard labor and competence. What most African Americans discover, however, is that the racial demons that have plagued them all their lives do not recognize business hours—that the stress of coping extends to a nonwork world that is chronically unwilling (or simply unable) to acknowledge the status their professions ought to confer.*
>
> *The coping effort, in some cases, is relatively minor. It means accepting the fact, for instance, that it is folly to compete for a taxi on a street corner with whites. It means realizing that prudence dictates dressing up whenever you are likely to encounter strangers (including clerks, cops, and doormen) who can make your life miserable by mistaking you for a tramp, a slut, or a crook. And it means tolerating the unctuous boor whose only topic of party conversation is blacks he happens to know. But the price of this continual coping is not insignificant. In addition to creating an unhealthy level of stress, it puts many in such a war state of mind that insults are seen where none were intended, often complicating communications even with sensitive, well-meaning whites who unwittingly stumble into the racial minefield.*

Source: Ellis Cose, *The Rage of a Privileged Class* (1993), pp. 55–56, New York: Harper-Collins.

Self-Reflexivity   In studying intercultural communication, it is vital to understand oneself and one's position in society. In learning about other cultures and cultural practices, we often learn much about ourselves. Many migrants note that they never felt so much like someone of their nationality until they left their homeland.

Many cultural attitudes and ideas are instilled in you; these things are difficult to unravel and identify. Knowing who you are is never a simple process; it is an ongoing process that can never capture the ever-emerging person. Not only do you grow older, but your intercultural experiences will change who you are and who you think you are.

It is also important to reflect on your place in society. By knowing what social categories you belong to, and the implications of those categories, you will be in a better position to understand how to communicate. For example, your position as an undergraduate student positions you to communicate your ideas on specific subjects and in particular ways to members of faculty or staff at the university. You might want to communicate to the registrar your desire to change majors. That would be an appropriate topic to address to that person. On the other hand, you would not be well positioned to communicate your frustration with your pet dog to your chemistry professor during an exam.

Learning About Others   It is important to remember that the study of cultures is actually the study of other *people*. Never lose sight of the humanity of the topic of study. Try not to observe people as if they are zoo animals. Remember that you are studying real people who have real lives, and your conclusions about them may have very real consequences for them and for you. Cultural studies scholar Linda Alcoff acknowledges the ethical issue involved when students of culture try to describe cultural patterns of others. She acknowledges the difficulty of speaking "for" and "about" others who have different lives. Instead, she claims, students of cultures should try to speak "with" and "to" others. Rather than just describe others in a distant way, it's better to listen and engage others in dialogue about their cultural realities.

Learn to listen to the voices of others. We learn much from experiential knowledge. Hearing about the experiences of people who are different from you can lead to different ways of viewing the world. Many differences—based on race, gender, sexual orientation, nationality, ethnicity, age, and so on—deeply affect the everyday lives of people. Listening carefully as people relate their experiences and their ways of knowing helps us learn about the many aspects of intercultural communication.

Applying Knowledge About Cultures

There are no easy rules to follow to become an ethical intercultural communicator. The following guidelines, though, may help you think about what it means to be an ethical communicator and what your responsibilities might be.

1. Learn to respect others. This is not as simple as it might seem. It involves learning to respect cultures and cultural differences.

2. Strive for empathy. Recognizing that people are different means that you must strive to understand how these differences affect their everyday lives. The ideal is to know what it's like to "walk in their shoes." That's true empathy. A practical approach considers in an empathic manner how these differences shape their lives.

3. Strive to eliminate oppression. This guideline extends beyond respect and empathy. As an intercultural communicator, you have a social responsibility to recognize patterns of domination in society and to avoid enacting them. This means more than simply empathizing with the oppressed.

4. Share the responsibility for ethics: Ethics are complicated in that one's own behavior does not make a situation ethical. Because communication occurs between at least two people, the responsibility for ethical (as well as competent) communication lies with all interactants.

French writer Antoine de Saint-Exupéry describes a dialectic tension between comradeship and the need to bond with others. This tension also fuels the ability to hate others and go to war. Think about the implications of this dialectic for intercultural communication.

> *In a world become a desert we thirst for comradeship. It is the savor of broken bread with comrades that makes us accept the values of war. But there are other ways than war to bring us the warmth of a race, shoulder to shoulder, towards an identical goal. War has tricked us. It is not true that hatred adds anything new to the exaltation of the race.*
>
> *Why should we hate one another? We all live in the same cause, are borne through life on the same planet, form the crew of the same ship. Civilizations may, indeed, compete to bring forth new syntheses, but it is monstrous that they should devour one another.*
>
> *To set man free it is enough that we help one another to realize that there does exist a goal towards which all mankind is striving. Why should we not strive towards that goal together, since it is what unites us all?*

Source: Antoine de Saint-Exupéry, *Wind, Sand, and Stars* (translated by Lewis Galantière), 1967, p. 235, New York: Harcourt, Brace & World.

THINKING DIALECTICALLY ABOUT INTERCULTURAL COMMUNICATION

Now that we have taken you down the path of intercultural communication, we want to introduce a way to juggle all of these contexts and perspectives and ethical imperatives. We believe that this approach can help you navigate through intercultural interactions. It is called thinking dialectically about intercultural communication.

As children, we learn to classify things into categories according to various conventional rules. You might be asked in a logical thinking exercise, for example, to select one of the following objects that does not fit in the group: horse, cow, pig, book. You probably would select "book" because it isn't an animal—a category into which the other objects fit.

In contrast, a dialectical way of thinking does not emphasize rigid categories. Instead it encourages relational thinking. Let's review some dialectical tensions that run through intercultural communication (Figure 12.1).

When we think about intercultural communication, we sometimes overemphasize the *culture* of the other communicator. Culture certainly is an important component in the communication process, but we must not overlook that the communicator is also an *individual*. Someone may be a member of a particular cultural group, but that membership does not reduce the person to that culture. Although the person has been influenced by that culture, he or she is still an individual and may not exhibit the cultural behaviors you are expecting. A dialec-

Figure 12-1   Dialectics in Intercultural Communication

tical perspective balances the presence of both the individual and his or her culture in intercultural communication. During an interaction, people may alternately express their individuality and their cultural backgrounds.

The personal–social dialectic, likewise, emphasizes the relationship between someone's personal characteristics and social characteristics. In some contexts, we enact particular social roles that give meaning to our messages. For example, when lawyers, financial planners, or physicians communicate on specific topics, their messages may be interpreted in particular ways. People are their social roles and their personal identities.

The differences–similarities dialectic emphasizes the tension that exists between observing ways in which people are different and noting the similarities. Much social science work on intercultural communication has tended to stress the cultural differences that exist in communication patterns, rather than emphasizing the similarities. The authors of this book believe that difference and similarity can coexist in intercultural communication interactions. It is important to see how differences and similarities work in cooperation or in opposition.

The static–dynamic dialectic highlights the ever-changing nature of culture and cultural practices, but also underscores our tendency to think about these things as constant. For example, we might assume that whatever we learn about table manners in Myanmar will be true when we find ourselves in that cultural context. Thinking about cultures and cultural practices as both static and dynamic helps us navigate through a diverse world.

You may recall from Chapter 5 the dialectic that exists between history/past and present/future. This dialectic describes how the past influences the present and future, and how our view of the past is influenced by our present perspective. One half of the dialectic cannot be understood without the other. Many influential factors precede and succeed any intercultural interaction that gives meaning to that interaction.

Finally, there is the privilege–disadvantage dialectic. As individuals, we carry and communicate many types of privilege and disadvantage. These may be in the form of economic, political, social position, or status. Hierarchical relations are important to intercultural interactions. For example, when a wealthy foreign tourist communicates with a poor merchant, the elements of economics and status will certainly guide their interests and interactions. Privileges and disadvantages will also influence any interactions between a rich, powerful nation and a poorer dependent nation. The hierarchies may not always be this clear-cut. In some instances, both parties (whether they're individuals or nations) may experience privilege on some topics and disadvantage on others. The two halves of the dialectic are not mutually exclusive.

We have introduced these dialectics to help you coordinate the vast amounts of information that are important in intercultural communication. Sometimes the information may seem to be contradictory . . . but, then, life is full of contradictions. Find new dialectics from other opposing forces. Many more will be evident. Once you begin to seek out these dialectics, you will be on the road to learning more about intercultural communication, about yourself, and about others.

SUMMARY

In this chapter, we first focused on individual components of intercultural communication competence—motivation, knowledge, attitudes, behaviors, and skills—as well as the different levels and approaches to competence. We also looked at the contextual components of competence and emphasized the dynamic and multiple nature of contexts.

Intercultural communicators are concerned with how students and practitioners in this field assess cultural behavior and study culture in an ethical way. Being an ethical student of culture involves being self-reflexive about one's social position and cultural identity. It also entails learning to listen to the voices of others who are different from you. Applying cultural knowledge involves respecting others, striving for empathy, striving for the elimination of oppression, and sharing responsibility for ethics.

One strategy for being an ethical communicator is to begin thinking dialectically about intercultural communication. This means moving away from thinking about communication with others in categorical ways to realizing that there are often two contradictory but equally important dimensions. Understanding comes from holding both dimensions simultaneously. Intercultural communication recognizes an individual–cultural dialectic. It also recognizes a personal–social dialectic, a differences–similarities dialectic, a static–dynamic dialectic, and a privilege–disadvantage dialectic.

REFERENCES

Alcoff, L. (1991/1992). The problem of speaking for others. *Cultural Critique,* *20,* 5–32.

Collier, M. J. (1988). A comparison of conversations among and between domestic culture groups: How intra- and intercultural competencies vary. *Communication Quarterly, 36,* 122–144.

———. (1989). Cultural and intercultural communication competence: Current approaches and directions for future research. *International Journal of Intercultural Relations, 13,* 287–302.

Cose, E. (1993). *The rage of a privileged class.* New York: HarperCollins.

Detweiler, R. A. (1980). Intercultural interaction and the categorization process: A conceptual analysis and behavioral outcome. *International Journal of Intercultural Relations, 4,* 275–295.

Dinges, N. (1996). Intercultural competence. In D. Landis & R. Bhagat (Eds.), *Handbook of intercultural training* (2nd ed.). Thousand Oaks, CA: Sage.

Hammer, M. R. (1987). Behavioral dimensions of intercultural effectiveness: A replication and extension. *International Journal of Intercultural Relations, 11,* 65–88.

———. (1989). Intercultural competence. In M. K. Asante & W. B. Gudykunst (Eds.), *Handbook of international and intercultural communication.* Newbury Park, CA: Sage.

Hammer, M. R., Gudykunst, W. B., & Wiseman, R. L. (1978). Dimensions of intercultural effectiveness: An exploratory study. *International Journal of Intercultural Relations, 2,* 383–392.

Hammer, M. R., Martin, J. N., Otani, M., & Koyama, M. (1990, March). *Analyzing intercultural competence: Evaluating communication skills of Japanese and American managers.* Paper presented to the First Annual Intercultural and International Communication Conference, California State University, Fullerton.

Hatch, E. (1983). *Culture and morality: The relativity of values in anthropology.* New York: Columbia University Press.

Howell, W. (1979). Theoretical directions in intercultural communication. In M. Asante, E. Newmark, & C. Blake (Eds.), *Handbook of intercultural communication.* Beverly Hills, CA: Sage.

Howell, W. S. (1982). *The empathic communicator.* Belmont, CA: Wadsworth.

Imahori, T., & Lanigan, M. L. (1989). Relational model of intercultural communication competence. *International Journal of Intercultural Relations, 13,* 269–286.

Johanesen, R. L. (1990). *Ethics in human communication* (3rd ed.). Prospect Heights, IL: Waveland Press.

Kale, D. W. (1994). Peace as an ethic for intercultural communication. In L. Samovar & R. E. Porter (Eds.), *Intercultural communication: A reader* (7th ed., pp. 435–441). Belmont, CA: Wadsworth.

Kant, I. (1949). *Fundamental principles of the metaphysics of morals* (T. Abbott, Trans.). Indianapolis: Library of Liberal Arts/Bobbs Merrill.

Koester, J., & Olebe, M. (1988). The behavioral assessment scale for intercultural communication effectiveness. *International Journal of Intercultural Relations, 12,* 233–246.

Martin, J. N. (1993). Intercultural competence: A review. In R. L. Wiseman & J. Koester (Eds.), *Intercultural communication competence* (pp. 16–29). Newbury Park, CA: Sage.

Martin, J. N., & Hammer, M. R. (1989). Behavioral categories of intercultural communication competence: Everyday communicators' perceptions. *International Journal of Intercultural Relations, 13,* 303–332.

Martin, J. N., Hammer, M. R., & Bradford, L. (1994). The influence of cultural and situational contexts on Hispanic and non-Hispanic communication competence behaviors. *Communication Quarterly, 42,* 160–179.

Maruyama, M. (1970). *Toward a cultural futurology.* Paper presented at the annual meeting of the American Anthropological Association, published by the Training Center for Community Programs, University of Minnesota, Minneapolis.

Monette, P. (1994). *Last watch of the night.* New York: Harcourt Brace.

Olebe, M., & Koester, J. (1989). Exploring the cross-cultural equivalence of the behavioral assessment scale for intercultural communication. *International Journal of Intercultural Relations, 13,* 333–347.

Ruben, B. D. (1976). Assessing communication competency for intercultural adaptation. *Group and Organization Studies, 1,* 334–354.

———. (1977). Guidelines for cross cultural communication effectiveness. *Group and Organization Studies, 2,* 470–479.

Ruben, B. D., & Kealey, D. J. (1979). Behavioral assessment of communication competence and the prediction of cross-cultural adaptation. *International Journal of Intercultural Relations, 3,* 15–47.

Saint-Exupéry, A. de (1967). *Wind, sand, and stars* (L. Galantière, Trans.). New York: Harcourt, Brace & World.

Spitzberg, B. H. (1989). Issues in the development of theory of interpersonal competence in the intercultural context. *International Journal of Intercultural Relations, 3,* 241–268.

Spitzberg, B. H., & Cupach, W. R. (1989). *Handbook of interpersonal communication competence research.* New York: Springer-Verlag.

Wendt, J. (1984). D.I.E.: A way to improve communication. *Communication Education, 33,* 397–401.

TEXT CREDITS

Page 129: From L. J. Daniel and G. Smitherman, *How I Got Over: Communication in the Black Community*, in D. Carbaugh, ed., *Cultural Communication and Intercultural Contact*, pp. 27–40, Laurence Erlbaum, 1990. Used with permission of the publisher.

Page 198: From B. D. Merritt, *Our Voices: Essays in Culture, Ethnicity, and Communication*, Á. Gonzalez, M. Houston, V. Chen, eds. Copyright © 1994 by Roxbury Publishing Company. Reprinted by permission of the publisher.

Page 210: From "Racist Love" by Hoyt Sze, *Asian Week*, July 24, 1992. Reprinted by permission of the publisher.

Page 214: From "Cold Water," a film by Nariko Ogami, dialogue reprinted with permission of Intercultural Press, Inc., Yarmouth, ME. Copyright © 1987 by Intercultural Press, Inc.

Page 223: From "Against the Great Divide" by Brian Jarvis, *Newsweek*, May 3, 1993. All rights reserved. Reprinted by permission.

Page 253: Reprinted by arrangement with The Heirs to the Estate of Martin Luther King, Jr., c/o Writers House, Inc. as agent for the proprietor. Copyright © 1966 by Martin Luther King, Jr., copyright renewed 1994 by Coretta Scott King.

NAME INDEX

SUBJECT INDEX

Act sequence, 55–56
Adaptation. *See* Cultural adaptation
Affective communication style, 128
Affective conflict, 245
Affirmative action, 11
African Americans, 9
  communication problems with Whites, 129
  conflict and, 247, 249, 252, 254, 255, 256, 257–258
  core symbols of, 67–68
  cultural spaces and, 156–158
  hair of, 57
  identity labels for, 71, 77
  identity of, 73–74, 77, 82–83, 84
  intercultural relationships of, 227–228
  interracial relationships of, 223
  job interviews and, 198–199
  Kwanzaa holiday of, 54
  neighborhoods of, 157–158
  stereotypes of, 195, 197–199, 210
  unique qualities of preaching among, 34
African cultures
  cultural adaptation of, 178
  foreign images and, 202
  intercultural relationships in, 227–228

African Queen, The (film), 188
Afrocentricity, 33–34
Age identity, 72, 73
Algerian culture, 178
Ambiguity, in intercultural conflict, 256
American Society for Training and Development (ASTD), 24
Amish culture, 16–17, 18, 31, 75, 151, 243
Anxiety and uncertainty management model of cultural adaptation, 169–170
Apache culture, 151
Arab Americans
  nonverbal communication and, 152, 154
  perceptions of mainstream culture, 195–196
Arab culture, 15, 197, 266
Ascribed identities, 67, 70
Asian Americans
  history of, 7–8, 100, 104, 106–107
  identity labels for, 77
  identity of, 70
  intercultural awareness of, 16
  Korean Day holiday of, 69
  neighborhoods of, 158
  nonverbal communication and, 152
  popular culture and, 196–197

  stereotyping of, 198
Asian cultures
  romantic relationships in, 218–219, 220
  stereotyping of, 210, 224
  See also specific cultures
Assimilation, 181
Attitudes, 268–270
Autonomy-connection dialectic, 232
Avoiding conflict style, 243–244, 247
Avowal, 67

Behavior
  assessing, 273–275
  competence and, 270–272
Belgians, 76, 88
Beliefs, shared and learned patterns of, 47–48
Black(s). *See* African Americans
Black Atlantic, The (Gilroy), 107–108
Black Elk Speaks, Being the Life Story of a Holy Man of the Oglala Sioux, 102
Blindness, and nonverbal communication, 147
Bluffing, 15
Bounded identity, 75
Bribery, 17

Cable News Network (CNN), 200